BRAIN STAGES

HOW TO RAISE

SMART, CONFIDENT KIDS

AND HAVE FUN DOING IT

K–5

PATRICIA WILKINSON AND
JACQUELINE FRISCHKNECHT, PHD

SANDRA JONAS
PUBLISHING

Sandra Jonas Publishing
PO Box 20892
Boulder, CO 80308
sandrajonaspublishing.com

Printed in the United States of America
24 23 22 21 20   6 7 8 9 10 11

Book design by Sandra Jonas

Publisher's Cataloging-in-Publication Data

Names: Wilkinson, Patricia, 1962–, author. | Frischknecht, Jacqueline, 1932–2015, author.
Title: Brain stages : how to raise smart, confident kids and have fun doing it, K–5 / Patricia Wilkinson, Jacqueline Frischknecht.
Description: Boulder, CO : Sandra Jonas Publishing, 2018. | Includes bibliographical references and index.
Identifiers: LCCN 2018946049 | ISBN 9780985581503
Subjects: LCSH: Child development. | Education, Elementary—Activity programs. | Educational games. | BISAC: FAMILY & RELATIONSHIPS / Parenting / General | EDUCATION / Elementary.
Classification: LCC LB1029.G3 | DDC 371.337 — dc23
LC record available at http://lccn.loc.gov/2018946049

DISCLAIMER
The information contained in this book is designed for educational purposes only and is not intended to provide medical advice or any other professional services. The information should not be used for diagnosis or treatment, or as a substitute for professional care. If your child has a medical or behavioral problem or you suspect such a possibility, consult your health care provider. The stories are composites designed to illustrate common behaviors and situations. Names have been changed to protect parents' and children's identities.

ILLUSTRATIONS
Sljubisa/Adobe Stock, 5; Blamb/Shutterstock, 6; Olive 1976/Adobe Stock, 7; Adiano/Adobe Stock, 55; Pingebat/Adobe Stock (face icons)

To parents,
the guardians of how our children's brains
develop and learn

And in loving memory of
Jacqueline Frischknecht,
who passed away before Brain Stages
could be completed, and whose life's mission
was to get this information
to as many people as possible

Join the Brain Stages community!

Visit **theBrainStages.com** for:

- Free printables
- More research-based tips and activities
- Upcoming speaking events
- Brain Stages workshops

CONTENTS

AUTHOR'S NOTE

I can't wait to share with you what Jackie and I have learned through decades of research as well as professional and personal experience. Our work has both confirmed things we did right in raising our own children and revealed things we wish we had done differently—if only we had known what you're about to discover.

Jacqueline Frischknecht (Jackie) earned her PhD in human communication and was a professor at the University of Denver. While raising three kids into successful adults and teaching hundreds of students, she became interested in how brains function and develop. The cutting-edge research excited her, and she set upon a quest to use that information to help parents and teachers stimulate and nurture children's learning.

I spent 23 years in the classroom, where I had the rare, wonderful opportunity to teach all the elementary school grades. The treasure trove of games to facilitate learning that I've collected and developed fit in quite nicely with Jackie's brain research. My husband, Chuck, and I have also raised two amazing daughters. Both are loving, socially conscious adults who have earned college degrees and support themselves in fulfilling careers.

Sadly, Jackie passed away in 2015. It's my honor and pleasure to present our combined work. Special thanks to Jackie's children for their steadfast support in completing this project.

Trish Wilkinson

1

HOW TO USE THIS BOOK

Parents are powerful! Many of us don't realize how much influence we have over our children's brain development. Our actions speak louder than anything we say and even stimulate how parts of our kids' brains form.

Children are born with a set of genes, but the environment parents provide has a huge impact on whether children will live up to their potential. Scientists used to think kids' brains were pretty well sorted out by age three, but more recent studies show that brain development continues through our mid-20s (Guyer et al. 2018).

That means parents can do all kinds of great things for their children. Moms and dads who talk to and play with their kids, allow some independent exploration, kiss their scrapes, provide encouragement, and maintain consistent boundaries nurture the emotional, memory, and knowledge centers in their children's brains. Parents also set the tone for how much cortisol (stress hormone) their children's brains produce, which plays a key role in how they will respond to new or challenging situations.

For many of us, this knowledge may make parenting seem an even bigger, more daunting responsibility, especially because mistakes are unavoidable. The good news is that kids' brains are elastic. If you step on feelings or cause undue stress, you can admit you blew it, promise to do better, and move on. When you keep your commitments, your child will learn that she can trust you and that it's okay not to be perfect. She'll also learn how to forgive others as well as herself.

And you're in luck because this book will help you not only raise smart, confident children, but also reduce your stress and make your parenting journey a lot of fun! Supported by research and experience, *Brain Stages* provides a how-to for boosting brainpower while cultivating a love for learning and developing communication skills in each grade, kindergarten through fifth. The biggest bonus, though, is the large collection of activities that build and reinforce skills while bringing your family closer and keeping you connected. No doubt you've heard the saying "The family that plays together, stays together."

Even busy parents can play age-appropriate, challenging games for fun and learning. In fact, many of the activities included at each grade level are designed with versatility in mind. Most can be played while you're standing in line at the grocery store, driving in the car, waiting at the doctor's office, or doing household chores. You don't have to play every game in this book—choose the activities that suit your family. (To see many of the activities in action, visit thebrainstages.com.)

Just before your child enters a new grade, you can read the applicable chapter to get a sense of how neural pathways in the brain are connecting for upcoming physical, mental, and social changes your child will likely experience—or if you prefer, you can read sections of each chapter that pertain to your interests. You can also check the index to locate sections to meet immediate needs, such as games to improve math or reading or to keep sharp kids motivated.

Brain Stages is intended to be a dog-eared reference you can turn to again and again to facilitate learning, get homework help, understand social changes, and discover ways to effectively interact with teachers and school administrators. You'll also pick up tricks to get kids the sleep and hydration they need, along with fun nutrition and exercise tips that work even on a tight schedule.

We've included academic guidelines at each grade. To read the skills your child will be expected to master, type the name of your state and "education standards K–12" into a search engine. The activities in *Brain*

Stages develop higher thinking skills and apply universally, but some skills may appear in a different grade level in your state's standards.

THE REAL DEAL: SLICES OF LIFE

Throughout the book, you'll find "Real Deal" sections featuring true stories—about our own families and the families of friends—that illustrate salient points and themes. Some names have been changed for privacy because the best stories are often the most embarrassing. Rest assured, those surprising scenarios in your household will turn out to be some of the most important lessons—for both you and your child— and the most entertaining memories.

THREE KINDS OF PARENTS

Examples of three different parenting styles appear at the end of each chapter to help define what works for supporting kids in learning— and what doesn't:

"Harried Parents" get overwhelmed with their busy lives. They have too many things to think about as it is. Educating kids is the school's job.

"Helicopter Parents" hover. With the best of intentions, they shelter their kids from discomfort rather than allowing them the gift of negative consequences for their actions to teach them boundaries and responsibility. Often their children live at home into their mid-20s or even 30s. When their kids move out, they need help with finances and other obligations.

"Angel Parents" represent the ideal for knowing when and how to provide guidance while still letting children learn from their mistakes. Give yourself a pat on the back when you find yourself in this category, and strive for some of the things modeled in these scenarios when you believe you've fallen short.

Depending on the amount of sleep we're getting, demands at work, and a myriad of other factors, most of us look like a combination of the types. Give yourself a break if you recognize yourself in a less than favorable example—no one can do everything "right" all the time.

CAUTION: BRAINS GROW AT THEIR OWN PACE

Because brains grow at different rates, your child's abilities will probably appear in more than one grade, so you may want to read more than one chapter. For example, your son might have read picture books and counted the change in your wallet at age three (skills for ages five to seven), yet in third grade, he still struggles with waiting his turn or sharing his toys (kindergarten skills). The chapters will help you recognize signs of your child's brain growth and tailor activities to meet his needs.

Do your best not to push beyond readiness. Getting impatient with your child for not maturing at the "normal" rate can cause emotional damage that could continue into adulthood. You can nurture brain development, but you can't rush it, so enjoy the ride.

Your children have plenty of time to learn at their own pace. When you support them where they are—whether that means providing challenges or remediation—instead of where people think they should be, everyone will be a lot happier (Semrud-Clikeman, n.d.).

THE SECRET SAUCE OF SUCCESS

- Play together and have lots of conversations so when things get rough, your child will already know that you're on her side.

- Provide supportive guidance in accordance with your child's maturity.

- Set clear rules and be consistent with realistic consequences, for both breaking and following them.

- Enjoy the journey while you can—children grow up fast.

We hope you'll find everything you need within these pages to understand how to make the most of your child's brain development and enjoy building a healthy social, emotional, and academic foundation.

✦ 2 ✦

USEFUL STUFF ABOUT BRAINS

A brain makes up only 2 percent of our body weight, but it gobbles up 20 percent of the energy produced and requires even more when we read or solve problems. An average adult brain weighs about three pounds, is about the size of a large cauliflower, contains mostly water, and has the consistency of a bowl of Jell-O. Why do you need to know these things? So when your child asks if there's a little elf controlling things inside his brain, you know how to set him straight.

Before we're born, our brains produce trillions of neurons, the long strand-like cells that communicate with one another using electrical impulses. Dendrites bring information to the neurons, and axons pass it along via synapses, tiny gaps between the cells, wiring the brain for direct, rapid, immediate learning and growth. In the first three years of life, kids' brains make as many as 250,000 neurons every minute,

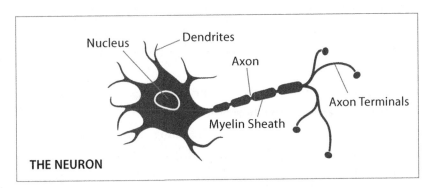

THE NEURON

and the majority are not yet connected into networks. With every experience, dendrites and axons migrate and connect with other neurons across synapses, becoming organized into circuits.

Brains decide within 18 seconds whether to create a memory path for new information. If the brain doesn't get the message "this is important," input can dissipate before a pathway gets generated. This is why building on familiar concepts and learning within the context of an activity has proven, over and over, most effective in acquiring new information (Peterson and Peterson 1959).

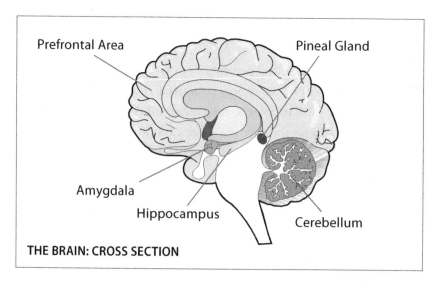

Prefrontal Area

Pineal Gland

Amygdala

Hippocampus

Cerebellum

THE BRAIN: CROSS SECTION

The hippocampus, a small organ in the temporal lobe, forms a critical part of the limbic system, the cluster in the center of the brain that regulates emotions and long-term memory (it's a big shot in the learning department). School-age kids who get consistent guidelines, sleep, exercise, and nutrition grow a larger hippocampus than those who don't (Simmons et al. 2017).

The brain is also hardwired for survival. Stress and fear generate cortisol and adrenaline, two hormones that help us get out of the way of an oncoming car but can impede learning. Daniel Goleman, author of *Social Intelligence*, explains it this way, "Cortisol stimulates the amygdala while it impairs the hippocampus, forcing our attention onto the emotions we feel, while restricting our ability to take in new information" (2006, 273–74).

The amygdala is the almond-shaped knob on the underside of the cluster responsible for processing emotions. The size of this area is proportional to the amount of stress in kids' lives: the safer they feel, the smaller the area. Those kids with smaller amygdalas tend to show more conscientious behaviors and openness to new experiences (Matsudaira et al. 2016). In a secure household—one with clear rules, a willingness to chat, and a sense of humor—children develop a healthy "fight or flight" response that keeps their hands out of the fireplace but gives them confidence and willingness to try new things.

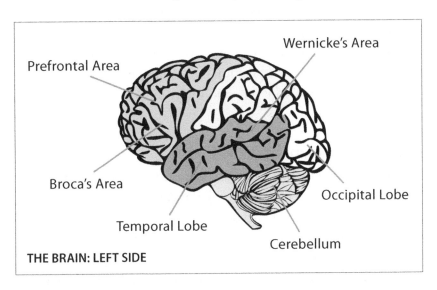

THE BRAIN: LEFT SIDE

In addition, moms and dads who have regular two-way conversations with their kids stimulate two parts of the brain—the Broca's area and the Wernicke's area—which work together to boost language abilities. As you are learning, parents are powerful, and sometimes it's simple—if you have lots of conversations with your child, you will give him a huge learning advantage, regardless of his IQ (Romeo et al. 2018).

Likewise, parents' marital status, socioeconomic status, and education don't matter as much as you might think. According to Pat Jones (2016), teacher of more than 35 years and owner of the website Teacher

Support Force, an online resource for educators using brain research to guide curriculum, "[Parents] don't even have to have a high school education. Just talking to your kids and answering their questions will develop their vocabulary and language skills." You can rest assured that your child's brain development is not affected by whether you are single or married, drive a Mercedes or a jalopy, or live in a mansion or an apartment in the projects. Talking with your child fosters a good relationship as well as creates and connects neural pathways.

And when you're with your child, be a good listener and try not to be quick to judge. The more he trusts you to guide with a loving, gentle hand, the more teachable moments you will enjoy together.

Your child can learn all kinds of things in everyday life. For example, his teacher may present a great explanation of fractions at school, but when you help him cut an apple into quarters to share with three friends, fractions become a practical tool. Almost everything you do to maintain your household is an opportunity to have fun while helping him build neural pathways.

A WORD ABOUT MULTITASKING

Lots of us get so busy that we try to do more than one thing at a time, and we convince ourselves that our brains can efficiently manage multiple activities at once. The studies beg to differ. According to functional magnetic resonance image (fMRI) tests, when we are given two tasks, our brains switch back and forth rather than focusing on actions simultaneously. Our brains are switch-tasking, not multitasking, and we don't do either task as well (Jeong and Hwang 2016).

In fact, while multitasking, we're about as effective as we are when we stay up all night. Research shows that the people who think they're good at multitasking are less effective than those who generally do one thing at a time and only try to do multiple things at once on occasion (Bradberry 2014). We even become less efficient while doing things we're used to, like making a meal, while we try to do something else at the same time (Bergmann et al. 2017). So just imagine how well your child is doing his homework while watching TV.

Learning involves concentrated attention as well as peripheral perception—that is, both conscious and subconscious processing. Although it's true that we can learn while dividing our attention between two or more activities, we better understand and remember those things requiring analysis or creativity if we focus on only one at a time. Multitasking may seem more productive, but the more we attempt to juggle mental efforts, the less efficient we become (Lin et al. 2016).

Knowing the truth about multitasking will help you as well as your child. When she swears she can do her homework in front of the TV, you'll know that though she may be able to complete the assignment, she won't learn or remember as much without paying full attention. Even if she has an easy assignment that day, allowing additional activities while she's doing her homework isn't a good habit to encourage.

BRAINPOWER AND POSITIVE PARENTING

Neuroimaging studies have revealed that a positive parenting style produces a higher volume of gray matter in children's brains—and the higher the volume, the better your child can store and apply what he learns.

A positive communication style is critical. A study based on fMRIs showed that young brains have trouble processing negative input before they're 11 years old. Scientists think that it takes more effort for our brains to interpret negative statements because they are more complex than positive ones. So encourage your kids by saying "You're on the right track. Now let's see if you can . . ." rather than "Oops, that's wrong" (Van Duijvenvoorde 2008).

Likewise, our brains can't process the word "don't." What do we do when someone says "Don't look!"? Try saying to your child "Please stop at the sidewalk" instead of "Don't run into the street."

In addition, children with parents who praise them tend to be more open to unfamiliar activities, new environments, and different ways of doing things. These kids produce less cortisol (the stress hormone) and are better at managing their emotions than kids whose parents focus on mistakes or withhold praise when their children fall short of their expectations (Matsudaira et al. 2016).

But the wrong kind of praise can cause more harm than good. If we tell kids they're smart when they do well, studies show that when they fail, they tend to doubt their intelligence. Once they lose confidence, they begin to quit projects at the first sign of trouble and can become reluctant to try new things. Rather than complimenting intelligence, praise your child for effort. Healthy self-esteem comes from accomplishment, which requires dedication to working through a problem until we find a solution (Klein 2000).

After crunching data from six case studies, researchers Claudia M. Mueller and Carol S. Dweck (1998, 33) from Columbia University conclude, "Fifth graders praised for intelligence . . . displayed less task persistence, less task enjoyment . . . and worse task performance than children praised for effort."

To acknowledge your child in an effective way, you can say, "Wow. You worked really hard on that problem. I wondered how you were going to solve it. Good for you for hanging in there." When a project comes up short, encourage your child to push past her comfort zone by saying something like "This is a good start. How do you think you could add to what you have done so far?"

Praise the energy and effort your child invests in projects, encourage participation, and gently guide toward improvement.

THE FOUR ESSENTIALS FOR A HEALTHY BRAIN

The four brain builders—sleep, exercise, water, and fuel—may sound obvious, but understanding what happens in your child's brain with adequate rest, plenty of physical activity, sufficient liquids, and wholesome eating will encourage you to be conscious of maintaining healthy habits—no matter how crazy your family's schedule gets.

1. Sleep

As you'll see in the next section on brain waves, a good night's sleep is critical for healthy function and development of the brain. Kids who get plenty of rest learn and apply information better than those who don't (Vermeulen et al. 2018). It's that simple.

2. Exercise

Getting enough exercise is almost as important as getting enough sleep. We generally hear that kids need more exercise to combat childhood obesity, but working up a sweat also boosts the size of the hippocampus—which in turn may improve memory and learning. A good workout also produces dopamine, a neurotransmitter that gives us a sense of well-being and also helps us remember.

Plus, exercise reduces insulin resistance, thereby increasing growth factors—chemicals that benefit the health of existing brain cells, stimulate the growth of lots of new ones, and send signals for the body to make more blood vessels for a well-oxygenated brain. Also, exercise improves mood and sleep, reducing stress and anxiety. Studies even show that the prefrontal cortex and medial temporal cortex, responsible for thinking and short-term memory, have greater volume in people who exercise compared to those who don't (Godman 2014).

To help your child get enough exercise, encourage her to try different physical activities, from baseball and soccer to martial arts and gymnastics. See if you can land on something she enjoys that will turn up her heart rate. The more fun she has with the exercise, the less coaxing you'll have to do to get her to practices.

Hint: If she changes her mind and wants to quit an activity, insist that she fulfill her commitment first. That is, if your child wants to switch from basketball to dance, make sure she finishes the season before doing something else. She can't let down her team, whether she's a starter or not. If you allow your kids to quit something they've committed to, you will teach them it's okay to shirk responsibilities.

Another big help is to get your child moving before school. I used to have my classes run laps, regardless of grade level, before we went to work. The kids always grumbled at the beginning of the school year, but most of them grew to absolutely love it. They earned a Popsicle stick for each lap, and many won awards for the number of miles run by the end of the year. And you wouldn't believe the difference it made to get their hearts pumping before diving into learning: better participation, brighter mood, sharper thinking, and higher test scores.

You can't make teachers send their students to run laps, but you can get your child moving in the morning. Hand him a jump rope, for example, and keep an ongoing tally of how many times he can jump. Praise his effort and make a big deal over when he breaks his record. Research tells us that engaging in rhythmic activities makes connections in the brain that contribute to building language and math skills (Sacheck et al. 2015).

If your child gets tired of jumping rope, switch it up by having him follow a workout for kids on YouTube. Better yet, get up a few minutes earlier and do it with him. Nothing says "this is important" like making exercise a priority for you too.

Maybe you'd rather follow a yoga or kickboxing video. If so, have your child do those activities with you instead. He may struggle to keep up at first, but it won't take him long to get the hang of whatever you want to do. If he doesn't like a certain activity, negotiate for one you can agree on or make a deal to rotate YouTube videos. Raising your child's heart rate before school will put him miles ahead in the learning game, and if you work out with him, you'll have a better day too.

3. Water

You've undoubtedly heard that drinking water is good for you, but did you know brains require hydration to do their best thinking? Studies show that kids who drink enough water can maintain focus, remember things, and apply what they learn better than kids who don't (Riebl and Davy 2013). Adequate hydration also reduces the tendency for afternoon sag and helps kids sleep better. A few more glasses of water may even alleviate headaches, weight gain, and attention deficit symptoms.

Forget sports drinks unless your child is soaked in sweat after an hour of strenuous physical activity. The salts and minerals are supposed to replace what heavy exercise has depleted. Although sports drinks often end up in lunch boxes, they aren't intended for general consumption.

Water is the best thirst quencher—it's inexpensive and readily available. If you want your child to do his best thinking, provide water rather than sugary drinks or beverages with sugar substitutes.

4. Fuel

Your child needs fuel for brain growth and development, and sometimes our busy lives get in the way of including enough B vitamins, zinc, and other brain foods in the family diet. Look for healthy, quick breakfasts, snacks, and lunches in the grade-level chapters to ensure your child receives all the nutrients she needs to develop her brain.

Protein foods are a must. The nutrients in eggs, lean meats, and fish are essential for producing and maintaining neurons, neurotransmitters, and a healthy hippocampus. If you're a vegetarian, be sure to do your homework to determine which foods supply the B vitamins, iron, omega-3s, omega-9s, and zinc your child needs for healthy brain growth.

Fruits and vegetables are also essential. If you aren't a big fruit and veggie eater or don't encourage your children to eat plant foods regularly, you're doing them a grave disservice because vitamins and minerals have a huge impact on how well the body and brain function. The studies are mixed on the effectiveness of supplementing with multivitamins, but the research community adamantly agrees there's no substitute for eating a balanced diet. It turns out we need the combination of elements in food for our bodies to absorb the nutrients involved in cell production and function of the nervous system. And to get kids to eat vegetables, Mom and Dad must eat them too.

Whenever possible, eat fresh foods and limit processed foods. Busy parents often get lured by the convenience of packaged, prepared items that can be thrown into a lunch box or microwaved for easy meals. The problem is that many processed foods are saturated with sugar and salt, a terrible combination for robust brain development. The American Heart Association (2011) reported that the average child eats three times the amount of sugar recommended for good learning and growth.

But beware—some food items we think are healthy really aren't, so read labels. For example, I used to give our girls yogurt cups because yogurt is supposed to be good for you, right? And it's easy to eat in the car on the way to school or to throw into a lunch box. When I got around to reading the label, I discovered each cup contained 18 to 26 grams of sugar—as much as some candy bars!

Another stealthy junk food is fruit juice. A 12-ounce can of soda contains 9 teaspoons of sugar, whereas the same amount of orange juice has up to 12 teaspoons! The amount of vitamin C and other nutrients in juice aren't worth the sugar bomb, even in 100 percent natural brands. Instead, hand your child an orange, an apple, or a handful of grapes. Eating the actual fruit delivers far less sugar, still provides vitamins, minerals, and soluble fiber, and retains the insoluble fiber removed during the juicing process. (The insoluble fiber slows the body's absorption of sugar which makes the job of the pancreas to process the sugar more manageable.)

Occasional pizzas, burgers, or ice cream won't have catastrophic effects on your child's brain development. And eating junk food once in a while keeps kids from going to friends' houses and gorging on brownies. Make no mistake, though, too many junk calories do more damage than adding belly rolls. They deprive your child's brain of the nutrients needed for thinking and memory. Children who don't regularly eat fresh fruit, vegetables, and protein often have trouble paying attention, learning, sleeping, and being active. According to the Children's Defense Fund (2010), children who don't eat healthy also suffer from a higher rate of psychological disorders, such as anxiety or learning disabilities.

Sadly, lots of school cafeterias don't cook anymore. They warm up prepared food loaded with salt, sugar, and preservatives. Allowing your child to eat cafeteria food occasionally won't be a game changer for hearty brain development, but providing nutritious breakfasts and lunches will be well worth your time.

The secret to a healthy, balanced diet is to eat a variety of nutritious, fresh food most of the time and to follow the rule that sweets, fast food, and potato chips are "an occasional treat."

★THE REAL DEAL★
What Worked for Us in Healthy Eating
Like most kids, mine liked junk food (and still do). Throughout grade school, my husband and I set a rule that the girls could have one dessert

after dinner—if they ate their whole meal. We didn't overfeed them and made sure regular exercise was part of the routine. Their "one thing" after dinner could be a cookie or two, a scoop of ice cream, a cupcake, or whatever looked good the last time we went grocery shopping.

Here is an example of a typical conversation at our house:

"I'm full. Do I have to eat the rest of my green beans?"
We'd say, "No, you never have to eat anything you don't want to."
The next question would often be, "Will I still get dessert?"
"You know the rule," we'd tell them. "If you're too full to finish dinner, you're too full for dessert."

We got lots of clever arguments in the early years, to which we'd say, "We wouldn't be doing our job as your parents if we let you leave your vegetables and then gave you goodies. Your body needs the stuff you're eating for dinner. It doesn't need a thing in those cookies."

Fair warning: Both of our daughters tested us near the end of kindergarten, two years apart. Assuring us that they wouldn't be hungry later, each one left the dinner table without finishing her meal. Soon after, they wanted to have dessert with the rest of the family, but we said, "We're so sorry. You know that an unfinished dinner means no dessert or 'second dinner' later." Tears and tantrums ensued.

Our hugs and words of understanding didn't calm either of them. But we held firm. We had learned that if we ignored a rule just one time, it would take us months of concerted effort to reestablish the boundary, so we committed to being consistent.

We put them to bed with extra hugs and let them cry themselves to sleep. Listening to the wailing through the door, my husband and I, teary ourselves, reminded each other that no one ever starved from skipping a snack after dinner. And we had to prevail only once with each child.

After that, we sometimes heard "If I don't finish my [fill in the blank], will I still get dessert?" But the girls knew the answer, and we all looked forward to meals together—catching up, making jokes, and enjoying deep conversations.

BRAIN WAVE BASICS

Millions of neurons communicate via electrical impulses we call brain waves because of their cyclical, wavelike nature. These impulses can be measured and mapped by a machine to create what's called an electro-encephalogram, or EEG—but you don't need to run to your pediatrician and request an EEG printout for your child. Simply understanding a bit about the different kinds of brain waves can help you know what activities will suit your child's needs at any given time.

Brain waves vary in frequency depending on our level of consciousness. These frequencies are measured in cycles per second, or hertz (Hz). The lower the hertz, the slower the wave. In order from slowest to fastest, brain waves are categorized as *delta, theta, alpha, beta,* and, the most recently discovered, *gamma.*

Delta Brain Waves: Unconscious Rejuvenation

Delta brain waves, the slowest of the five brain waves, are essential for everything from basic life functions to high-level cognitive tasks. Sleep, the magic elixir, produces languid, healing delta brain waves to remove waste as well as repair and rejuvenate the mind and body for a new day. You know how cranky or scattered you feel and how overwhelming the simplest tasks can seem when you haven't gotten enough sleep. Your child has similar experiences plus the added stress of extraordinary energy requirements for physical and mental growth.

One thing parents can do to help their children get adequate, high-quality sleep (and those precious delta waves) is to establish a consistent bedtime ritual. For example, at a regular hour, kids change into pajamas and brush their teeth, and then parents read with them before turning out the lights. Studies show that children who have optimal bedtime routines perform better in terms of executive brain function than those who don't. That is, a consistent routine helps kids get the sleep they need, so they have an easier time paying attention, remembering information and applying it to new things, and using reason to solve problems (Kitsaras et al. 2018). Delta waves are imperative for mental, emotional, and physical health.

Studies show that skimping on sleep has the opposite effect: impaired attention, alertness, concentration, and reasoning, which, for kids, often puts absorbing new concepts—or even building on familiar ones—into the too-hard basket. One of the best gifts you can give to your child (and to yourself, for that matter) is a good night's sleep. School-age children need between 9 and 12 hours of sleep each night to make enough delta waves to do their best learning.

Having a consistent bedtime ritual, including getting home from activities on time for your child to get a solid night's sleep, will give you some downtime too. And making sure your child gets enough rest may help you get more sleep as well. Not only will your household be happier and more alert, but your own brain will also be healthier. Scientists are discovering that long-term adequate sleep is a key element in avoiding Alzheimer's, Parkinson's, and Huntington's diseases as we age (Musiek and Holtzman 2016).

GETTING ENOUGH MUCH-NEEDED DELTA WAVES

1. **Develop a drinking habit.** Make it a family ritual to drink an eight-ounce glass of water in the afternoon and another one shortly after dinner to cool the brain and hydrate the body for healthy sleep.

2. **Get moving.** A study in New Zealand found that sedentary children can take up to two hours longer to fall asleep than active ones. At least one hour of daily exercise kicks brain chemicals into gear to help kids nod off at bedtime (Reinberg 2009). Adults can do as little as 20 minutes of exercise three days per week to fall asleep faster and get higher-quality rest (Kredlow et al. 2015).

3. **Set a specific bedtime and wake-up time.** Be consistent, even on the weekends, because extra hours of sleep can keep kids (and adults) from feeling sleepy the night before they have to get up early again.

4. **Create a bedtime routine.** A habitual relaxation time triggers the secretion of melatonin from the pineal gland in the center of the brain. This hormone slows brain waves, causing drowsiness and relaxation. Snuggling with a stuffed animal or special blanket can add comfort (but be sure to discourage additional toys, especially ones that are stimulating). Soft sheets, room-darkening shades, and relative quiet can also send signals to the brain that it's time for sleep.

5. **Turn off the TV, e-tablet, cell phone, and computer two hours before bed.** Research indicates the light from electronic devices can interfere with the production of melatonin. Even a half hour of TV before bed can rob your child of up to two hours of sleep (Figueiro et al. 2009).

6. **Turn down the heat.** Melatonin also regulates the drop in body temperature needed for sleep. You can help by setting the room temperature between 65 and 70 degrees, cover your child with a light blanket, and make sure pajamas aren't too hot. (*Hint:* Cut the feet off pajama bottoms to help your child maintain a comfortable sleeping temperature.)

7. **Wait until morning to approach stressful subjects.** The stress hormone cortisol is produced in the brain to regulate blood sugar and immune response, among other things. Confronting your child right before bed can raise cortisol levels, keeping her wired all night. Besides, she'll be fresher and more able to deal with the uncomfortable topic you need to discuss with her after a good night's sleep.

8. **Respect bedtime fears.** Sometimes all it takes to decrease your child's monster-induced cortisol levels is for you to give the closet and the space under the bed a thorough check. If she still worries, try using a favorite toy to "stand guard" after the lights go out. Another option: Get a lavender spray made with essential oil and call it "monster repellent." Not only will the lavender ward off imaginary

beasts, but this oil is also thought to help people sleep. (Avoid commercial bathroom fresheners—the chemicals can be toxic.)

9. **Spend a minute breathing with your child.** This calming yoga practice can help: ask your child to inhale slowly to the count of four and then exhale as you count backward. Repeat the process four to six times, kiss your child on the forehead, whisper "Good night," and leave the room.

10. **Try white noise.** Play music with ocean waves, raindrops, or other calming sounds, or have your child wear foam earplugs. The distraction from outside sounds can help relax your child into sleep.

11. **Talk to your pediatrician if nothing works.** Ongoing trouble with falling asleep, staying asleep, or nightmares may indicate a sleep disorder and require medical attention.

THE REAL DEAL

The Thing That Wouldn't Sleep

Our older daughter had problems sleeping from the time she was born. She was the only infant I knew who slept, at most, eight hours in a 24-hour period. This pattern continued as she got older, yet she needed more sleep. Heck, we needed her to log more z-time to keep us from going insane when she became ultrasensitive, stubborn, and short-tempered from lack of sleep.

We followed every suggestion on the list of strategies to help kids get enough sleep for healthy growth and learning. Her nightly ritual remained the same throughout elementary school—take a bath, brush teeth, read a book and sing prayers together, and then turn out the lights. But we had to experiment with a number of things, like rotating stuffed toys for our daughter to sleep with—her lamb one night, her teddy bear the next. We played white noise, such as ocean surf or steady rain, to slow her brain waves enough to allow her to drift into sleep.

During the day, we tired her out as much as possible with physi-

cal exercise. She played basketball and club soccer, and practiced tae-
kwondo martial arts (eventually becoming a black belt), which also
helped her learn to focus better in school. Our daughter was a sweet-
heart when she got the rest she needed, so we put a lot of effort into
bedtime for her—but she, and we, still suffered after occasional nights
when she woke up often or lay awake into the wee hours.

If you have a child who has difficulty falling or staying asleep, what
works for a while to lull your little one into healing delta waves may
not be effective forever. Be ready to try new things, or similar things in
different combinations, throughout the months and years.

Theta Brain Waves: Slightly Faster Than Delta Waves

Theta waves occur as we fall asleep, dream, wake up, and doze. Meditation also brings about periods of theta brain wave activity. Some of our
best ideas spark in this twilight consciousness because receptivity can
increase. Have you ever rested your eyes for 15 minutes and found yourself rejuvenated with the energy to get through the rest of the day? Or
has a thought come to you while you were dozing and made you jump
up to take care of whatever your subconscious mind solved for you?

That's the power of theta waves.

Your child's mind continually processes information. Theta waves
aid in relaxation and rejuvenation, and researchers think they may help
on a subliminal level to generate new ideas that children can apply to
what they already know.

STIMULATE THETA WAVES FOR CREATIVE, WELL-ADJUSTED KIDS

1. **Listen to music.** Nearly all kinds of music stimulate the areas of the
   brain responsible for creative, abstract thought. Relaxing while
   listening to music can lull brain waves into slower theta cycles, a
   great way to end the day or to recharge in the car on the way to
   gymnastics.

2. **Create a visualization.** Induce theta brain waves by guiding your child on a mental journey. Maybe she's worried about an upcoming test. Ask her to close her eyes, and talk her through what it would look and feel like to be calm and answer questions with ease. Media mogul Oprah Winfrey, Olympians Kerri Walsh Jennings and Misty May-Treanor, actor Jim Carrey, and business giant Andrew Carnegie, to name a few, used creative visualization to program their brains for success.

   Modeling this technique with your child could be the gift that transforms dreams to realized goals throughout her entire life. And if your child gets curious about skydiving, for example, taking her on a mental adventure is a lot safer than jumping out of an airplane!

3. **Get plenty of sleep.** Here's that magic elixir again. Getting enough z's helps the body grow and rejuvenate muscles, bones, and organs. Dream sleep also produces theta waves that some scientists believe promote memory retrieval when learning something new (Payne et al. 2012).

Alpha Brain Waves: Total Physical and Mental Relaxation

When we're in a relaxed, restful state, alpha waves dominate the brain. Scientists agree that these waves are optimal for learning both technical concepts, typically left-brain-hemisphere activities such as math and science, and creative skills, typically right-brain-hemisphere activities such as painting or singing.

Connecting the conscious with the unconscious mind, these waves also transfer information from short-term to long-term memory. It follows then that kids who skimp on alpha waves—that is, those who don't get enough downtime—have trouble remembering things (Payne et al. 2012).

3 WAYS TO GENERATE ALPHA WAVES FOR BETTER LEARNING

1. **Listen to classical or calm music.** Research supports playing mellow music to settle brain waves into a relaxed alpha state to prepare kids for learning. Play a little Mozart, Native American flute, or other calming music during breakfast; in the car on the way to school, a doctor's appointment, or soccer practice; or before homework.

2. **Practice rhythmic breathing.** Some schools in Baltimore have found that yoga meditation—children sitting quietly and listening to their breathing—provides an excellent replacement for detention when kids get into trouble. The rest and relaxation have helped students pay attention in class, and behavior has vastly improved (Gaines 2016). Use focused breathing to help your child hit the reset button after school or during any times of stress. If you breathe together, this could be a good break for you too.

3. **Pause before going to sleep and when awakening.** At the end of a busy day, bedtime rituals that include quiet activities, such as reading a story, help to slow brain waves, improve memory, and prepare for a good night's sleep. Evidence also suggests that waking to soft music or a gentle nudge from Mom or Dad and having a couple of minutes to ease into the morning instead of jumping right out of bed produces alpha waves, optimal for learning.

Beta Brain Waves: The "Thinking" Waves

Beta brain waves occur during daily activities, when attention is directed toward cognitive tasks. Considered the "normal" rhythm, beta waves are generated by the logic centers in the left-brain hemisphere. Being in a beta brain wave state enhances our ability to do the following:

- Think quickly
- Focus
- Set and work toward goals

- Solve problems
- Complete tasks
- Write
- Interact with other people

In other words, we need beta brain waves to conduct our lives, but without alpha-wave downtime, cortisol levels can get too high (the stress hormone, remember?). Your kids are as susceptible to stress caused by beta brain wave overload as you are, possibly more so. On the most elemental level, this is an illustration of the importance of life balance.

Did you get a little stressed reading the last few sentences? Luckily, the solution is simple: choose a couple of activities for generating theta and alpha brain waves from the suggestions above and add them to your family's daily routine. Experiment until you develop a couple of regular habits to slow brain waves for mental and physical well-being. You'll also get to enjoy a little brain wave settling and stress reduction when you slow down to read to your child before bedtime.

6 BETA WAVE BOOSTERS

1. **Pump up your child's heart rate.** Regular exercise gets more oxygen to the brain. Lots of studies show better learning, memory, and concept application in kids who consistently work up a sweat (Sacheck et al. 2015).

2. **Keep your child hydrated.** Drinking water helps the brain regulate temperature, puts kids in a better mood, and keeps them alert for better thinking (Riebl and Davy 2013). When your child gets up in the morning, have him drink water. We're all a little dehydrated after going so many hours without liquids during a good night's sleep. Offer more water when your child gets home from school and after dinner. At first, you may notice lots of bathroom breaks, but after a while, kids' bladders usually adjust.

3. **Get a good night's sleep.** Yep, you guessed it. Sleep is the best possible way to rejuvenate beta brain wave cycles for a new day. Parents who set consistent bedtimes and nighttime rituals reap consistent rewards for both themselves and their kids (see "Getting Enough Much-Needed Delta Waves" on page 17).

4. **Do independent reading, puzzles, or crafts of any kind.** These activities get a healthy set of beta waves cycling because they tend to be relaxing at the same time the brain is actively thinking.

5. **Play "brainpower" games included in each chapter.** The games will assist your child in learning a boatload of practical skills, and you'll have lots of fun, hear very little whining, and deal with far fewer arguments—with you or between siblings.

6. **Help your child set a homework routine.** Working on math problems, reading, and writing are jobs for beta brain waves. The purpose of after-school assignments is to solidify new concepts and practice familiar ones. Kids are habitual creatures and do their best thinking when they sit down to work at about the same time of day in a comfortable environment they're used to.

Gamma Brain Waves: The "Insight Waves"

Although we know little about the speedy gamma brain waves, initial studies show that they're associated with flashes of insight and high-level mental processing. Some say meditation can stimulate short bursts of gamma activity, but more research is required to make any definitive claims. When new information on gamma brain waves is available, you can find it on the *Brain Stages* website: thebrainstages.com.

Brain Waves and Technology: Not as Bad as You Think

Technology is here to stay. We're not going back to lighting our homes with candles, and we're not going back to card catalogs and long days at the library to gather information.

Yes, too much time playing electronic games can tweak your child's brain. Recent studies indicate that long periods of playing video games generate slow theta brain waves. The escape into fantasy from the real world may be part of the allure. People who play a lot of video games produce excess dopamine, the chemical released by the brain that mediates pleasure. So the brain of someone playing a computer game for hours looks the same on an fMRI as the brain of a drug addict.

In addition, brain wave activity shuts down in the prefrontal cortex, an area responsible for producing beta brain waves that help keep people focused. Not surprisingly, an inordinate number of kids who spend a lot time playing electronic games end up on medication for attention deficit hyperactivity disorder (ADHD) (Sheikholeslami et al. 2007).

According to researchers summarizing neuroimaging findings, internet gaming addiction is "associated with structural and functional changes in brain regions involving emotional processing, executive attention, decision making, and cognitive control" (Lin et al. 2012, 2).

But like so many things, video games aren't damaging if played in moderation. Even games kids love that have little or no educational value won't turn their brains to mush if parents set limits to prevent overuse. And lots of games out there can actually help. Many teach new skills, offer interesting information in creative ways, and gradually increase in difficulty as kids master an activity.

In terms of computers in general, there's no doubt they have become more useful in school. In fact, more and more classrooms have students using e-tablets for assignments, and many homeschoolers follow internet curriculums. Computers give kids immediate access to information, games, and exercises that are leveled in accordance with their abilities, and sometimes personalized assignments provided by teachers. Electronics offer convenient ways for students to turn in projects and for teachers to keep records of grades and tests that can be shared with students and parents.

As important as they've become, however, e-readers have been surrounded by controversy regarding comprehension. But Ferris Jabr (2013), writer for *Scientific American,* points out, "Before 1992 most studies concluded that people read slower, less accurately, and less comprehensively on screens than on paper. Studies published since the early 1990s, however, have produced more inconsistent results: a slight majority has confirmed earlier conclusions, but almost as many have found few significant differences in reading speed or comprehension between paper and screens."

Scientists think the gap between the effectiveness of paper versus screens is closing because today's kids use electronic devices from an early age, and their brains are getting wired differently. It's valuable to note that kids who read both print and electronic books seem to end up with the best comprehension (Myrberg and Wiberg 2015).

The important thing to realize as a parent is that children learn language, logic, and social skills best in real-time interaction with the people who care about them (Romeo et al. 2018). But used in moderation, computers can serve many positive purposes—more on that later.

Pediatricians and researchers generally agree that *kids ages 5 to 18 can safely spend up to two hours of cumulative time fixated on screens daily*, including television, e-tablets, cell phones, and any other electronic devices (Jary 2018). So set a timer. That way, you won't forget about your pleasingly occupied child. If you establish screen limits now, the middle and high school years will likely be more pleasant too.

If you haven't yet placed controls on home computers and e-tablets to shield your children from inappropriate web content, consider installing Net Nanny or Symantec Norton Family Premier (Rubenking and Moore 2018). For other highly rated software, check out *PC Magazine*'s latest list of favorites online.

★THE REAL DEAL★
Something Else We Didn't See Coming
When our daughters were in third and fifth grade, my husband and I noticed that arguments broke out between them more often, and they began to snap at us as well. They started calling each other names and using disrespectful phrases that we assumed came from the playground. We knew they hadn't heard that rude language at home—or had they?

One evening after dinner, the girls cleared the table and then went into the family room to turn on the TV while I put the dishes in the dishwasher. When snippets of the show reached me in the kitchen, I discovered where their recent rudeness had come from. Studies point out that kids copy behavior they see and hear, and our daughters were no exception. My husband, Chuck, heard the show too, a kids' program we'd thought was innocuous. It was then we realized that unless we sat with the girls and watched every show with them, we couldn't monitor the language and content for appropriateness.

Instead, we turned off the television from Sunday through Thursday (school nights) and paid more attention to the programs our kids watched on the weekends. Their ridiculous squabbles, name-calling, and disrespectful attitudes stopped. Just like that. Homework was easier to get done too.

The moral of the story: keep the two-hour limit in mind and experiment with screen time as well as program content in your household to see what works best for your family.

LET'S GET STARTED

Now you know some brain basics, including the functions for various brain waves and the ways sleep, exercise, water, and food affect brain growth. Equipped with research to back up *praising effort* rather than smarts, you're ready to embark on your child's journey through elementary school.

Enjoy the ride. It goes fast.

⋆ 3 ⋆

KINDERGARTEN
Beginning Big-Kid School

K indergartners have a lot of energy—they hop, skip, run, or wiggle whenever possible—and they like to play with words or make silly sounds. They don't understand the abstract yet, so wordplay or puns often baffle them. In fact, be careful with teasing and sarcasm because children this age take things literally. If you call your kindergartner "Goofy Face," you'll likely find him stealing into the bathroom to look in the mirror to see what you're talking about.

YOUR KINDERGARTNER'S BRAIN

At the beginning of kindergarten, your child's brain will be close to its adult size and volume. This means your five-year-old is ready for experiences and influences to shape the person she will become. Parts of the brain that control motor function, learning, memory, thought, and creativity are set by your child's fifth birthday, but new neural connections and pathways are still forming and becoming more intricate with every new experience and piece of information. At this stage, either networks continue to grow and become more intricate—or they atrophy.

Since most kindergartners' brains are just beginning to interpret symbols like numerals, they learn best through concrete examples. For instance, counting mixed nuts or multicolored cereal offers yummy incentive for this age group to learn about numbers in context. Forget buying flash cards or workbooks for math practice. You can have much more fun together and build greater understanding using tasty snacks (see pages 57–58 for fun games that teach math concepts).

Similarly, activities like reading together, singing songs, and using the pictures in a story to predict what will happen are effective ways to support your child in learning to read and write (see pages 54–57 for fun language activities). Take advantage of these little folks' curiosity and joy of discovery as often as you can to create lasting, positive memories for you both.

KINDERGARTEN SOCIAL TRAITS

Viewing the world in black and white, five- and six-year-olds begin to develop a firm sense of right and wrong. Don't be surprised if your child starts giving you a hard time for letting a bad word slip or doing other things that don't align with the values he's been learning at home and at school. Leading by example has never been so important in helping him make sense of the world.

Your Relationship

Your kindergartner will look for your approval and want to be taken seriously. Remember, kids this age can't process negative language, so whenever possible, use positive statements and acknowledge your child for a clever thought, a valiant effort, or a job well done. Receiving regular positive feedback builds confidence, a key ingredient in enabling kids to accept constructive criticism and unfavorable consequences for breaking a rule. When sincere compliments become more the norm than the exception, your child's overall behavior will likely improve because he won't want to disappoint you.

Friends

At this age, kids are now able to make simple decisions on their own and can play alone or with other kids without constant parental supervision. Kindergartners take school rules to heart, and they become better at sharing and taking turns with peers. This means they also tend to like to point out when others do something that, in their view, is "against the rules"—even at home. You may have to define how your home life is different from their classroom environment.

Your kindergartner will likely play with lots of different kids this year. Favorite friends will come and go as your child tries new things and finds new interests. As you realize you're no longer at the center of your child's universe, his developing independence may make you feel wistful. Still, this fledgling autonomy is particularly important in a classroom of 20 to 30 kids.

KINDERGARTEN ACADEMICS

Generally speaking, in kindergarten through third grade, kids work hard to learn to read, and from fourth grade on, they read to learn. Remember when kindergarten was a place to do fun projects and learn to take turns? Expectations have changed. The current climate of grade-level education standards, reinforced with national and state tests, requires little folks to reach specified competencies in each subject. Veteran teachers compare today's kindergarten curriculum with first-grade skills of the past.

Bobbie Hatfield (2008), kindergarten teacher of 35 years, points out, "Gone are the days when kindergartners spent their time at school learning how to share, recognize the letters and sounds, and count to 10. Now children have to learn to read and write, and we don't have as much time to spend on skipping, jumping rope, and kids getting along with one another."

When people question whether these young children should be expected to learn academics in kindergarten, Denise Mikkonen (2010), a National Board Certified teacher, says,

If your heart surgeon said "I've been doing everything the same way for the last 20 years," that wouldn't be a good thing. Parents didn't have . . . all this media when they were going to school. The world is different now. Education and expectations are changing because our kids come to school knowing and being able to do more things because of the world we live in.

Due to increased academic expectations (see the list of skills on pages 36–37), half-day programs can no longer take the time to provide the socialization kids received a generation ago. Nowadays, a year or two of preschool experience helps kids adjust to the rigors of kindergarten.

If you are a parent who had the means to take sole care of your child for the first five years, don't worry. Meeting kids for playdates, reading picture books, talking about life, and working on projects like cooking and painting are also great preparation for kindergarten.

To help accommodate children's scholastic and social needs, full-day kindergarten programs are cropping up all over the country. Longer school days help with childcare, and the extra hours in class give kids more time to practice new skills and solve problems using words instead of fists or flying toys.

What kindergarten schedules are available in your area? Find out if your local public school has a program to suit your family's needs. If not, take a field trip to the district office. Most districts have several kinds of programs and will allow children to transfer to another school, space permitting.

Also ask about charter schools, which are publicly funded but run by a group independent of the school board—for example, teachers and parents can operate a charter. These schools generally follow a nontraditional curriculum or focus. Magnet schools may be another option. They emphasize specific areas, such as fine arts or science. Private schools also offer a variety of programs and sometimes give scholarships or allow for reduced tuition arrangements.

Some families educate their children at home due to religious or philosophical reasons, special needs, or skill-related pursuits, such as extra time required for a sport or a musical instrument. You can find a myriad of free programs and curriculums online.

Birthdays Make a Difference

Kindergarten for kids in the United States typically begins at age five, with birthday cutoffs ranging from July 31 (examples: Hawaii, Missouri, Nebraska, and North Dakota) to New Year's Day of the same school year (example: Connecticut). With such a large difference in policies, up to a 16-month gap in age can occur when children move to another state.

Parents' choices can also contribute to a significant age disparity. In the hectic world of work and expensive day care, some parents eagerly enroll children into kindergarten before they turn five. At the same time, other parents opt to give kids with late birthdays an extra year before starting kindergarten, a practice known as "redshirting" (borrowed from college sports giving players a year to mature before adding them to the roster). Children in the same classroom can be more than a year apart in age, and often a world apart in development and maturity.

Why are parents waiting to enroll their children into school in increasing numbers? Some of them simply want to give their kids more time to mature. Kelly Bedard and Elizabeth Dhuey (2006), economists at the University of California, Santa Barbara, published a study that looked at how age affects kids in the long term. After poring over math and science test scores for almost a quarter-million students across 19 countries, they found that younger students not only scored lower overall on standardized tests, but were also less likely to attend college—two powerful incentives for parents to tough out the extra year of preschool or full-time day care.

You might be thinking that late birthday or not, your younger child will do fine in school. After all, your four-year-old knows all the letters and sounds and has a decent vocabulary from all the conversations you've had with her and the many stories you've read together. She may even be reading on her own.

But even if academics in elementary school turn out to be a breeze, social issues often arise in middle school. Those early adolescent years are tough enough without being one of the youngest students in the class. If we go one step further, suppose your son or daughter makes it through middle and high school with flying colors, he or she will likely be at a social and maturity disadvantage in college too.

If the potential for social issues isn't compelling to you, consider this—depending on school district policies, which vary a great deal, promoting intellectually precocious kids to a higher grade (in other words, skipping kindergarten altogether) or starting children early in kindergarten may result in repeating a grade. Here is the worst part: in a study where children were asked what they feared most, they rated repeating a grade just after losing a parent and going blind (Anderson et al. 2003). Though lots of studies emphasize the hit kids take to their self-esteem, the National Association of School Psychologists estimates 30 to 50 percent of American students repeat a grade before high school (Jimerson 2001).

7 SIGNS YOUR CHILD IS READY FOR KINDERGARTEN

1. Listens to simple instructions and then follows them.

2. Puts on a coat and goes to the bathroom without help.

3. Says the alphabet and counts to 20.

4. Holds a pencil and cuts with scissors.

5. Expresses interest in books and retells stories using the pictures.

6. Demonstrates eagerness to learn new things.

7. Takes turns, shares, and plays games with other children.

If you answered "yes" to most and "sometimes" for the rest, your child will probably do fine in kindergarten. But be wary of starting a young child early. Studies show that down the road, children with late birthdays are at a clear disadvantage when their social and academic skills are compared with those of their older same-grade peers.

THE REAL DEAL
Caught Between Principle and Circumstance

Full disclosure. I believe children shouldn't be rushed into kindergarten. At the beginning of every school year, my younger students with late birthdays stood out as less mature. Throughout my 23 years in the classroom, those younger kids tended to struggle—if not academically, then on the playground and in cooperative groups.

But it's not always simple, and I didn't have years of experience when I was faced with this decision myself. At the time our younger daughter was approaching school age, the California cutoff date was December 1. Although her birthday is in late September, my husband and I agreed to hold off on kindergarten, sending her instead to a pre-school with a reputation for fun and playful learning. It seemed like a smart decision, but a month later, we noticed that our little one had lost her ready giggle and the bounce in her step.

"What was the best part of your day at school?" Chuck asked, trying to be positive.

"When you picked me up," she said, her bottom lip quivering. "These kids can't read. They don't even know their letters and sounds. I feel weird there."

My husband and I agonized over what to do. Our daughter could already read and write when the school year began, but she still wet her pants occasionally, and small altercations could lead to dramatic sob fests. We could answer "yes" to all seven kindergarten-readiness criteria, but would she suffer from being one of the youngest in her class?

After talking to several teacher friends, discussing further with my husband, and shedding a few tears of my own, we enrolled her in kindergarten—a week after the school year had started. She did great academically, but truthfully, throughout grade school and even most of high school, she never connected particularly well with her peers.

Once she got to college, she made amazing friends (interestingly, most of them have late birthdays). Near the end of the fall quarter of her senior year, she landed a good job for after graduation. Although she has since changed positions, she continues to support herself in a fulfilling career.

The moral of the story: Children are individuals. As parents, we have to do research to make an informed decision. There will be pros and cons in every situation.

Make It Official

If you've decided to postpone kindergarten a year, it is best to make sure the school district is on board. To make it official, go to the school where you intend to send your child and meet with the principal.

A word of caution: Some principals get pressure from higher administrators to start children in kindergarten by the cutoff date set by the state, the district, or a private school's board of directors. Be kind, but firm. Remember, you and your child are the clients at an elementary school and you know your child better than anyone. Parents have more power than they realize.

Barring specific directives from superiors, most principals will agree to allow parents to start their children a year later, especially if a child's birthday falls after September 1. (In recent years, half the US elementary schools have chosen September 1, or earlier, as the cutoff date to start kindergarten anyway [Education Commission of the States 2014].)

Don't give up on your quest in the face of an uncooperative administrator. In a public system, check with the district office to find out which principals will allow children to enter kindergarten later. Most private schools are willing to negotiate. After all, you have the option to decline to send your child there. In fact, you could get a phone call from a formerly less-than-flexible principal with a change of heart.

Redshirting Parents, Beware!

In several states, kindergarten is not a mandatory grade, so if you don't sign an agreement with the school ahead of time, you could show up a year later to register your child for kindergarten and get a shock. With a change in principals, a faulty memory, or a changed mind, the school may insist on enrolling your child in first grade, skipping kindergarten entirely.

How is this possible when kindergarten has become so academically oriented? Educators have been puzzling over that one for years.

Luckily, many public as well as private schools have figured out that these arbitrary cutoff dates don't mean kids are ready to blend sounds and begin learning to read, or that little fingers are strong and nimble enough to hold a pencil and write something legible. Kindergarten-readiness programs (a step between preschool and kindergarten that gives children an extra year to mature) that "graduate" students to kindergarten have surfaced in many districts throughout the country. Spending another year on the smaller playground beats failing kindergarten.

Visit the websites of your local school district and area private schools to find out what kindergarten-readiness programs are available in your area.

KINDERGARTEN ACADEMIC SKILLS

Language Arts

- Know the letters in the alphabet and the basic sound of each letter.

- Name the author and illustrator of a story and define the role of each in telling the story.

- Talk about the pictures in a story and understand their relationship to the text.

- Compare the adventures and experiences of characters in familiar stories.

- Ask and answer questions about text, and retell familiar stories.

- Identify characters, settings, and major events in a story.

- Ask about unknown words in a text.

- Actively engage in group reading activities with purpose and understanding.

Mathematics

- Know numeral names from 1 to 100, count up to 20 items accurately, and compare groups of objects.

- Understand addition as putting together and subtraction as taking from.

- Work with numbers 11–19, understanding their values and the repetition of numbers 1–9.

- Identify, describe, and create geometric shapes.

- Compare lengths, sizes, and shapes of objects (e.g., buttons, blocks, coins) and classify and count them.

To find out what your child will be expected to master in your area, type into a search engine the name of your state and "education standards K–12." Skills may appear in a different grade in your state's standards.

A Little Time Goes a Long Way

Having limited time during the day doesn't have to keep you from having fun while supporting your child's brain development. You can play the games in this book while running errands and doing household chores. Researchers at MIT found the best thing you can do to boost brainpower is have give-and-take conversations with your kids—nothing formal or planned, just the regular exchange of ideas (Romeo et al. 2018).

Another beneficial thing you can do is reinforce the concepts your child is learning, both by playing games and by helping with homework assignments, to give those new neural pathways a work out. And, yes, kids have homework in kindergarten nowadays.

Check out the simple steps below to establish good habits early and make your precious time together count.

6 SIMPLE STEPS TO GREAT HOMEWORK RESULTS

1. Find out what stories are being read at school and read them yourself. You'll avoid the "How was school?" / "Fine" conversation killer because you'll know something about what your child has been learning and be able to ask open-ended questions.

2. Set up a place for your son or daughter to do homework that has plenty of light and table space and no distractions like the television.

3. Get your child in the habit of doing schoolwork around the same time every day.

4. Check assignments to catch careless mistakes, blank lines that require an answer, or misinterpreted directions.

5. Model desired behavior, such as reading for pleasure.

6. Never *do* your child's homework.

Are you rolling your eyes at the last one on the list? Stress makes people do weird things. In my two-plus decades of teaching kindergarten through sixth grades, every year I received assignments completed in parents' handwriting. They weren't bad parents—just crazy busy.

On their own, kids often wait until the last minute to do homework, so they become tired and uncooperative. Time gets short, and parents do the homework out of desperation. Worse, teachers often dismiss it as an isolated breech of sanity, so when the next race against the clock hits, the parent decides to slap down the answers again real quick.

Your child is better off turning in unfinished work with a promise of a specific time for completion. Help by making sure she keeps that promise. Catch bad habits early or they will haunt you in later grades.

FAMILY COMMUNICATION: POWER TO THE WHITEBOARD!

Your child is starting big-kid school where life will get more hectic: school events, classroom performances, fund-raiser deadlines, and dance or baseball practice. If you haven't already started a family organization system or you'd like a new one, the whiteboard was an indispensable tool in our family. Feel free to make modifications to meet your needs.

- Get a split whiteboard/bulletin board to hang in a prominent place in the house (ours was in the kitchen). Make sure your kindergartner can reach it or provide a stool.

- With a dry-erase marker, list the days of the week on the whiteboard side with plenty of room for family members to write under the name of each day.

- Write in regular weekly activities under the appropriate day in blue. Draw symbols (e.g., a baseball bat, a stick figure dancer) next to the words so your child can "read" the board.

- Add events or appointments specific to a particular day in red. Use symbols next to the words whenever possible.

- Use the bulletin board side to pin up flyers, phone lists, and important reminders.

- Encourage your kindergartner to note birthday parties or other activities on the board using a combination of letters and pictures. This will help your child become more invested in the family schedule and improve his reading and writing skills.

THE REAL DEAL
The Tragedy Before the Whiteboard

My husband and I waited six years to have our first child. Two and a half years later, our second little girl arrived. I had thought I was quite the authority on parent/child relationships early on in my teaching career as a childless, 20-something. Problems seemed black and white. Once our daughters entered elementary school, at the same school where I taught, they helped me discover the gray, sometimes psychedelic, reality of raising children.

Despite my 10 years in teaching, I was a nervous parent when my older daughter started kindergarten. I began to understand that things most teachers insisted were "common sense" weren't always obvious.

For example, the importance of family communication became a glaring beacon in December of that year. My daughter gave her dad a flyer from school to inform parents of the upcoming winter pageant her class had been working on for the past couple of months. She had talked about the songs she was learning at school, but I didn't realize there was a formal presentation. I never saw the announcement, and Chuck assumed two things: I worked at the school, so I must have known about the event, and I wouldn't be able to make it since I would be teaching first grade during the scheduled time.

My daughter's teacher came into the staff room that day, beaming and gushing about how beautifully the children had performed. Then she told me my daughter looked sad and asked why I wasn't there. The teacher would have been happy to have my whole class come in to watch the kids sing. Somehow, none of this was mentioned before that moment, and I burst into tears.

After that painful experience, we put together the whiteboard system to make sure we never missed another important event—and it worked!

Busy Parents Can Go to School Too

Parents who spend a little time at school can make a big difference in their children's education. Show up for parent conferences and follow up with your child by sharing the information you learn from the teacher. If you can, juggle obligations and squeeze in an hour a week (or month or semester) to volunteer in your kindergartner's classroom. Arrange ahead of time to chaperone on a field trip, attend an awards ceremony, visit the book fair, help at the school carnival, or do whatever may be important to your child. Participating in the school environment sends a positive message about the importance of education and keeps you up to date on class themes and projects.

Annie Stencil (2008), kindergarten teacher of 10 years and mother of three sons in Southern California, says, "Make the effort to go to at least one event during the year. It shows that you care, that what your children do matters, and makes kids feel important when their peers and teachers see their parents at school."

How Much Is Too Much?

Support for learning at home and at school gives kids an enormous advantage, but parents who catch or cushion every fall or who shelter their child from every possible physical, emotional, or social bruise do more harm than good.

Our job as parents is to work ourselves out of a job—that is, to raise well-adjusted, independent members of society. Beginning in kindergarten, if moms and dads constantly make sure the library book goes into the backpack on library day, do the last few problems on the math worksheet, or second-guess the teacher when their child receives a poor mark or gets disciplined, how can kids learn to take personal responsibility?

If you teach your child how to be accountable now, you'll invest more time and energy in the short term, but those early practiced skills have amazing sticking power. You still remember songs, sayings, and poems you learned when you were five or six years old, right? That's because neural pathways are forming, connecting, and pruning away unused neurons at top speed.

Responsible, busy parents sometimes do everything for their kids because it's easier and faster. Teaching five- and six-year-olds how to take care of their own things requires time and patience. It can be exhausting to constantly supervise little folks in checking for specific items in the homework folder or remind them to put a library book in a special spot in the house.

Studies show it takes between three weeks and several months to practice an action consistently to form a new habit. Since a child grows and changes so much, parents may have to help their kids get organized at the beginning of every school year for several years running before kids begin to organize themselves. But if children have had sufficient practice and support in the early years, a true understanding of personal accountability will empower them into adulthood.

In the primary grades (K–3), some children take longer than a few weeks to develop independence. Parents may also have to step in periodically for refreshers or to reinforce good homework habits. But if you consistently practice for a few weeks at the beginning of each school year, you'll avoid frantic searches for homework or books the morning they're due, saving yourself time and headaches.

Be prepared, though. Even with support from home, sometimes kindergartners still forget to take their homework folders out of their backpacks and turn them in. That gets extra wearisome after you've spent precious energy to help with and check work during the week. Usually teachers remind students to turn in homework, but occasionally these young ones still miss the cue. Most children learn the lesson after they suffer the consequences, whatever those may be in any given classroom. Whether it's a time-out at recess or a missed opportunity to check out a new library book for the week, your child will survive and learn in the process.

Keep an Open Dialogue at Home

In our fast-paced lives, we have to create space for our children to talk about what happens at school and home to help them mentally process experiences. Kids' neural pathways at this age are actively forming, but they are still incomplete. Kindergartners also see the world through a lens of limited experience. Without regular conversations with you in a safe environment, an issue with a classmate or the teacher may not become apparent until your child starts mouthing off to adults or hitting other kids. Worse, hurt feelings can cause silent maladies, such as withdrawal from social situations and a loss of confidence.

Ask open-ended questions, ones that require your child to respond with a phrase or a few sentences rather than "yes" or "no" or another one-word answer like "fine" or "good." Actively listen to find out as much as possible to resolve problems as they arise. And if a situation at school sounds outlandish or serious, be aware that kindergartners can wildly misconstrue events.

At Back-to-School Night, when I would present my education program for the year, I always promised parents I wouldn't believe questionable stories their children told me about what goes on at home without talking to them first—and I've heard some crazy ones. Likewise, please investigate disturbing tales your child brings home about other students or the teacher before getting upset or taking action.

THE REAL DEAL

Kindergarten Nightmare

As I drove into the parking lot of the school where I taught first grade and our daughter went to kindergarten, Jessica announced from the booster seat behind me, "Mommy, I think I should kill Mr. Harold."

"You what?" I knew I must have heard her wrong.

"I want to kill Mr. Harold," she said in her chipmunk voice.

I barely jammed on the brakes in time to avoid hitting the SUV in front of us. How could my baby be thinking of snuffing out the kindly old grandfather who brought her best friend to school?

"She's five. She can't mean this," I muttered to myself, watching Mr. Harold take Madeline's hand in the parking lot.

"Madeline would be terribly sad to lose her grandpa," I pointed out, squelching the urge to scream. "And lucky for us, we don't have to decide when someone dies."

I looked at Jessica in the rearview mirror, and goose bumps spread on my arms as I watched her gaze follow Mr. Harold and Madeline walking toward the hallway to the kindergarten classroom.

"But, Mom, he's old and—"

"We're not killing anyone!" I almost shouted as I pulled into a parking space. "Now, grab your backpack."

My mind reeled as I walked to Jessica's classroom with her skipping next to me, like she always did. And who happened to come around the corner, directly toward us in the hallway?

"Hi, Mr. Harold!" Jessica stopped skipping and gave him a hearty wave. I cringed, fearing she'd tell him his time was up.

"Good morning, you two." His warm grin deepened the creases around his eyes and mouth in his pleasantly weathered face.

"Nice to see you." I forced a smile as he turned to leave.

I held my breath the rest of the way down the hall and around the corner, bracing myself for another death threat, but Jessica just started skipping again and didn't say a word. At the door to her classroom, she gave me a quick hug and hung her backpack on the hook with her number.

"Love you, Mommy. See you after school," was all she said before she scampered inside to take her place on the rug next to Madeline.

I prayed under my breath, "God, please don't let Jessica tell Madeline what she told me this morning." Through the door, I saw Jessica sitting on the carpet, her head tilted, her eyes glazed in thought amid the chattering children.

Alone in my classroom, before the bell rang to bring in my students, I called my husband to give him the latest installment of *Raising a Child: Things We Had No Clue Were Coming.*

"Why would she say something like that?" Chuck asked.

"I don't know. I'm freaked."

"They sure missed this one in the parenting books," Chuck said. "Let's talk to her about it at dinner. I'll see you tonight."

After work, I went to pick up our daughter at day care, hoping whatever had been going on in her head that morning had been forgotten. In the kitchen of the converted house, on my way outside to the playground, I ran into Mrs. Elliott, the director. "Is something wrong with Jessica, Mrs. Wilkinson?" she asked.

"Um . . . Why?" I hoped my face didn't give away how much I wanted to crawl under the table.

"She's washed her hands at least 10 times today," Mrs. Elliott said. "When I asked her why, she told me they were dirty, and she couldn't get them clean. I checked to see if she'd gotten ink or glue on them, but her hands looked spotless to me."

"I'll . . . ask her about it."

Our little girl seemed to be becoming unhinged, but at least she hadn't stabbed anyone with a pencil.

On the way home in the van, I glanced over my shoulder to see Jessica closely inspecting her palms. I wondered who this crazy child was and where she had hidden our daughter.

"Can I push the button on the garage door opener?" she asked as we pulled into the driveway.

"Sure." I was grateful for the normal request and handed her the small plastic box.

While we waited for the door to slide up, she said, "I should kill Madeline's grandma too. Mrs. Harold would be all alone without Mr. Harold."

"No one's killing anyone!"

The van screeched into the garage, and I slammed on the brakes. My heart pounded. I'd somehow failed as a parent. Already. Before she even hit puberty. I thought seriously about running away from home. I sucked in a deep, shaky breath to keep the tears from spilling down my face as we made our way into the kitchen.

Chuck greeted us with outstretched arms. "How's my little bear?"

"Daddy!" Jessica yelled and slammed into his legs in a full-body hug.

He bent down to embrace her and then poked at her ribs. I listened to her giggle as I set the table for us to eat the veggie and chicken dish Chuck had whipped up in the wok.

"Let's eat," I said, feeling better with the hug and tickle ritual.

"I gotta wash my hands!" Jessica shouted and darted from the room.

I gave Chuck a quick summary of my conversation with the day care director before Jessica dashed back into the kitchen and plopped onto her chair at the table.

"Hey, why the big hurry to wash your hands, Jess?" Chuck asked, spooning chicken and vegetables onto her plate. "I'm glad you remembered without being reminded, but you seemed like you were scared."

"Mommy read me a book about yucky germs last night. It said you can get sick if you don't wash your hands. And I'm not getting sick." She shook her head hard enough to get dizzy. "No way."

Chuck stole a confused glance at me. "That must have been some book."

"Daddy?" Jessica's doe eyes gazed up at him in earnest. "Is Licorice ever coming home?" She hadn't mentioned our beloved mutt since that heart-wrenching talk a couple months ago, just after we had him put to sleep.

"No, Little Bear." Chuck's chest deflated as he put a gentle hand on her arm. "Licorice can't come home, remember?"

Jessica's eyes filled with tears. "But I want him to lick my face and wake me up in the morning." She folded her arms on the table and laid her head on them.

"Licorice was old and sick," Chuck reminded her. "It would've been cruel to keep our doggie alive when he was in so much pain."

"I miss him too, sweetie," I said and stroked her hair.

My breath caught. That was it—the reason she'd been acting like such a nut. "Jess, are you afraid doctors put people who get sick or grow old to sleep forever, like our dog?"

She covered her head with her little hands and nodded into her arms.

"Come here." Chuck pulled her onto his lap. "We all loved Licorice, but animals are different from people. It's even against the law to put a person to sleep like that, no matter how sick."

She looked up at her dad with serious eyes, then at me, and back at Chuck. "You promise you and Mommy won't get put to sleep?"

"We're going to be around for a long time. I promise." He tightened his big daddy arms around her, and she pressed her cheek against his chest.

*   *   *

Years later, we all laugh about Jessica's childhood thoughts of offing the elderly, and we have a lovable golden retriever mix named Alice. But our daughter's belated reaction over the loss of our beloved dog, in her kindergartner's head, made perfect sense: If a dog could be put to sleep in old age, an elderly person could undergo the same fate.

Jonathan Gale (2009), clinical psychologist in La Jolla, California, advises,

> When serious changes occur within the family, such as a death
> or divorce, if a child isolates [himself], has trouble focusing in

school or getting along with peers, or displays a disturbing consistent change in behavior over a period of a few weeks, parents should seek professional help. Sometimes an outside person, especially if parents struggle with their own grief and turmoil over a loss, can clarify problems and lend support to get children through a difficult transition.

Although Jessica's example is extreme, misinterpretation of comments or events is common for kindergartners. If your child struggles with a problem at school, make an appointment with the teacher to get another perspective.

5 QUESTIONS TO ASK ABOUT SCHOOL TO GET REAL ANSWERS

Many parents complain that when they ask their children what happened in school, they say, "Nothing." Try asking these specific questions to get the conversation going and gain some insight into the school day:

1. What songs did you sing (or stories did you read) at rug time today?

2. Who did you play with at recess, and what did you do together?

3. Which school project did you like best today, and what did you like about it?

4. Who did you work with in class today, and what did you work on?

5. What do you wish you could do better?

Parent-Teacher Communication

Call and leave a message at the school, or email the teacher to set up a time to talk. Remember, unless the teacher prepares for a change in the schedule, a meeting right before the school day begins or during school hours takes time away from preparation for the day's activities or from the students. Usually teachers will gladly meet with parents or speak with them on the phone after their students leave for the day.

Ask innocuous, nonthreatening questions. For example: "My child tells me [fill in the blank]. Can you tell me your take on what happened in the classroom today?"

The teacher might fill in a missing piece of information—such as a misunderstood direction from the teacher or a hurtful comment (intentional or not) by another child—that will put things into perspective and shed light on how to solve a social issue. Once parents understand the full story, usually things can be worked out.

But what about when your child misbehaves or has some other problem at school?

The Dreaded Phone Call

It's hard to hear bad news, especially about our children. In kindergarten, the most common behavior problems get handled in the classroom—trouble with sharing, taking turns, self-control, or completing assignments. Generally, a teacher won't make a phone call unless your support is needed to solve a problem. For instance, your child may get overwhelmed with certain academic activities and shut down, so the teacher might want to modify projects and enlist your help to finish them at home.

A close friend of mine got a call from the principal at her son's school. Her normally mild-mannered tyke smashed a banana into another kindergartner's back. The kids, parents, and teacher got together to talk out the situation.

If you should get a call about an incident or a negative pattern at school, it's important to remember that you and the teacher are on the same side. The teacher's intention is not to tattle or blame you for problem behavior, but to get your help.

Make an appointment to meet and discuss the situation in depth. Together, you can come up with a plan for modifying troubling behavior that can be consistently implemented at home and at school. I am happy to report that after some talking and a review of the school rules, my friend's son now keeps his bananas to himself, and the kids are good friends.

THE BEHAVIOR CONTRACT

Gasp. Your child's teacher calls to tell you your little angel hasn't been so angelic. This does *not* mean you are a terrible parent! Children are individuals who make decisions. Your job is to redirect negative behavior and turn this into a learning opportunity. Besides, with a positive outcome, you'll have a fun story to tell your grandchildren.

To break negative patterns at school, I have found the most effective method is a behavior contract, developed by the teacher, the parents (both Mom and Dad, if possible), and the child.

Contract Details

For the best results, do the following:

- List no more than three desired behaviors.

- Make a chart (teacher or parents) to be passed daily from school to home and back.

- Break the school day into bite-size, doable blocks of time.

- Use symbols to denote success or failure in given periods of time.

- Sign the agreement—all parties, including the child.

- Give rewards for success, different for two, three, four, or five good marks in a day (e.g., after-dinner board game, special video time, or a Mommy or Daddy date at the park). *Note:* Do not offer material incentives such as junk food, toys, or money. "Payment" for fulfilling normal responsibilities sets a dangerous precedent.

- Quickly impose consistent negative consequences for failure to achieve the goals (e.g., impose something the child does not like, such as extra chores, or take away something the child does like, such as recreational screen time). *Note:* You'll need to make the distinction between the roles of technology—as entertainment and as a tool to find information or complete school assignments—and treat these uses differently.

- Be patient. If you communicate with the teacher daily, the process will take several weeks since new habits take time.

- Be kind to yourself. Don't beat yourself up if mistakes get made along the way. Just do your best to fix them and move on.

Sample Behavior Contract

1. Brandy raises her hand and waits to be called before giving answers to questions in class.

2. Brandy keeps her hands and materials to herself.

3. Brandy finishes her work.

Behavior	Mon	Tues	Wed	Thurs	Fri	Initials
Rug time a.m.	☺	☺	☺	☺	😐	PW
Small group #1	☺	☹	☺	☺	☺	PW
Small group #2	☹	☹	☺	☺	☺	PW
Snack/recess	😐	☹	☹	😐	☺	PW
Rug time p.m.	☺	☺	😐	😐	☺	PW

Teacher/Parent Comments:

Mon. Good day, but during group #2, wrote on another child's paper.

Tues. Rough day outside of rug time, had to sit alone during group work and take a time-out at recess for poking other kids.

Wed. Best day so far! Still working on taking turns at recess.

Thurs. Nice start, getting better.

Fri. Looks like we're getting the hang of things, no pushing or yelling and shared materials nicely.

Teacher Signature_____ Parent Signature_____

Child Signature_____

Attention Deficit Hyperactivity Disorder

People used to talk about spirited and scatterbrained kids in the classroom. Since then, with the help of positron emission tomography (PET) scans and other imaging tests, scientists have discovered that neurotransmitters and electrical impulses behave differently in some people's brains.

One in 10 kids in the United States is diagnosed with attention deficit hyperactivity disorder (ADHD). Symptoms include difficulty attending to conversations, staying on task, sitting still, remembering things, and falling asleep. Although a classroom behavior contract helps develop firm, consistent boundaries coordinated between home and school, sometimes more help is needed.

Often educators recognize ADHD symptoms, but they aren't qualified to diagnose the disorder. They can merely suggest parents seek a pediatrician's opinion. Only a medical professional can legally identify the condition. Due to maturity issues, doctors are reluctant to diagnose ADHD before age six.

Most pediatricians (or specialists such as psychiatrists) ask parents to fill out a questionnaire to determine if a child has an attention disorder. Each answer to a question is assigned a point value. If the total score falls within a given range, a child might be diagnosed with ADHD. One treatment or intervention for the disorder is medication that helps a child focus or relax enough to participate more appropriately in the classroom. The doctor might also recommend other treatment modalities for improving focus, such as behavior therapy and education strategies.

Before handing over medication, you may want to see a "map" of your child's brain that shows the electrical activity in various parts. You may be surprised to discover that your child's brain works fine. In that case, allowing time to grow as well as setting specific rules with consistent consequences, both positive and negative, may help your child's focusing issues and self-control. On the other hand, if there is a problem, a brain map can help determine the best course of action to alleviate attention and impulsivity issues.

To learn more about attention deficit disorders, visit the *ADDi-tude* magazine website: additudemag.com. Everything a parent needs to know about symptoms, diagnosis, medication, parenting tips, and help for your marriage while raising ADHD kids is included on the site. Parents can also subscribe to a monthly e-letter and the magazine via the website.

THE REAL DEAL

Sometimes Things Aren't What They Seem

My oldest daughter showed signs of ADHD in kindergarten. Her teacher suggested I talk to our pediatrician because our little girl spaced out during class and missed directions, lost concentration during projects, and forgot to turn in completed assignments. When we took her to the doctor, he gave Chuck and me diagnostic forms to fill out independently of each other. Using this method, we discovered that my daughter was a clear candidate for prescription drugs.

But giving our five-year-old psychotropic medication seemed like a big step. Her dad and I decided we needed more conclusive evidence than behavioral observations and scores we'd recorded on forms. Because our medical insurance didn't cover it, we paid the extra money for a "brain map" to show us what was going on inside our daughter's head.

Although counterintuitive, medications for ADHD are stimulants that cause neurons to fire faster and more efficiently, thus controlling impulsivity and improving the ability to concentrate for longer periods. My daughter, however, did not have areas in her brain where electrical activity moved slowly. Instead, her neurons fired too fast, causing her to become distracted, to lose focus to the point of forgetting what she was doing in the middle of a task. Had we given her the stimulant the doctor would have prescribed, Chuck and I could have caused much greater problems for our daughter. Revving up a brain that's already in high gear can't be a good thing.

Based on the results, we were able to choose effective therapies, along with strategies we could easily implement at home. For example, we color-coded folders to make assignments easier to find, helped our daughter make checklists to go over before turning in assignments, and encouraged her to ask questions when she didn't catch the directions, rather than guessing at how the teacher wanted projects to be done.

The process helped our daughter learn how to cope in school with less frustration in the classroom as well as in other areas of her life. This is not to say that medication is always a bad thing. In some cases, prescription drugs can be a salvation. Just make sure to do some homework to figure out what will work best for your child.

Keeping Kinders' Interest

Keeping almost any kindergartner's mind on task can be a challenge, in or out of the classroom. At this age, kids are curious about everything and ask questions like "Where does the sun go at night?" But it is not uncommon for a five- or six-year-old to take off after a moth while you're answering his question.

To keep an active, young mind focused and engaged, try involving your child in the explanation. For example, to explain how day turns into night, have him direct a flashlight beam onto your body and watch what happens as you turn around. Then switch places. Shine the light on your little "planet" for him to see the change from light to dark as he turns in place. If that moth still upstages you, don't worry. There's plenty of time to absorb life's little truths.

Watch for what renowned physician, educator, and philosopher Maria Montessori called a "sensitive period." She pointed out that a subject sparking a child's curiosity will take learning to new heights if that interest is fed. Parents are the perfect catalysts to provide concepts about space, zoo animals, dinosaurs, reading, counting money, or whatever excites their children. At home, there is more flexibility to nourish immediate interests than at school with a room full of kids. And fun activities that sharpen skills, like the ones on the following pages, will bring you closer and never seem like work.

5 WAYS TO KICK-START KINDER KIDS IN LANGUAGE ARTS

1. **Read!** Picture books, to-do lists, cereal boxes, street signs—any printed material. Have fun with expression, and use your finger to track the words as you read picture books. For favorite books you've read a gazillion times, invite your child to retell you the story using the pictures. This activity builds vocabulary and comprehension, and before you know it, your kindergartner will recognize the words!

2. **Play I Spy on car rides.** Decide on an object you see—for example, a train whizzing by—and use the first letter sound to start the game. Say: "I spy, with my big [green] eyes, something that starts with the letter *T*." Other passengers in the car may ask collectively for three more clues like "Does it have wheels?" or "Is it alive?" Players have three chances to guess the object. The player who comes up with the correct object chooses the next item. If all three guesses are wrong, the original player reveals the object and takes another turn. This game keeps kids occupied, builds observation skills, and polishes letter/sound recognition.

3. **Have fun with "The Name Game" song.** Originally recorded by Shirley Ellis in 1964, "The Name Game" sets the stage for people to make up songs using family members' and friends' names with nonsensical syllables. For example:

   Ruben, Ruben, bo-bu-ben / Bo-na-na fanna fo-fuben / Fee fi mo-mu-ben / Ruben!

   Shanda, Shanda, bo-ban-da / Bo-na-na fanna fo-fanda / Fee fi mo-man-da / Shanda!

   Jenny, Jenny, bo-ben-ny / Bo-na-na fanna fo-fen-ny / Fee fi mo-men-ny / Jenny!

   This game creates phonemic awareness, or consciousness of sounds. Eventually kids put letter sounds together to read and write words. But making up songs with everyone's name is fun even if your child can already read. Visit thenamegame-generator.com to get started.

4. **Put on some children's music.** It's hard to be "on" all the time, so use some tools. Music is a great one! Kids' songs offer humor and information that sticks in children's minds along with the melodies.

5. **Rhyme your hearts out.** For a great pastime in the car or as you wait in the dentist's office, make up nonsense rhymes and invite your child to add to the list. For example:

You: "I lost my mitt down the pit."

Child: "Here I sit and have a fit."

Or you and your kindergartner can take turns listing as many words (real or made up) as you can with the same ending and new beginning sounds—for example, yellow, mellow, wellow, cello, bellow, dellow, fellow, hello, kello, Jell-O. This game also helps kids differentiate sounds and prepares them for reading.

PINKY PUSH-UPS: WHEN WHEATIES AREN'T ENOUGH

One of my big gripes about schools is that teachers are forced to make kindergartners write before they've developed enough strength or coordination to grip a pencil correctly—between the thumb and index finger, resting on the middle finger.

Five- and six-year-olds are expected to write numbers, sentences, and simple stories nowadays, but achy hands, with two or three fingers bunched to support the pencil against the thumb, can make writing physically and mentally exhausting. Luckily, the fun activities below can connect neural pathways and build dexterity for holding pencils, pens, and crayons.

1. **Writing in salt.** Put a thin layer of salt on a cookie sheet or at the bottom of a baking pan and have your child practice "finger writing" the letters and words they're practicing in class that week. The tactile grains of salt and the large movements will help solidify your child's ability to form the letters while strengthening finger muscles.

   Note: It's fun to make play dough out of the salt when your child finishes. Here's the recipe: 1 cup flour, 1 cup warm water, 2 teaspoons cream of tartar, 1 teaspoon oil, ¼ cup salt, food coloring. Mix all ingredients, adding food coloring last. Stir over medium heat until smooth. Remove from pan and knead until blended smooth. Place in plastic bag or airtight container when cooled.

2. **Roll snakes.** Speaking of dough, your child can roll "snakes" to spell out words. Even molding figures strengthens fingers to make writing numbers and letters a breeze. If you don't have dough or modeling clay already, and you don't have time to make some, it's inexpensive and available in stores where toys are sold.

3. **Build.** Your son or daughter can use playing cards, Legos, blocks, cereal boxes, cans, or anything else in the pantry to build houses, cities—whatever strikes your child's imagination! Picking up, stacking, balancing, and snapping objects together give those manual muscles a good workout.

4. **Make jewelry.** Have your child string plastic or wooden beads to create sentimental gifts for grandmas, aunts, cousins, and friends. Stringing beads steadies little hands—and melts hearts.

5. **Sew.** Invite your kinder kid to stitch with a kid-sized needle and thread (available where toys are sold) while you mend socks and replace missing buttons or do other chores. Sewing builds fine motor coordination and is a good skill to know.

50 HIGH-FREQUENCY WORDS: THE LEG UP IN LANGUAGE ARTS

Knowing high-frequency words helps in both reading and writing—a simple task with big results. Spell the words aloud in the car or in line at the grocery store, and ask your child to "guess" the word. Once your child knows quite a few, ask him to spell words for you to "guess."

At night when you read together, point out some of these words, but don't interrupt the story too much or your kindergartner could get frustrated. In time, he may point out words on his own. When that happens, have him choose a couple of pages to do a treasure hunt to find all the words he knows. He can mark dots next to the words in the grid below.

When he can read and spell all the words, do something special to celebrate, like take a trip to the library, the park, or a local museum.

a	all	an	and	are
as	at	be	but	by
can	each	for	from	had
have	he	his	how	I
in	is	it	not	of
on	one	or	other	out
said	see	some	that	the
there	they	this	to	up
use	was	we	were	what
when	with	word	you	your

4 FUN WAYS TO KICK-START KINDER KIDS IN MATH

When there are so many convenient items available to discover math in the spirit of play, why risk burning out a kindergartner on worksheets? Skills books from the drugstore provide some drill and practice, but even if your child enthusiastically fills out pages at first, once the novelty wears off, attitudes can sour on doing homework and completing school projects. Extra paperwork is completely unnecessary when motivating math materials are available at your fingertips. Once your child learns how to play the following games, she can play while you do family chores.

1. **Make delicious patterns.** Fruit Loops, mixed nuts, or any yummy items that can be categorized, put into color groups, or set into repeating patterns make a good afternoon snack and the perfect tool for learning math concepts. (*Hint:* Math is full of repeating patterns. Putting cashews, almonds, and pecans into a certain order will form neural pathways that will connect as number patterns later.)

2. **Put together stealthy fact families.** Start with five raisins, Cheerios, or gummy bears. Have your child put those objects on a flat surface and cover different amounts of objects with her hand. Then ask her how many she's hiding given the number of objects she can see. At first, she'll guess, but soon, she'll count. If she needs a little push, model counting up on your fingers. At the end of the game, she gets to enjoy the fun snack as a reward!

   On another day, have her pick a number between 1 and 10 (give help if needed) and have her play the hiding game again. At first, she may need help with covering different numbers of objects, but she'll be an expert in no time. Manipulating objects to understand how numbers work provides a strong base for learning math concepts.

3. **Take advantage of those pesky coins.** When your wallet or family jar fills with coins, ask your kindergartner to group them. This easy activity is good for learning how to compare and categorize objects.

4. **Sort anything.** Toys, shoes, socks, storage containers, fruit, vegetables, crayons, buttons—use any items that can be put into groups with similar attributes. This activity sharpens grouping skills that follow kids all the way to algebra and beyond!

Note: These activities also strengthen hand muscles for better writing.

The Best Things in Life Are Free!

Some of your child's best learning will occur when you are out together and you stumble upon occasions for him to apply concepts introduced at school. Most cities and towns have websites and at least one regional publication that lists fun places for families to go for free or for minimal cost: concerts in public parks, story times in libraries, community centers with all kinds of activities, and nature preserves with hiking trails, to name a few.

Find out what activities your community offers and take advantage of that wide-eyed kindergarten curiosity. You never know where your child's next "sensitive period" or passion for learning will take you. And while tagging along on your child's road to discovery, you'll also expand your own world.

KINDERGARTEN OUTSIDE THE NORM

What if your kindergartner struggles with picking up letter sounds or counting pennies? Or what about the flip side of the equation? Your child already reads picture books aloud at home, and if you promise five M&Ms and pull two out of the bag, you get an automatic demand for three more. Will the teacher give assignments that keep your son or daughter interested in school?

Remember, human beings learn new skills at different rates, so don't panic. There is a lot you can do to help your kindergartner either catch up or stay excited about learning.

The Tortoise

If your kindergartner is behind many of her peers in school, be patient. She may grapple for months with a task in kindergarten that she masters within a few days in first grade because the neural pathways have formed to support learning the concept.

If you read to your child daily, play games sometimes, and help with homework consistently, you can relax. Just do your best to keep the activities fun. Kids operate on their own timetable, not always the schedules adults set for them. Besides, slow and steady often wins the race.

RED LIGHT, GREEN LIGHT: END *B* AND *D* CONFUSION

Follow these simple steps to help your child make a habit of forming these two tricky letters correctly and you will save a world of frustration for both of you! Play Red Light, Green Light for several days in a row, and watch your child's handwriting transform!

1. Use lined paper with extra wide spaces if possible. Use a green crayon to put a dot where the letter begins (the "green light" for go) and use a red crayon to place a dot where forming the letter ends (the "red light" for stop). Crayons work best because kids can feel wax on the paper better than they can feel graphite from a pencil or ink from a pen.

   A lowercase *b* starts at the top line, goes down to the bottom line, and then back up to the middle line and around to form the "belly." As your child practices the letter, say together "down, up, and around." A lowercase *d* begins just below the middle line, goes up to the middle line and around to form the "derriere," and then reaches all the way up to the top line and goes back down to the bottom line. Have your child say with you "around, up, and down."

2. Write green dots to form the whole letter in the beginning for your child to trace and place only one red dot where to stop. Watch to make sure your child begins and ends the letter in the right place.

3. When your child feels comfortable with tracing the letters, drop most of the dots. Place only a green dot to mark where the letter begins and a red dot where the letter is to end. *Hint:* Get a crayon sharpener (pencil sharpeners work too). Making red and green lights with dull crayons can make them bigger than optimal.

4. If your child still reverses a letter using green and red lights, help create a tactile memory by writing the entire letter with a green crayon. Then gently guide the pencil in his hand to trace the letter 10 times as consistently as possible.

RED LIGHT, GREEN LIGHT VARIATION
GET WORDS AND SENTENCES GOING LEFT TO RIGHT

1. Use lined paper and remind your child that green means "go."

2. With a green crayon and a ruler, draw a heavy vertical line down the left margin of the paper or put a green dot at the beginning of each line on the page.

3. With a red crayon, draw a heavy vertical line down the right margin of the paper or put a red dot at the end of each line on the page. *Note:* Use a crayon because kids can feel the wax—it makes a tactile boundary, unlike pencil, marker, or pen.

4. The green dot or line is the "green light." Ask your child to begin writing, or to go, next to the green light.

5. When your child gets to the red dot or line on the right side of the page say, "Stop. Red light." *Hint:* Using sound effects—revving a pretend car engine to go and mimicking squeaky brakes to stop— helps some kids get into the game.

6. Ask your child to go (start writing again) at the green light on the next line and keep practicing so long as your child is interested. You might be surprised at how many lines your little student will fill.

7. For fill-in-the-blank or individual word answers on homework papers, put a green light or dot at the beginning of the space and a red light or dot at the end of the space.

8. As soon as you think your child is ready, put the crayons in her hand, and have her place the green and red lights on the lined paper or homework paper.

Note: Red Light, Green Light helps in grasping directionality. Truly understanding left and right is a huge help in learning to read. The game also gets children to put margins in the right places on their papers, which will make writing paragraphs, essays, and stories easier in the future too.

Cookin' with Gas: What to Do with Those Brilliant Little Kids

Few people excel at everything. Some kids perform well in academics but struggle with holding a pencil, spend more time arguing with classmates about whose turn it is than they do playing, or avoid interacting much with peers altogether. Jumping rope or catching a ball may elude them.

If your five-year-old is ahead of the other kids now, before you campaign to promote him to first grade, keep in mind that many of his fellow kindergartners will catch up academically and that there is much more to learn in school than math and reading. Going to school with peers of the same age can contribute to the development of the whole child, socially and emotionally as well as academically. Still, skipping a grade to be with intellectual peers instead can be beneficial for some gifted, socially mature children (Makel et al. 2016).

Important: Remember to praise your sharp child for effort rather than achievement. Children who are praised for intelligence rather than tenacity to solve problems often doubt their abilities and want to give up when they run into difficulties (Klein 2000). Convincing a frustrated gifted child that having to work through complications is normal (if he hasn't needed to do it before) is tough but doable. More dangerous is the child who quietly decides he must not be as smart as everyone thought and stops putting effort into assignments or tests.

Teachers look at students' educational needs and plan accordingly as much as possible. Most teachers understand the concept of providing differentiated instruction—that is, kids who can handle harder work receive more challenging assignments within the framework of whatever subject is being taught. The truth is, however, planning activities for varying ability levels presents other problems, such as accusations of "tracking" students or complaints from parents who feel slighted because their child didn't get to do the same activity as their friend's child.

If your kindergartner needs more challenging work than the school provides, try the activities on the next page. A contract can also help you, your child, and his teacher work together as a team to meet your child's needs (see "Contracts for Quick Kids," page 64).

9 WAYS TO KEEP SMART KIDS ENGAGED AT SCHOOL

If your child shows signs of needing more challenging assignments at school, you can do things at home to enrich what she's learning. Find out from the teacher what themes are planned for the year—for example, walking safety, an upcoming holiday, or community workers, such as peace officers, firefighters, and librarians. Then use some of these ideas to expand on the themes and keep your kindergartner engaged.

1. **Enlist the teacher.** Ask for activities you and your child can do together at home in line with the curriculum. If you include the teacher, she may even allow your child to share those projects with the class.

2. **Bring classroom topics to life.** Take your child to a local museum and surf the internet together, affording the opportunity to apply what's presented in the classroom.

3. **Hunt for discovery.** Visit the library to explore books on classroom themes.

4. **Cut and paste.** If you subscribe to magazines, cut out pictures to make a collage of topical pictures.

5. **Conduct home experiments.** Here is a good one for fall: When you carve your jack-o'-lantern for Halloween, keep some of the pumpkin seeds to watch them sprout. Dampen a paper towel, add a few seeds, and press the towel against the inside of a drinking glass. If you add a little water daily, the towel will remain damp, allowing the seeds to germinate. Keep the seeds in a spot that gets some sunlight, and in a few weeks, the seeds will have grown enough roots for your child to plant them in the yard. By next fall, your family will have your own pumpkin patch. For more experiments, visit "Kindergarten Science Activities and Experiments" on education.com.

6. **Keep an art cupboard.** Have lots of different materials on hand so your child has what he needs to do a project when the fancy

strikes—beads, play dough, stickers, paints, scissors, glue, markers, crayons, construction paper.

7. **Make a treasure map.** Write simple directions or draw picture hints, and ask your child to use the information to find a hidden object in your home, in the backyard, or at the public park.

8. **Brainstorm new story endings.** When you read to your child before bedtime, ask her, "What would happen if . . .?" and come up with a different circumstance than in the story. Before long, your child won't need a question to make up a new ending.

9. **Tell the same story in a different setting.** Here is an example based on a classic: Little Red Riding Hood walks through the big city to get to Grandma's house. Who does she meet along the way? Who dresses up as Grandma?

CONTRACTS FOR QUICK KIDS

A concrete set of expectations will support your child, you, and the teacher in keeping your brainy kid engaged at school.

What to Do

1. Make an appointment to meet with the teacher.

2. At the conference, explain the need for enrichment to keep your child involved in school.

3. Find out about the classroom themes for instruction. Consider discussing several themes so you don't have to meet often.

4. Brainstorm with the teacher to create a list of activities to do at home that can be linked to school.

5. Set up a routine for how your child will complete enrichment assignments and ways those projects may be shared with the rest of the

class. *Important:* Your child may take a week or a month to complete activities. No pressure! The object is to keep your child engaged, not burdened or overwhelmed.

6. Invite everyone who participates in the enrichment projects to make quick written comments on the contract. This will encourage investment in accomplishing activities. *Note:* Your child's teacher may do as much or as little as she wishes with the contract. Remember, your child's teacher has many other students to think about.

Example Contract

Theme: Pumpkins

Home	School	Comments
Buy a small pumpkin and guess the number of seeds inside. Write down your prediction.	Take the pumpkin to school and ask kids to guess the number of seeds inside.	Monday (child): I drew a face on my pumpkin.
Cut it open and count the seeds. Check to see how close your guess was to the actual number.	Take the seeds to school in a plastic container. Tell how you counted the seeds and the actual number.	Tuesday (teacher): Thanks for bringing your seeds to class. It was fun to find out how many seeds were in the pumpkin.
Plant some pumpkin seeds in a small container of potting soil and place other seeds on a wet paper towel in a glass.	Share both models with class and have kids predict which will grow better.	Wednesday (child): This was messy, but we got it done.
Bake remaining pumpkin seeds at 350° for 5 minutes, sprinkle salt over them and bake 15 more minutes.	Share baked seeds at snack time with class. Check for sprouts in both the soil and the moist towel.	Thursday (teacher): Yummy snack! Thanks for sharing. Give the seeds a few more days to sprout, okay?

Look up fun facts about pumpkins and print or draw pictures on a piece of paper.	Post the paper in the room for the rest of the class to see and share if time. Check for seed growth.	Friday (child): This was my best week so far. ☺

Note: If your child isn't writing yet, he can dictate comments for you to write.

Also look for fun enrichment pursuits for kids at community centers, libraries, museums, and nature facilities. Parks and recreation departments often present entertaining educational opportunities as well. And online, lots of websites offer thinking games and activities for every possible interest in science, geography, history, music, and art.

If you've tried several of the ideas for engaging smart kids here, yet you still feel your child's needs aren't being met, and you think she is socially mature and would be comfortable going to school with older children, consider talking to the administration about advancing your kindergartner to the first grade. A study in the Netherlands found that children academically advanced compared to their peers who skipped a grade fared comparably socially and emotionally (Hoogeveen 2012), though that isn't always the case. Provided your child's brain is truly ahead and not just in front of other kids because of all the fun stuff you've done together for the past five years, moving up may be a viable option. Bear in mind that there may not be a single right answer or a perfect solution—you may have to weigh a myriad of considerations to determine what's best for your child.

KINDERGARTEN CARE AND FEEDING

Let's talk about the four brain essentials—sleep, fuel, water, and exercise—and some tips about homework and hygiene. You really can comfortably meet your child's needs—and your own—while keeping your sanity. A little routine and a few time-saving ways of doing things can make all the difference.

Sleep: The Ingredient That Can Make or Break School

We already talked about the importance of z-time for your child to produce the delta and theta brain waves needed to build, rejuvenate, and keep her brain healthy (see page 16). Be aware that kindergartners may be thinking more like three-year-olds at school during those busy weeks when they can't get enough sleep. You'll be doing yourself and your child a huge favor if you develop a bedtime routine that begins at the same time most evenings, including weekends.

Dr. Avi Sadeh of Tel Aviv University found that 30 minutes less sleep for three consecutive nights caused the cognitive function of elementary children to operate at two years below their grade levels (2007). Worse, a study found that sleep problems in childhood could predict mental health issues in adolescence (Gregory et al. 2009). Researchers at the Sleep Medicine Laboratory at Technion, Israel Institute of Technology, a world-renowned network of sleep laboratories in Haifa, Israel, found that in addition to lacking brainpower, sleep-deprived children can also suffer from symptoms associated with ADHD (Golan and Pillar 2004). How can kids learn to read, write, and count when they're too tired to think?

Take little Chet: He sleeps about 12 hours at night and needs to crash for an hour or two after he gets home from kindergarten. His mom works at home, and his parents enjoy the alone time in the evening, so it's easy for him to get the sleep he needs.

Araceli, on the other hand, sleeps late on Saturdays to make up for lost sleep on school nights. Her whole family sleeps in on Sunday mornings and goes to the late church service. During the week, no matter what herbal tea Araceli drinks, the bedtime stories her mom reads, or the restful music played in her room, she doesn't drift off to sleep until 10 or 11 o'clock. She must get up at 6 o'clock so her mom can get to work on time, and kindergarten lasts a full day at her school. By lunchtime, her eyelids droop at the picnic table, and she can barely eat. At recess, Araceli perks up to play, but she gets spacey in the afternoons. On Friday, Mrs. Day lets her put her head on the desk after lunch because she gets teary and miserable at the end of the week.

Cary needs more sleep than she gets, too, but her older siblings keep her up with their music or TV shows. Her family also goes to her cousin's house a lot, and they get home after Cary's bedtime. Her parents think she gets along fine at school, but thinking or remembering new things sometimes gets hard, and Cary often misses the teacher's instructions. When she gets crabby, Mrs. Day asks Cary to put her head on a desk during rug time, and she doesn't like that because she misses singing songs with the other kids.

Sean needs 10 hours of sleep every night, and he gets it. There's a strict rule in his house: The TV is off by eight o'clock, and his big brother can listen to music only on headphones. Sean is a high-energy kid during the day, always on the move, but when his head hits the pillow at night, it's like cutting the strings on a marionette. He's out. At school the next day, he's almost always fresh, perky, and ready to learn.

Your child's sleep patterns may be similar to or completely different from those above. *The important thing to know is that the amount of sleep your child gets has a powerful impact on his brain development.*

What about the increasing numbers of pudgy little people? In February 2008, researchers reviewed the results of 17 studies across the United States and Europe and concluded that a consistent lack of sleep also contributes to childhood obesity (Chen et al.). To stave off those junk food cravings and extra pounds, one of the researchers, Youfa Wang, MD, PhD, at the Center for Human Nutrition at Johns Hopkins University, recommends children 5 to 10 years old get at least 10 hours of sleep a day, including naps (Hitti 2008).

Wang acknowledges that some children, because of biological needs or differences in sleep quality, may need fewer hours. More research needs to be done to figure out the connection between the amount of z-time and the extra belly rolls, but Dr. Wang points to three contributing factors: (1) more awake time means more munch time, (2) sleepiness makes for lazy days without exercise, and (3) lack of sleep may cause certain hormones to increase hunger pangs. In short, do everything you can to help your child get enough sleep (Hitti 2008).

Refer to "Getting Enough Much-Needed Delta Waves" on page 17 for ways to support your child in getting the sleep she needs.

After-School Family Routine for Success

Annie Stencil (2008), kindergarten teacher and mom, shares the after-school ritual that works for her family. She admits occasionally life gets in the way, but the family stays as close to the routine as possible.

Annie's son Jaime comes home from kindergarten in the afternoon, has a glass of milk, and eats a snack—cookies, apple slices, or celery sticks slathered with peanut butter. With a full tummy, he plays with his toys or with his little brother, Bryant, for about an hour.

Then Jaime goes to the bathroom, washes his hands, and sits at the kitchen table to do his homework. Stencil begins making dinner as her son takes 20 to 30 minutes to do the math and language assignments for the day. If Jamie gets stuck on something, Annie takes a break from cooking and explains the directions. They do a sample or two together, and Jaime finishes the rest. When he's all done, Stencil checks the work, and they correct mistakes together.

Jaime and Bryant watch TV for 30 minutes to an hour before dinner, depending on how well Jaime stayed on task to finish his homework. He hardly ever misses his favorite afternoon shows anymore because he's lost his TV time more than once for messing around. The boys turn off the television when Stencil calls them to eat. They learned to do this after Dad took away their watching privileges for two days the last time they didn't turn it off and come to the table.

The family sits down to eat dinner together and each member takes a turn to tell about their day. "That family time is what makes all the work of raising kids worth it—for my husband and me to get to *enjoy* our children," Stencil says. "After dinner, we like to play a board game, take the dog for a walk, or just goof around."

Then it's time to take a bath or shower and get ready for bed, complete with Batman pajamas, glow-in-the-dark toothbrushes, and story time. Depending on whose turn it is, one of the boys chooses a book from the shelf for Daddy or Mommy to read. At the end of the story, the little guys get tucked into bed, say their prayers, and the lights go out—except for the night-light that scares off the monsters in the closet.

The Stencils' routine may not work for your family, but you get the idea. Set up your own activities, done in a specific order before bedtime. If you're having trouble sticking to a schedule, sit down as a family and write one out together. Tape it up on the bathroom mirror or the bedroom wall for easy reference. Remember, it takes several weeks to form a new habit. Save yourself a lot of headaches by getting the homework done ahead of bedtime. You'll appreciate the time for yourself after your child goes to bed.

3 WAYS BUSY FAMILIES CAN GET HOMEWORK DONE

1. **Enlist help at day care.** If your child goes to day care after school, ask the provider to make sure the homework gets done before you pick up your son or daughter. You still have to check the work and help make corrections when you get home, but it will take less time than doing the whole assignment. Family time and dinner together is important too!

2. **Keep a toolbox in the car.** If you're on the go, keep a homework kit in a box or bag in the car with pencils, erasers, scissors, a glue stick, and crayons or colored pencils. That way, homework can get done anytime, anywhere. Be sure to check the work together when you get home!

3. **Read before bed, no matter what.** This ritual nurtures a love for books, ensures the daily reading homework gets done, gives you precious time together, and sets the mood for relaxation into sleep.

You Are What You Eat, and Your Kids Are Too

Like it or not, our kids watch us closely. The food we put into our mouths, like everything else we do, is scrutinized under detective-like surveillance. Parents who want their kids to eat healthy have to model the behavior. Be conscious of the food you eat and acknowledge junk food as a treat, so your kids learn the difference between unhealthy eating and occasional indulgences.

Breakfast

Did you know a lot of kids skip breakfast before going to school? Some kids aren't hungry, or they run out of time to eat in the morning (I had one of each). You can't drive a car without putting gas in it, and kids can't do their best thinking without fuel either. Plus, it's a little-known fact that going without breakfast puts on weight. The body's metabolism doesn't kick into gear in the morning without food to break the fast from the night's sleep, so calories burn more slowly. That also means the body, and by extension, the brain, moves sluggishly until it gets revved up with food. No kidding.

An egg, half a piece of wheat toast, and half an orange or apple is an excellent breakfast for a kinder kid, but lots of parents don't have time to prepare a meal in the morning. If cold cereal and milk are on the menu, check the nutrition information for the lowest sugar and highest fiber content possible, and be sure your child drinks the milk left in the bowl. For most processed cereals, the vitamins are sprayed onto the food in the factory. If the milk stays in the bowl, so do the vitamins.

And if you don't have time for your child to eat a bowl of cereal, try giving your kinder kid a banana or apple slices along with a low-sugar, high-fiber granola bar with moderate protein, such as one of the Kashi products. Easy to eat in the car on the way to school, they have the nutrients your child needs for learning.

Be careful not to give your child a sugar rush that will last about 20 minutes and then practically turn off his brain. This happens because sugar hinders the body's absorption of B vitamins, necessary for cognitive thinking, coordination, and memory.

6 QUICK BREAKFASTS TO HELP KINDER KIDS THINK AT SCHOOL

The choices below have carbohydrates for quick energy, fat for vitamin absorption, and fiber and protein for staying power—most can be eaten in the car if you're running late.

1. Half a peanut or nut butter and jelly sandwich and milk or water.

2. A Kashi Chocolate Almond & Sea Salt Chewy Granola Bar (or other brand with low-sugar, high-fiber content) and a banana—the banana provides bulk to stay fuller longer and potassium, an electrolyte required for keeping the brain, heart, kidney, muscle tissue, and other organ systems in good condition.

3. Apple or banana slices slathered with peanut or nut butter and milk.

4. Plain instant oatmeal sweetened with fresh fruit (berries, apple, or banana pieces) and a cup of milk or water. Zap the oatmeal in the microwave for a minute, and toss in the fruit with a few nuts for added nutrition. A splash of maple syrup makes it extra yummy.

5. A hard-boiled egg (it has omega vitamins—brain food) and a banana or an easy-peel mandarin orange.

6. Who says kids have to eat traditional breakfast foods in the morning? If your child likes leftovers, offer spaghetti and meatballs or chicken fingers from dinner the night before.

What's for Lunch?

Do you see glimpses of your children or their classmates in the following story?

"Hey look!" Monica holds up a plastic bag to show off her treat inside. "Chocolate chip cookies!"

"Remember," Mrs. Day says, "your mom said you have to eat the rest of your food before you can eat the goodies." She spends every break period passing out these little reminders, but often they fall on deaf ears—or selective ones.

Both of the blue picnic benches outside the classroom are full of kindergartners eating snacks or lunches under a wooden canopy.

"I got a sandwich with meat in it too." Monica smiles at her discovery in the container and picks up one of the triangle halves her mom lovingly made fresh that morning.

"My mom makes me peanut butter and jelly because that's all I'll eat." Ruben picks up his rectangular half sandwich on Wonder Bread and takes a big bite. His chipmunk cheeks make Jake and Monica laugh.

Jessica's dad was in a hurry, so he sent a tuna pack with her to spread on a small stack of crackers. She quietly eats what her dad calls "the good stuff" first, but she can barely stand to wait to eat the small chocolate mint that comes with the tuna package. The candy is the best part.

Brandon sits quietly with a bag of chips, drinking something called "fruit punch" and munching on a chocolate cupcake. He learned the first week of school not to brag about his daily treasures. Mrs. Day might hand him some peanuts and make him choose between the punch and the dessert. She thinks too much sugar wipes him out, but Brandon likes his lunches.

"What did you get?" Monica asks Jake.

"I hab a cut ub apple."

"Jake, swallow your food before speaking, okay?" Mrs. Day reminds him.

Jake swallows. "'K." He points to each item in his lunch box. "I got pieces of apple, some grapes, a string cheese, and chocolate milk with a straw. See?" He holds up the small box to show his friends.

"You didn't get a sandwich?" Monica nibbles a second bite off the first half of her turkey and cheese on wheat.

"Nope. I eat one of those when I get home. Here is just a snack."

Monica gets tired of her sandwich after the second bite and moves on to a plastic baggie. "Look! I have purple grapes too!" she tells Jake, and she chomps on a few.

"Can I have some?" Ruben is done with his PB&J and his orange sections don't look nearly as good as Monica's grapes.

"Here." Monica gives Ruben the bag. He pulls two grapes out and hands it back.

"No, you can keep it," Monica says.

"Thanks!"

Monica's grapes are gone and she's eaten a few bites of her sandwich. She puts the remaining three-quarters of her sandwich back in the container, plops it into her SpongeBob lunch box, and closes the lid. She's ready for her chocolate chip cookies. Every crumb disappears. It's funny how desserts are so much easier to eat than other foods. Then a cherry drink, with 10 percent real fruit juice, washes down her yummy treat.

To go out to the playground, Monica has to clean up so she dumps everything left in her lunch box (including most of her sandwich) into the trash, puts SpongeBob against the wall with the other lunch boxes, and runs to the climbing structure to get in some playtime before the break ends.

Brandon finished eating his sugar-saturated, caloric Armageddon several minutes earlier and is whipping down the slide. At the bottom, he sprints around the structure and slams his hefty body into Monica. She goes flying off the stairs onto the spongy surface below, designed just for such occasions. The impact still hurts and scares her, so Monica bursts into tears.

"Brandon Wenkle!" Mrs. Day comes rushing over. "What do you need to say to Monica?"

"Sorry?" Brandon shrugs as if he didn't realize he caused a problem until his teacher asked the question.

"Yes. I think that would be a good start."

"Sorry, Monica."

"Please be careful, Brandon," Mrs. Day warns, "or you'll have to sit out for a while."

"Okay."

Mrs. Day checks out Monica's knee. It's a bit banged up but nothing serious. "Alla-kazam-alla-kazee, make feel better this cute little knee," the teacher says, waving her hand over the boo-boo. Then she blows on it to finish the "magic spell" as is her custom, the recipe for making almost any owie feel better. "How's that?" she asks her patient.

"I think it's better," Monica says with wide eyes. Is her teacher really magic?

"Are you ready to go play?" Mrs. Day asks.

"Yeah!" Monica is off to the playground, but this time she decides to jump rope.

Jake and Ruben have finished their snacks, cleaned up, and joined the rest of the kids on the playground. They are racing tricycles with red rims on the two-lane track when Mrs. Day rings the bell to line up.

It's time to go inside and learn how to use five pennies to figure out how many combinations of "families" they can come up with and make up a story about them. Jake and Ruben are alert and ready to work after refueling their growing bodies with protein from foods like peanut butter, string cheese, and chocolate milk. Vitamins from the grapes and apples give them a kick-start, and the exercise they got running around and riding tricycles gets their brains moving too. Working together, the two boys come up with all the combinations to make five and a great story about Spider-Man and the five people he saves.

Poor Brandon is out of gas. His 20-minute sugar rush fizzled, and his eyelids droop. Walking from the rug to the table with Shanda seems like harder work than he can take right now. She talks so much Brandon wants to cry.

Jessica partners up with Monica to make up a penny story. The protein, omega-3s, and omega-9s in the tuna that Jessica ate for lunch have primed her brain for some penny action. Monica looks like a rag doll. Those couple of bites of sandwich couldn't keep her brain going, and the sugar rush-and-crush from the cookies and cherry drink have left her without the energy she needs to make sense of the pennies on the table.

* * *

You may or may not see your kinder kid in that group. The point is that young minds need lasting fuel to learn new things. School is no place for junk food. Parents often think a cookie, bag of chips, or fruit drink puts a little pizzazz into a lunch box. As you saw with Monica, though, the healthy food often gets neglected in favor of treats, so brainpower sputters and fizzles out.

But as an after-school snack, coming home to cookies and milk is an age-old tradition.

Stencil says, "An example of a great pick-me-up snack for half-day kinders would be half a sliced apple, a string cheese, and a small water bottle or some milk, assuming the kids have eaten breakfast." For full-day kindergarten, include a full sliced apple so the extra wedges can be eaten at snack time later in the day.

If your child comes home starving, talk to the teacher to see if food is getting traded for cookies or thrown away in favor of playtime. If not, add something to your child's lunch pail from Mrs. Stencil's list of nutritious energizers to get the most out of the school day.

MRS. STENCIL'S FAVORITE FOODS TO RECHARGE KINDER BRAINS

5 Carbohydrates for a Slow, Steady Flow of Energy

1. Half an apple, sliced into four wedges—a whole apple is hard to eat and is too much for most kindergartners.

2. Orange wedges—start the peel on a couple of mandarin oranges so your kinder kid can peel the fruit herself, or cut half of a regular-sized orange into four slices for easy eating. (Teachers have to help with inserting straws in milk boxes and other chores, so try to set up your child to be independent.)

3. A few baby carrots—a crunchy, healthy snack full of vitamin A and fiber.

4. Smaller fruits—grapes, cherries (pitted), and strawberries (tops removed) are thirst quenching and nutritious too.

5. A snack-sized box of raisins—will do in a pinch with a nice drink of water.

7 Proteins for Lasting Nutrition

1. String cheese—easy and fun to eat.

2. A hard-boiled egg—recent studies have redefined the egg, once shunned as unhealthy, as primo nutrition (Wallace and Fulgoni 2017). *Hint:* Buy extra coloring kits at Easter for fun throughout the year.

3. Half sandwich—peanut butter and jelly, meat, or tuna provide omega-3s and omega-9s to boost brainpower.

4. Crackers with tuna, meat, or cheese (about four)—recharge kids' brains for solid thinking.

5. Leftovers from dinner—last night's meatloaf cut into bite-sized pieces, a chicken leg, or a small container of casserole or mac and cheese. Lots of kids enjoy the homey feeling of eating food at school that the family ate together.

6. A handful of nuts or dried soybeans—provide some crunch and support brain function.

7. A small container of cottage cheese with fruit pieces or applesauce—offers a balanced snack for better thinking.

2 Good Drinks to Hydrate Young Bodies

1. Milk—if your child is sensitive to dairy, try almond, soy, or coconut milk.

2. Small water bottle—don't refill the bottle more than once because bacteria builds up and the plastic breaks down.

Treats: LEAVE THEM AT HOME!

Easy Healthy Dinners on a Tight Schedule

When life gets busy, overwhelming at times, parents are often tempted to grab whatever is easiest. Boxed macaroni and cheese or pizza once in a while won't hurt, but these foods should be fairly rare. Your child's brain needs omega-3s, omega-9s, and B vitamins. Kids don't have to eat fancy—their brains and bodies just need vitamins, minerals, and healthy fats, proteins, and carbohydrates they can use to grow and mature.

Rather than eating out of a window, or picking up a pizza, you're better off boiling a bunch of eggs on the weekend or buying them already cooked and handing them out along with a piece of whole wheat toast and apple or orange slices. The prep time is about the same as cooking a pot of pasta, and breakfast for dinner is a much healthier option. You can also buy precut veggies and fruit in the produce section to eat at mealtimes. They're more expensive, but no higher than hitting a takeout place to pick up enough junk food to fill hungry bellies. If you're on a tight budget, check the labels for wholesome, inexpensive canned soups that are quick to prepare.

Whenever possible, make extra food so you can repurpose or repeat a meal later in the week. I used to make a big pot of chicken and vegetable soup or a large meat and veggie stew on Sunday afternoons, when we weren't busy running around. There's nothing better, or easier, than warming up yummy homemade soup or stew for dinner on a winter's day—several days, in fact.

To drink, hand your child a glass of milk or container of water—the best thirst quencher ever. If you can squeeze in the time before or after dinner, let your child run around, dance, work out to a video, jump rope, or take a brisk walk with you—anything that gets her to work up a sweat. With a bit of exercise and nutrients in her tummy, she can enjoy clearer thinking, better memory, and more quality sleep.

Kindergartners' Teeth

Children are individuals, and wiggly teeth can happen earlier or later, but their two front bottom teeth generally fall out at age six or seven, followed by their top two front teeth.

Drs. Christopher Hughes and Jeffrey Dean (2016, 134–35), specialists in pediatric dentistry, advise dentists to tell parents and caregivers to brush children's teeth until at least age six. Once a child makes the transition from brushee to brusher, they say the job becomes one of "active supervision."

You may need to remind and occasionally demonstrate how to clean certain areas in your child's mouth all the way to age 12, according to Hughes and Dean, depending on dexterity and sense of responsibility. Several months before handing off the task, start using a two-minute timer, often included with kids' toothbrushes, to ensure you're spending the minimum amount of time necessary to adequately clean those little choppers. Then when your child is ready to take on the brushing duties, the timer will already be part of the teeth-cleaning habit.

This may seem extreme, bordering on helicopter parenting, but studies show that before age six, most kids don't manage to clean all the nooks and crannies. According to the American Medical Association, tooth decay is the most common long-term childhood disease because cavities in primary teeth can affect the permanent teeth underneath.

And baby teeth are more important than many of us realize. They help children establish good chewing habits, make room for and guide permanent teeth into the correct position, and provide a barrier for the tongue so kids can form sounds such as /d/, /l/, /s/, and /t/. Besides, cavities can be painful, and crooked permanent teeth can make children self-conscious.

About a month before your child's sixth birthday, make a big deal out of the rite of passage for taking over toothbrushing duties, a step toward independence. Begin talking through the process for how to do a thorough cleaning, step-by-step. Explain that you put a pea-sized dab of toothpaste on the brush so your child will be less likely to swallow the suds. Fluoride helps make teeth stronger, but the chemicals in most toothpastes aren't healthy to digest (just like drinking soapy bath water isn't good for you).

Show how you wet the brush before putting it into your child's mouth, the up and down movements for best removal of sugar and plaque, and establish an order for brushing each area to make sure every tooth gets clean. When the process has gotten familiar enough, begin asking what to do first, then what comes next, and so on. Give your child turns to put on the toothpaste, wet the toothbrush, and brush areas in his mouth with your supervision.

On your child's sixth birthday, include brushing his own teeth, all by himself, as part of the celebration, and make this noble responsibility the reward after eating cake and ice cream. This is a declaration that he is truly older and more capable of taking care of himself.

Even so, the International Association of Pediatric Dentistry (IAPD) recommends that parents still floss kids' teeth until they're eight or nine years old. Most children don't have the dexterity to do a good job cleaning between their teeth before then. The IAPD also advises parents to have sealants put on kids' first molars that come in at about age six. The teeth come in soft, have deep grooves that are hard to get clean with a brush, and are cavity prone.

Paying attention to how much candy your child eats may seem obvious, but did you know fruit juices and processed carbohydrates—pizza crust, bagels, pasta, and muffins—are just as bad? These foods mix with bacteria in the mouth to produce the acid that erodes teeth and causes cavities as much as brownies and ice cream. Establishing how to eat these foods in moderation, along with conscientious brushing every morning and evening, will give your child healthy habits and strong teeth for a lifetime.

WHERE DO YOU SEE YOURSELF?

"Turn off the TV. It's time to go!" Mrs. Durango shouts on her way to the kitchen.

"Okay," five-year-old Janice answers and realizes she forgot to brush her teeth. But her mom is in a big hurry, so she can't do it now.

Mrs. Durango throws a bag of chips, a string cheese, and a juice pouch into the lunch box and grabs her briefcase. She'll make sure she does a better job with dinner. Where does the time go? "Janice! We gotta get out of here. We're going to be late!"

"Coming!" Janice pushes the "off" button on the TV remote control, picks up her backpack, and rushes out the door.

"Shoot. I forgot something," Mrs. Durango says. "Get in the car. I'll be right there."

Janice climbs into the backseat and buckles her safety belt. Her backpack feels light, so she opens it to see if something's missing. In a panic, she unhooks her belt and bolts out of the car.

"Where are you going?" screeches Mrs. Durango, grabbing Janice's arm. "We're going to be late!"

"I have to get my homework folder and my library book!"

"You should have gotten your stuff together instead of turning on the TV." Mrs. Durango drags her daughter back to the car.

"But, Mom—"

"Sorry, honey. We don't have time to go back and find all your things." The words are clipped and final. "Next time you'll know better." Mrs. Durango winces at herself. She knows she's being a hypocrite, but she must get to that meeting at work.

Janice sits quietly on the way to school with tears in her eyes while her mom listens to the radio to calm her nerves.

At the sidewalk in front of the school, Mrs. Durango drops off Janice. There's no time to walk her daughter to class today. Her client will be waiting as it is.

"Bye, Janice. I'll see you tonight," she yells out the window.

Her five-year-old shuffles down the sidewalk as she drives away.

"Let's go brush your teeth, Jeremy," Mrs. Steiner says.

"Okay." Her kindergartner gets up from the table and leaves his cereal bowl for her to take to the sink.

They go to the bathroom, and Mrs. Steiner pull's Jeremy's toothbrush off the stand, puts on the toothpaste, and brushes his teeth for him.

"It's time to go," she says as she wipes his mouth with a hand towel. Then she leaves the bathroom to pick up her son's backpack next to the front door. She knows his homework, reading log, and library book are inside because she put them there the night before.

"Oh. We forgot your lunch box." She scurries off to get Jeremy's lunch out of the refrigerator and puts it into his backpack for him, and they get in the car.

After the short trip to the school, Mrs. Steiner parks in the lot, takes her son's hand, and walks him to his classroom.

"Bye, Mom." Jeremy hugs her.

"I'll see you after school at the ice cream social," she says.

"Oh yeah! I forgot about that," he says with a smile as he walks away to go sit on the carpet.

Mrs. Steiner takes Jeremy's folder out of his backpack and puts it in the basket. She feels a little guilty because she had a hard time getting him to finish his homework the night before, so she filled in the last several spaces for him. But it's better than turning in unfinished work, right? Then she puts his library book into the red wagon that the classroom monitor will roll to the library to return the books and hangs the backpack on a peg on her way out the door.

😇 "Bring your bowl to the sink please, Jeanne," Mr. Davis says as he puts his own cereal bowl in the sink. "Did you take your vitamin?"

Jeanne pops the purple multivitamin into her mouth as she walks the bowl across the room. "Yep," she says with a smirk.

"Good job." Her daddy smiles. "Let's go brush your teeth. We have to leave in about five minutes."

"Okay." Jeanne scampers to the bathroom, and Mr. Davis follows.

He lets her put a pea-sized dollop of toothpaste on her child-sized toothbrush and wet it under the faucet. She hands him the toothbrush and he begins the routine, counting eight strokes in each section of her teeth, cleaning the insides, outsides, and eating surfaces. He's looking forward to his daughter taking over this job on her sixth birthday.

"Did you see anything on the board that you have to do after school today?" Mr. Davis asks Jeanne on the way to the front door.

"I have the ice cream social at day care," Jeanne says, grabbing her backpack at the front door. "And Mom is picking me up for my dance lesson after that."

"Oh, right. The dance lesson."

Mr. Davis got a whiteboard to hang on the wall in the kitchen. As family activities come to his and his wife's attention, they mark them on the appropriate day. They draw simple pictures to go with entries, like an ice cream cone and a stick-figure dancer, so Jeanne can "read" the board too. In the last couple of weeks, their daughter has drawn some of her own pictures to make sure the family doesn't miss events.

"Let's do the backpack check," Mr. Davis says.

"All right." Jeanne unzips her Hello Kitty backpack and peers inside.

"What do you need?" her father asks.

Jeanne takes out her homework folder. "I have my homework packet right here. And my reading log is on top. Look, you and Mommy signed it every day." The five-year-old holds up the paper to show him with a wide smile.

"You did a really good job this week." Mr. Davis arcs his eyebrows with a slight turn of his head. "Are you missing anything?"

"What?"

"It's Friday," he hints.

"Oh! My library book!" Jeanne runs to the living room to find the book in its special spot on the end table next to the couch. "Here it is!" She grabs *Clifford the Big Red Dog* and brings it back with her.

"Good job," Mr. Davis says. "Let's see if you can remember to put your book in the red wagon this week so you can pick out a new one at the library today."

"I will." Jeanne looks up at her dad with happy brown eyes. "Can you help me read it tonight?"

"You bet." He kisses his little girl on the head. "Come on. Let's go."

After the quick ride to school, Jeanne's dad parks the car and walks his daughter to the classroom, glancing at his watch. Mr. Davis has plenty of time to get to work, even with traffic. He fights the urge to remind his daughter to put her homework folder in the basket and her book in the red wagon. How will his daughter learn to do those things unless she makes a few mistakes? Instead, he hugs his little one and says, "Have a great day, Chicken Pop."

Jeanne laughs at their inside joke. "You too, Daddy."

Mr. Davis peeks through the window to watch his daughter remember, on her own, how to put away her folder and library book. He smiles and goes off to work a happy dad.

* * *

We can look like any of these three parents in varying degrees, depending on the situation. That bit of additional time to be an "angel parent," though, will pay off many times over. Ask questions to make sure your child has what she needs. Your kindergartner won't learn how to be responsible if you put her books in the backpack for her. Making sure she gets her homework folder off the couch and into her backpack the night before will also save a lot of headaches. Who needs more stress? Not you or your child, so why not set up routines now that will create a happier future for the whole family, throughout your child's school years?

As our kids get bigger, their mistakes can get bigger too, and bigger mistakes can be harder to fix. Kindergarten is a great place to solve problems before they get out of hand. But you're not going to be perfect all the time. The object is to recognize parent-child dynamics, smile at ourselves for the things we do well, and do our best to improve our shortcomings.

CONCLUSION

By now, you probably feel like you're getting the hang of playing with your child at the same time you're building the best possible foundation. Your family has a central way to communicate, either with a whiteboard or with something that works better in your house (which we hope you'll share on thebrainstages.com).

You've established a routine for your child to get downtime after school, complete homework assignments, and do fun things with the family. The bedtime ritual is set, and your child usually gets enough sleep to produce essential rejuvenating delta and theta brain waves.

After some experimentation, you have come up with combinations of healthy foods for your child to eat, even in a hurry, and you have a working relationship with your child's teacher or homeschool advisor.

Then kindergarten ends—much too quickly.

Your family will be happier if you continue to play games during the vacation break between grades. Not only will you have a good time sorting, chanting, cooking, and guessing what will happen next in a new library book, these activities will keep your child's neural pathways growing and maturing, rather than atrophying from lack of use.

Soon your child will go to first grade, which is considerably more demanding than kindergarten. Don't worry, though. We'll make sure you'll both be ready for this huge year of mental, social, and physical changes.

FIRST GRADE
Little People, Big Changes

First-graders often have a veritable thirst for understanding their environment. Your child will likely go from being generally curious to needing specific details about how the world works. You'll get to share fun facts and have surprisingly philosophical discussions with your six- or seven-year-old. This intense desire to understand will serve your child in the transition from the social environment in the kindergarten classroom to the more academic focus of first grade.

YOUR FIRST-GRADER'S BRAIN

First-graders' neural pathways become more efficient at communicating—that is, signals between neurons and sections of the brain get more synchronized. This means that gross motor control (regulated in the frontal lobes) becomes smoother and better integrated, so you'll likely notice your six- or seven-year-old better able to jump rope, catch and kick balls, and ride a bike.

Similarly, fine motor skills improve. Hands become more agile, especially if your child has spent time connecting neurons and strengthening small muscles by molding clay and sorting small objects (see "Pinky Push-Ups: When Wheaties Aren't Enough," page 55).

Activities such as writing, drawing, cutting with scissors, typing on a keyboard, and manipulating a touch screen will get easier in first grade. The occipital region (the back area) of the brain also becomes more adept at handling visual stimulation, so your child will likely find print, whether digital or on paper, easier to track and interpret.

If you worried that your friend's kid read by the end of kindergarten but yours still didn't know all the letter sounds, you were probably anxious for nothing. Keep reading together regularly and soon your child's neural pathways will allow him to put phonemes, or letter sounds, together to make words. Helping your son or daughter learn the high-frequency words in each chapter will also add vocabulary to long-term memory in the hippocampus.

Remember, brains mature at different rates. In the meantime, you'll find lots of games here to stimulate neural connections while keeping reading fun. On the other hand, if you've been feeling proud that your little one started reading before others in her age group, you should know there's a good chance her peers will catch up. The good news is she'll enjoy sharing and talking about stories with classmates.

You may have noticed that it works best to give one instruction at a time. As soon as you add a second or third direction to the list, your child will either complain or forget all but one thing anyway. Although neural pathways are becoming more defined in first grade, your child's ability to remember and process a sequence of instructions won't develop for a couple more years—and it's no wonder. After extensive analysis of functional magnetic resonance imaging (fMRI) test results, neuroscientist Harris Georgiou (2017) from the National and Kapodistrian University of Athens in Greece reported that about 50 independent processes are simultaneously at work in human brains performing visual-motor tasks.

That's a lot of mental activity for a six-year-old to contend with and then keep track of another instruction besides.

FIRST-GRADE SOCIAL TRAITS

Your first-grader may strive for independence and look outside the family for validation from other adults, such as teachers, coaches, aunts, and uncles, so you may not feel like a best friend anymore. Don't worry. This social extension is normal, even healthy.

Your Relationship

Your child will likely still thrive on your praise—but remember to compliment effort, creativity, and problem-solving, not intellect. You don't want your child to question his intelligence every time he struggles with a concept or project. If he's commended for things like staying with a task to completion, even when it gets tough or tedious, you'll set him up for a successful life. Also, continue to make encouraging comments ("Well done!") since his brain hasn't yet learned to process negative feedback ("You did that wrong").

Friends

First-graders value their friends as much as they do their parents or teachers. You'll find that the weird putt-putt sound your son makes lately came from another boy in his class, or your daughter's latest favorite slang word came from her new best friend. First-grade kids are highly conscious of gender differences, so boys tend to play with boys and girls with girls.

Boys can bounce from buddy to buddy or bond with one or more classmates for the rest of the school year. Their friend choices usually come from proximity and the games they like to play at recess. If a playmate steals a turn at the kickball diamond, he may get called out or socked on the arm, but the group usually forgets the infraction quickly.

Girls, on the other hand, are much more fickle. One day they're best friends, and then the next day they get their feelings hurt or become distracted by other classmates and claim new BFFs. Although it's important to keep an open dialogue with your son or daughter, don't worry about a bit of friend swapping. Both boys and girls at this age don't seem to concern themselves with playmates coming and going.

Another thing the genders have in common is the tendency to think everyone sees the world the way they do. For example, first-graders agree rules are necessary to play a game, but they choose which ones to follow, mostly because they hate to lose, and they assume playmates will fall in line. Trying to slant or change rules happens often and tempers flare.

Fortunately, by age six or seven, most kids have learned to talk—

more like yell—over what's "fair" rather than throwing punches or pulling hair. Before intervening, see if they can work it out. Solving such conflicts on their own teaches them how to cooperate and compromise. But it's a good idea to keep an eye on a playgroup in case someone gets bullied or arguments get out of control and fists start flying.

Once friends have gone home, you can use the "teachable moment" to talk about critical social skills, which are just as necessary to teach as any other skill. Your child may need your help to see others' perspectives. For example, you may have to explain why a friend might have gotten upset when your child didn't hold her spot in the four square line while she went to the bathroom.

Instead of pointing out that letting the friend back into the line would have been the nice thing to do, ask questions to help your child realize how she might have contributed to a problem (see the questions below). That way, she can process what happened and make better decisions in the future. Such conversations with you will engender empathy, teach your child about courtesy, and develop self-confidence—all important attributes for your child's introduction to real-world peer pressure.

HELP FIRST-GRADERS TAKE RESPONSIBILITY IN CONFLICTS

If you ask the following four questions without judgment—including in your tone of voice—and patiently listen, your child will likely glean his part in an unpleasant interaction with peers or teachers:

- What do you think made your friend/teacher/classmate react like that?

- If you were the one involved, do you think you'd feel the same way? Why?

- What do you think you'd do in the same situation?

- Is there anything you could have done or said to help solve the problem? If so, what?

FIRST-GRADE ACADEMICS

First grade presents the largest transition between school years until middle school. This year, your child will be expected to read and talk about picture books as well as social studies and science articles, and write responses to questions in complete sentences. Numbers will take on new meaning, as will geometric shapes, coins, and time. This is an exciting time of discovery!

Physical exercise is important all the time, but particularly at this age because it helps with self-control. Make sure your child works up a sweat every day to balance sitting at a desk for hours, especially if he is adjusting from a half day in kindergarten to a full day in first grade.

FIRST-GRADE ACADEMIC SKILLS

Language Arts

- Ask and answer questions about stories and articles.

- Retell stories and understand their central message.

- Identify words and phrases that suggest feelings or appeal to the senses.

- Identify who is telling the story (point of view).

- Compare the experiences of characters in stories.

- Read stories, articles, and poetry leveled for first grade.

- Explain the differences between fiction and nonfiction.

- Describe connections between individuals, events, ideas, or information.

- Ask and answer questions to clarify the meaning of words and phrases.

- Use headings, glossaries, and electronic menus to locate information.

- Use illustrations and details in a text to define main ideas.

- Identify the reasons an author gives to support his or her ideas.

- Compare two articles on the same topic.

- Use a capital letter to begin sentences and use ending punctuation.

- Capitalize common proper nouns, such as names of people and days of the week.

- Use grade-level phonics in writing and decoding unfamiliar words.

- Read with enough fluency to understand the text.

- Participate in conversations about first-grade topics and texts.

- Describe people, places, things, and events.

- Use drawings to illustrate ideas, thoughts, and feelings.

- Write opinion, informative, and narrative paragraphs (with adult support).

- Figure out the meaning of words and phrases using context or a reference guide.

- Use words and phrases heard in conversations and learned from text.

Mathematics

- Solve addition and subtraction problems.

- Understand the relationship between addition and subtraction.

- Know the fact families from 1 to 20.

- Count and write numerals from 1 to 100.

- Understand 1s, 10s, and 100s place value.

- Measure lengths by using equal units, such as blocks or paperclips.

- Represent and interpret data, such as a bar graph to depict kids' favorite colors.

- Tell and write time to the hour—1:00, 2:00 . . . 12:00.

- Reason with shapes, such as knowing how to construct a square that has four sides of the same length.

- Use math concepts to argue a point in conversation.

- Keep trying new things to find a solution until a problem is solved.

- Solve problems using drawings or objects.

- Look for and make use of structure and repeated reasoning.

To find out what your child will be expected to master in your area, type into a search engine the name of your state and "education standards K–12." Skills may appear in a different grade in your state's standards.

HIGH-FREQUENCY WORDS—FIRST GRADE

Make a copy of the list or keep this book in the car. While you drive and run errands together, your first-grader can "go on a scavenger hunt" to find the words below. You'll be amazed where she finds them—on street signs, posters, cereal boxes—anywhere she sees print. Have fun celebrating when your child can read and spell all the high-frequency words.

50 Words First Grade, First Semester

am	ate	away	big	black
blue	brown	but	came	come
did	do	down	eat	find
four	from	funny	get	go
good	help	here	into	jump
like	little	look	make	me
must	my	new	no	now
our	play	please	pretty	ran
red	ride	run	saw	say
she	so	soon	too	want

40 Words First Grade, Second Semester

box	by	could	every	fly
give	going	has	her	him
just	know	let	live	may
next	old	once	open	over
put	round	stop	take	thank
them	then	think	three	two
under	walk	well	went	where
white	who	will	year	yellow

4 WAYS TO BOOST YOUR FIRST-GRADER'S SKILLS IN LANGUAGE ARTS

1. **Take a picture walk.** Whenever you and your child read a new book, go through the pages and guess what will happen in the story based on the illustrations. Whether you guess right doesn't matter. Good readers make predictions and confirm or correct them semiconsciously. This game will improve your first-grader's comprehension.

2. **Make words.** If your first-grader gets spelling lists or new words from stories read in class, a great way to cement new vocabulary into his brain is to "make the words" using Scrabble tiles. The physical act of assembling the appropriate tiles adds tactile and visual stimulus associated with the words. If the homework assignment requires the words to be written, cover the tiles to see if your child can remember the order of the letters. Casually use the words in context during conversations to help internalize meanings.

3. **Do a quick share.** Tell your child your thoughts on the story or chapter you read, paying attention to how the characters deal with the

conflicts and how you might have handled a similar issue. Most of the time, kids will respond with their own opinions, but if not, ask open-ended questions: "What do you think about how Hansel and Gretel handled getting dropped off in the forest?" or "What do you think we would do if we got left in the forest?" (You don't want to leave your child alone in any scenario because this can cause bad dreams—and worse. Kids are still literal at this age.)

4. **Guess what's next.** Your child may want to read the picture books and have you read chapter books before bedtime. Try some of the entertaining books listed below. After you read a while, before turning the page, ask your child to guess what might happen next. Again, whether the guess is right or wrong doesn't matter. You'll add fun to bedtime reading while painlessly building comprehension skills. When your first-grader is ready to try reading a chapter book on his own, these familiar stories will be a good place to start.

10 BOOK SERIES AND STORIES TO MOTIVATE YOUNG READERS

The best way we know to get first-graders reading is to provide them with fun early-reader books to enjoy with you until they can recognize and decode words on their own. Listed below are some well-loved series and stories that have excellent track records for sparking a love for reading.

1. Frog and Toad series by Arnold Lobel (4 books)—each has five simple, funny, sometimes instructive and touching stories about a frog and his friend, a toad.

2. Henry and Mudge series by Cynthia Rylant (29 books at last count)—stories of Henry, a young boy, and his experiences with his huge dog, Mudge.

3. You Read to Me, I'll Read to You series by Mary Ann Hoberman (5 books)—collections of simple short fairy-tales, fables, scary stories, and more.

4. Young Cam Jansen series by David Adler (20 books)—young-reader mysteries solved by a child detective who has a photographic memory.

5. Tacky the Penguin series by Helen Lester (7 books)—a funny, unique penguin saves the day and becomes accepted by his community.

6. *I Wish That I Had Duck Feet* by Theo. LeSieg (aka Dr. Seuss), and lots of other Dr. Seuss books—kids love LeSieg/Seuss's strange characters and silly rhymes.

7. *Emily's First 100 Days of School* by Rosemary Wells—fun, adventure, and math—what's not to like in the bunny's early school days?

8. *The Boy Who Loved Words* by Roni Schotter—a boy plays with words in silly, fun ways that introduce vocabulary and word patterns.

9. *Miss Smith's Incredible Storybook* by Michael Garland—when a teacher tells stories from her magic book, characters come alive and go on fun adventures with students.

10. *There Was an Old Lady Who Swallowed Fly Guy* by Tedd Arnold—a funny story that builds on itself with a twist that first-graders love, in context that kids can decode.

NAMES FOR 10 GAME: A FUN WAY TO KICK-START FIRST-GRADE MATH

This seems like a small thing, but if your child knows all the combinations of numbers that make 10, or the "names" for 10 (0 + 10, 1 + 9, 2 + 8, 3 + 7, 4 + 6, 5 + 5, 6 + 4, 7 + 3, 8 + 2, 9 + 1, 10 + 0), many other math concepts will come easily. We live in a world of base 10 where these combinations appear relentlessly—repeating in 1s, 10s, 100s, and so on—in money, percentages, decimals, fractions, metric measurement, and even time.

If your child learns the names for 10 and truly understands the pattern, you'll probably notice him blurting out answers to whatever calculations arise in family situations.

Here's how to solidify the names for 10 in your child's brain and give him a leg up for life:

1. Set out a pile of something fun to be counted—nuts, cereal, raisins, buttons, pennies—and have your child count out 10 items.

2. Separate one item to the right of the group and count the objects in each location. Have him say out loud "9 + 1 = 10."

3. Continue the previous step with one more item moving to the pile on the right until your child reaches "0 + 10 = 10."

4. Now repeat the process starting with "10 + 0 = 10," and continue having your child slide one object to the left this time, vocalizing the name for 10: 9 + 1 = 10, 8 + 2 =10, . . . 0 + 10 = 10. This will tactually and visually illustrate the commutative property of equality ($a + b = b + a$). You don't need to point out the property—the experience is more important. *Note:* If your child seems finished with the game and wants to eat the Cheerios, you're done for the day. The next time you play, repeat the first four steps before continuing with step five. If your child is enjoying the game, keep going!

5. Grab a clear cup so your child can see the objects inside. Have him repeat steps two through four, placing the cup upside down over the pile the items move to. Challenge him to say the names for 10 aloud without looking inside the cup.

6. Now comes the best part: Choose a random number of items to cover with the clear cup, and see if your child can "guess" how many objects are under the cup without looking. *Note:* In the event of a

wrong guess, have your child count the objects through the clear cup first and then turn to the ones on the table and continue counting to 10. For example, if there are 6 objects under the cup, he would start on 7 to count the objects in the exposed pile. This will provide experience in "counting up," another first-grade skill.

7. If your child is ready to move on to something else, the Names for 10 game can end here and pick up on another day. But if your child wants to keep playing, replace the clear cup with an opaque one. Challenge your child to tell you how many objects are hidden under the cup given the number of items in the exposed pile and pick up the cup to confirm or correct the answers.

8. After you've played this game together a few times, you'll start to notice numbers coming up in real life. Maybe you'll see a 7 on an apartment or office door. You can point out the number and ask your child for "7's partner" to make a name for 10. Encourage your first-grader to find numbers that can be paired as well. You won't believe the cool places your child will notice numbers!

9. Model names for 10 aloud to calculate change at the store, for instance.

7 MORE FIRST-GRADE MATH GAMES FOR FUN AND FOUNDATION

1. **O'Clock Time Travel.** Throughout the day, when you notice the time near an o'clock, mention the time to your child and talk about what you're doing at that moment. For example, around 7 a.m. bring attention to the short hand pointing to the 7, or the numeral 7 in the hour position on a digital clock, and the activity you're doing (getting up in the morning or having breakfast). Once you've mentioned several activities, take turns asking each other what time it was when

you did certain things. This game reinforces the o'clock concept, time orientation, and strengthens memory.

2. **Shape Up!** This game is a modification of I Spy. You and your kids guess an item in the room or other setting by describing the shapes. For example, "I spy a square on the top and four rectangular prisms, one on each corner." (*Answer:* dining table.) Their creative descriptions may surprise you. Kids learn two- and three-dimensional shapes and can apply descriptive skills to reading and writing.

3. **Delicious Fact Families.** Similar to the Names for 10 game (page 95), get out some small, yummy items that your child can move around to show fact families from 2 to 10. For example, a fact family for 5 would look like this: 2 + 3 = 5, 3 + 2 = 5, 5 - 3 = 2, and 5 - 2 = 3. Moving physical objects to show these mathematical relationships gives kids a huge advantage in understanding numbers and how they work. (*Hint:* Finding missing numbers when they get to algebra is a lot easier for kids who have played this game.)

4. **Popsicle-Stick Bundles to 100.** Popsicle sticks are inexpensive, can be purchased in any craft or variety store, and are great for helping kids understand how base 10 works.

   a. Have your child count out 10 sticks and bind them together with a rubber band.

   b. Next, have him count 11, 12, 13 . . . and bundle the next batch of 10 sticks when he gets to 20.

   c. Then have him count 21, 22, 23 . . . and bundle that batch of 10 sticks when he gets to 30, and so on up to 100.

   d. Once he bundles the sticks to 100, have him unbundle a group of 10 and experiment with adding and subtracting different numbers of sticks with 10s and 1s for a concrete view of what's happening during addition and subtraction. For example,

2 bundles and 6, or 26, + 4 bundles and 3, or 43, equals 69. Bundling, unbundling, and moving the sticks around clears up any confusion kids might have—not to mention, the game makes learning new math concepts so much more fun.

5. **Coin Combos.** Dump the change out of your wallet or coin jar and have your child see how many ways coins can go together to make 10¢. In time, when she can assemble those combinations easily, show her a quarter, tell her it's worth 25¢, and coach her to put together coins that make 25¢. You might be surprised how quickly she transfers the skill to a larger number, like 50¢. In addition to teaching about money, this game develops logic and number sense.

6. **Jump to 100.** Ask your child to see if he can count to 100 while jumping rope, without missing. For a good workout, take turns to see who can get to 100 without missing first. This game is good for coordination, number sense, and keeping fit. Teach your child to do the smaller hop between jumps over the rope. Interestingly, that rhythm seems to help get neural pathways geared up for reading.

   No kidding. Brain-based teacher Pat Jones (2016) in Georgia says she sees a significant bump in her students' reading, no matter their age, within a month of mastering that middle hop between jumps.

7. **Bounce to 100.** Similar to jumping rope, have your child see if she can bounce a ball 100 times without it ricocheting off her shoe and rolling away. Although more studies need to be done to determine the process that happens in the brain during physical movement while counting, kids seem to relate rhythm to numbers—sort of how music is comprised of tones, rhythm, and counting.

Passionate Learners

First-graders often become intrigued with a specific topic or activity. They may get excited about dinosaurs, the solar system, geography, or the Olympic Games. Sometimes reading a book or taking a field trip ignites a passion for a certain animal. They can't read enough stories about horses or see enough pictures of turtles.

If you happen to be the lucky parent of a child like this, take advantage of this powerful motivation for learning. Check out books, play games, and go places to fuel your first-grader's interest. Share your six- or seven-year-old's excitement over seeing dinosaur bones at a natural history museum or a replica of the universe at the planetarium and make memories that neither of you will ever forget.

First-graders are particularly sensitive to absorbing new things, especially if they can learn from life. While the two of you are taking a walk, grocery shopping, waiting at the doctor's office, or doing anything else together, point out things you notice in the environment. Ask questions, and encourage your child to do the same.

Sometimes, especially when six-year-olds get excited, their tongues will get ahead of their brains. Unless stuttering or stammering impedes communication, it's usually nothing to worry about. As your child gets older, his tongue will catch up with his mouth.

If a question arises that you don't know how to answer, you can set a great example by admitting your ignorance and looking it up together on your phone or computer. This sort of modeling conveys that it's okay not to know everything and demonstrates how to find information. As a bonus, your child may learn what it means to arrive at an informed opinion to make a decision.

Still Black and White

First-graders begin to understand that actions have consequences, sometimes ones that are unfavorable or unpleasant, so self-control begins to evolve on a higher level. However, kids this age can be even more judgmental than kindergartners. Forget understanding right and wrong in shades of gray. Their black-and-white interpretations usually become starker—well, at least for *other* people.

If something you do doesn't fit into your first-grader's idea of how the world should work, he'll make a disapproving face if he's the quiet type. A verbal child might let you know you've crossed the line in front of all your friends. The same may go for people he's just met, including adults.

Given how others' perceived mistakes seldom go unnoticed, it's funny how easily first-graders justify bending the rules themselves. For example, your child may know that the TV isn't supposed to go on after dinner, but he reasons that since the book fair ran late, surely you won't mind if he hits the power button and watches just one show. In your first-grader's mind, the rule doesn't count because there was no time to watch TV before dinner.

It's important to stay consistent with house rules because as soon as you allow exceptions, circumstances will crop up all over the place for modifying directives in your child's favor. Before you know it, homework will get done at the last second, and bedtime will creep later and later. And then you will have to start all over to recreate the routine, putting in all kinds of extra time and effort to get the family back on track.

Homework in First Grade

First grade will be packed with new concepts and skills. Somewhere on a sliding scale, your child learned the letters and sounds in kindergarten as well as how to blend them to decode simple words. She also learned a list of high-frequency words, such as "of" and "the."

By the end of first grade, she'll be expected to read entire picture books fluently and write complete sentences. She'll go from understanding the value of numbers from one to 20 and possibly counting to 100 to grasping fact families and place value. She'll *use* numbers through 100 and beyond—to figure out how much money her class must raise to pay for a special activity, for example—and much more.

Your first-grader's brain will be wildly busy developing and connecting neural pathways. For those pathways to form and store information in the hippocampus for long-term memory, new concepts require repetition. The old adage "Practice makes perfect" may be an exaggeration, but practice does make us better by giving us the repetition we need to anchor knowledge in our brains.

Homework provides practice and teaches kids responsibility. As the National Education Association (n.d.) points out, "At the elementary school level, homework can help students develop study skills and habits and can keep families informed about their child's learning."

Although opposing opinions fly regarding the validity of homework, a study at Duke University synthesized data over 16 years and found homework had a positive influence on achievement (Cooper et al. 2006). The results were more conclusive for middle and high school students, but if children don't begin doing assignments outside class until sixth or seventh grade, they won't have developed the skill or discipline to tackle them.

The National Parent Teachers' Association (NPTA) recommends 10 to 20 minutes of homework every school night for first-graders. Teachers are encouraged to give kids assignments that require them to apply what they learned in class rather than busy work, but a certain amount of drill and practice is necessary. Learning math facts, for example, allows children to absorb advanced problem-solving concepts without having to stop and count 5 + 3 on their fingers, which interrupts higher-level thinking skills, such as deductive reasoning.

Ask your child what story she's reading at school that week, and if you can, read the story yourself. You'll enjoy more meaningful conversations about what your child did in school that day as well as be able to expand on story themes and answer questions.

Make sure to take a few minutes to check homework. You'll not only catch and help with errors, but also spot misunderstandings about what your child learned in class. In addition, looking over your first-grader's assignments will inspire ideas for which games to select from this chapter to try on your next car ride or in line at the store.

If homework takes too long to complete, though, you may have to experiment to support your child in reinforcing skills and developing study habits. Try using a timing device to keep assignments from gobbling precious family time. If the problem persists, check in with your child's teacher. Struggling to complete homework could be a symptom of other issues that you and the teacher can address together.

KITCHEN-TIMER MAGIC FOR HAPPIER HOMEWORK

Have your child choose a special place to do homework around the same time every day (see "6 Simple Steps to Great Homework Results," page 37). But sometimes the routine isn't enough to keep first-graders from daydreaming and taking forever to finish assignments. To avoid lengthy homework sessions, give your child downtime after school or extracurricular activities before breaking out the homework folder. Remember, alpha brain waves occur in relaxed consciousness and are optimal for learning. Sometimes, all kids need is a thinking break to get refocused.

But if taking a breather from producing those active beta brain waves doesn't help your child get on task, use the kitchen timer to add some fun and get the job done. Here's how:

1. **Set the timer.** Start with a short amount of time for your child to complete the first task the homework requires—for example, 30 seconds or a minute to write a sentence using a new action word (verb).

2. **Say "Ready . . . Go."** Challenge your child to finish the sentence before the timer goes off. The contest will add excitement, and your child will understand how long the task should take to complete if the work is done with intention.

3. **Repeat as often as necessary.** You may have to set the timer for every sentence if it takes your child a while to buy into finishing the work. For stubborn or wiggly kids, you may expect to use a timer for each sentence or math problem for several after-school assignments. But usually after a couple of timed tasks, kids get into a rhythm. You'll likely be able to set the timer for several minutes, and the homework will get done before the bell or buzzer.

4. **Offer an incentive.** For days when your child is particularly tired or sleepy, offer a small but motivating prize for beating the timer—for example, playing catch or jumping rope for five extra minutes or an extra story at bedtime (or chapter if you read novels to him). Beware

of offering computer time or candy. Once kids receive such rewards, they often don't want to do homework without "payment."

5. **Be patient.** Once you've consistently used the timer a few times, kids typically stop needing the extra support, and they'll do the work on their own as part of their routine.

THE REAL DEAL
The Truth about Timers

For our older daughter, who was particularly distractible, my husband and I had to occasionally bring out the timer throughout elementary school to help her stay focused on assignments. We usually needed to revisit the timer when she didn't get enough sleep the night before or something emotional happened at school.

Our younger daughter, on the other hand, never needed the timer because she was determined to read as much, write as much, and be as good at math (at her grade level) as her big sister. Kids are individuals, so feel free to modify or mix and match any games or suggestions to suit your child.

Family Dynamics

As first-graders sift through so many new ideas and influences, they can make better social and academic decisions when they have a strong home rooted in regular family communication.

With each passing year, life becomes more demanding and complicated for children. Asking "What did you do in school today?" will often get you "Nothing" in response since mentally breaking the day into events can seem overwhelming.

Try asking your child specific open-ended questions to help him focus on activities instead of the whole day at once. You'll likely find your six- or seven-year-old much more capable of describing the day's experiences.

6 QUESTIONS TO GET REAL ANSWERS

1. Who did you work with in class today, and what did you do together?

2. What story are you reading right now? What's it about?

3. What did you do at recess time? Who did you play with?

4. What did you do in math today? How was it (fun, boring, easy, hard . . .)?

5. What was the best thing you learned today?

6. Is there anything you wish was easier for you?

Your child's answers will help you select games you can play in the car or while you're preparing dinner to sharpen skills and make learning even more fun.

As your child progresses through school, communication through the family whiteboard or wall calendar will gain importance (see "Family Communication: Power to the Whiteboard!" on page 38 for a refresher on how to set up a central point for family communication).

Not only will everyone's participation in tracking commitments be helpful, but allowing your child to contribute and creating a habit of checking the board will also keep the family connected—no matter how busy your lives become.

First grade is generally a good time to encourage written words on the whiteboard or calendar rather than picture symbols. Writing for a purpose gives kids a sense of power and responsibility while improving their skills. In this world of constant, instant communication via email and texts, it is more important than ever to be able to string words together in a coherent manner. In fact, whenever possible, ask your child to be the family scribe. For fun writing ideas, check out the list on the next page.

5 OPPORTUNITIES FOR YOUR FIRST-GRADER TO WRITE

1. **Birthday list.** Ask your child to write a list of possible presents he would appreciate for his birthday. This is a great motivator.

2. **The grocery list.** Keep a pad of paper in your car and brainstorm about the things you need to pick up at the store. Have him write the list for you. He can also write a list in the kitchen while you check recipes, the cabinets, and the refrigerator.

3. **To-do or errands list.** Before you leave or when you get into the car to run errands, have your child write the list of things you need to accomplish.

4. **Holiday list.** Whatever holiday your family celebrates, make sure your child writes a list of things he plans to give other people. This helps children participate in the joy of giving as well as receiving.

   One year, our two girls made tree ornaments for everyone in the extended family. One daughter wrote the list of ornaments going to the adults, and the other daughter wrote the list of ornaments going to the kids. Another year, we made and decorated gingerbread cookies for aunts, uncles, cousins, and grandparents. You get the idea.

5. **Personal notes.** Once again, there's no better teacher than you. Model the behavior that you want to see. If you write notes, your child will too. Kids love to find notes written to them on the kitchen counter or living room coffee table.

   You'll start to get scribbles in return. Some of my favorite keepsakes are messages our children wrote to my husband and me. The bonus is that if your kids are in the habit, you'll have better communication via text and Post-it notes once your children get to middle and high school. You may even find a few love notes addressed to you along the way.

Playing Organized Games as a Family: Much More Than a Good Time

Now that your child is a little older, you'll find a growing interest in participating in games as a family, whether it's playing a board game, jumping a long rope, or shooting hoops in the driveway. Break out a deck of cards and teach your first-grader how to play poker. Kids love to use plastic chips, and you'll be surprised how stealthy your six- or seven-year-old gets collecting those face cards. Games not only sharpen skills, but can also decrease tension in the household and give you an opportunity to simply enjoy one another's company.

10 GREAT GAMES FOR FIRST-GRADERS AND THEIR FAMILIES

1. **Tic-Tac-Toe.** This simple, readily available game provides practice in tactical planning.

2. **Monopoly Junior.** You still get to buy, trade, and pay rent, but the game has been simplified for younger players.

3. **Twister.** This hilarious physical game develops connections between brain hemispheres.

4. **Mancala.** This classic is good for fine motor coordination and strategic thinking. You can make a game using marbles and a milk carton or buy the wooden version where toys are sold.

5. **Checkers.** Who didn't love to play checkers when they were little?

6. **Trouble.** Kids love the Pop-O-Matic dice, and the game is great for counting practice and working strategic angles.

7. **Junior Scrabble.** The letter tiles can be a great tool and motivator to help children learn their weekly spelling words, and playing the game builds vocabulary.

8. **Uno.** This card game develops categorizing skills as well as number order. Kids love it because it is easy to learn and readily adapts to players' abilities.

9. **Jenga.** Remove small wooden pieces from a tower while trying to keep the structure from toppling—great for fine motor coordination and strategic thinking.

10. **Connect Four.** Great for patterns and strategy, but only two can play at a time.

FIRST-GRADE OUTSIDE THE NORM

Some kids take off in first grade and read everything in print, from books to street signs to cereal boxes, while others couldn't care less about deciphering words, much less reading stories. They'd rather be jumping rope, running, kicking a ball, or playing video games. (Remember: Scientists recommend that kids should spend no more than two hours a day staring at screens. See page 26.)

The Tortoise

If you find out during your fall parent-teacher conference that your child is struggling in various subject areas, try not to worry. Ask for specific ways you can help at home as well as the steps the teacher is taking in the classroom to support your child in developing the required first-grade skills. You may want to explore the possibility of setting up an academic contract with goals and objectives, similar to the behavior contract on pages 49–50. Chances are, with diligence and communication between you, your child, and the teacher, you'll discover approaches to motivate your child and fill in learning gaps.

Observe how your child does homework and reads at bedtime over the next several weeks as you employ interventions the teacher suggested. Jot down what you notice in a notebook and include the date. Has following directions become easier, for example? Has reading aloud become more fluent? Dates and written notes will help you remain realistic about your child's progress. Sometimes, we question whether our kids have learned anything, but when we go back to earlier observations, we realize their skills are developing, slowly but surely.

However, if your child doesn't show improvement within four to six weeks, you should contact the teacher again. Ask if your child still struggles in the classroom as well. If so, the teacher may have initiated a student study team evaluation with other teachers and education professionals, usually the speech specialist and school psychologist, to brainstorm ways to bolster your child's progress. If your child's teacher hasn't begun the process, you can ask her to arrange such a meeting. Once you request an evaluation, the teacher is legally required to act upon it.

First grade is too early for the school to conduct testing to determine possible learning disabilities (and many private schools don't provide this service), but getting started on the process will pave the way for getting your child help as early as possible.

According to Susan Cradduck (2016), a licensed educational psychologist in San Diego,

> The law states we can't diagnose kids with learning disabilities until they're at least two years behind, which would be preschool age in the case of a first-grader, where developmental lines overlap. Most schools don't provide resource specialist help and other special education services until second grade. If the student study team process has begun in first grade, students can get tested at the beginning of second and get help as early as late fall semester.

Remember, though, brains grow at different rates, and every kid is an individual. Your son's or daughter's neural pathways may not be connected yet for reading or solving equations. Give your child a chance to improve with some of the activities in this book before deciding a learning disability is the culprit for academic struggles.

If your child is having difficulty grasping math concepts, play the Names for 10 game on page 95 until those number values become automatic. For reading help, try the language arts games on page 93, practice the first-grade high-frequency words on page 92, and play the physical games on page 115 to work out wiggles and improve memory. A little extra time and practice may be all your first-grader needs to catch up.

⋆THE REAL DEAL⋆

"Slow" Might Be Something Else: Jackie's Personal Story

I first became interested in how brains work when I was teaching at the University of Denver. The different ways my students appeared to learn was fascinating. It wasn't long before my fascination moved closer to home.

When one of my daughters began first grade, she was placed in the "slow learners" class, and I was called in for a parent-teacher conference. According to her teacher, my daughter wasn't interested in learning how to read and caused all kinds of disturbances. I knew she wasn't a slow learner, so I talked the teacher into placing her in the "top class of learners" for a week to see what would happen.

I checked out library books at several reading levels and left them around the house. Over the weekend, she became quite excited about some of the books, and I could hardly get her to come to the table for a meal. Her excuse: "Don't bother me. I'm reading."

How did she learn so quickly?

She admitted she had been secretly reading her big sister's books for some time with a flashlight under the covers. Then the question became: How did she teach herself to read?

Her brain seemed to learn best by exploring on her own at her own pace. She didn't respond to traditional teaching because she was impatient with what she considered boring. Why did it take us all so long to figure out what was happening?

Her experience led me to begin researching how brains learn, and I discovered they are most ready to learn certain skills at certain times. My daughter required the independence to follow her own way.

My graduate students, not surprisingly, exhibited a wide variety of learning styles, from those preferring the freedom to learn autonomously to those favoring the explicit guidance of a professor.

Cookin' with Gas: Keeping Smart Kids Engaged at School

Have you been praising the energy, brainpower, problem-solving skills, and tenacity your child exhibits while doing projects? This type of acknowledgment makes sharp kids successful, as opposed to focusing on intelligence, which can have the opposite effect (Mueller and Dweck 1998). Gifted and talented education (GATE) and other such programs are usually funded with special education resources—being way ahead of peers can be just as awkward and isolating as limping from behind.

Sometimes smart first-graders lose interest in school, feeling like the activities done in class cover material they already know. If this happens in your family, revisit "9 Ways to Keep Smart Kids Engaged at School" on page 63. Plug in your first-grader by brainstorming projects together with the teacher to find ways to relate classroom themes to more in-depth projects.

If you can be organized enough to sustain a contract (page 64), this offers a way to connect ventures outside of school with activities done in the classroom. Sometimes, busy parents and teachers find it difficult to maintain a contract, but if you continue to engage your first-grader in tasks that go with stories read at school as well as science and social studies units, your child will feel more a part of the group rather than an outsider. In turn, your child will be able to engage more in classroom activities.

THE REAL DEAL

The Smartest Kid I Ever Knew

You may not realize it, but it's tough to be a genius. I once had a first-grader named Nick who would hide pencils and scissors from other kids or fiddle in his desk instead of engaging in class discussions or projects. But whenever I called on him, he knew the answers.

The problem was that while the other kids learned names for 10 and how to read picture books, he read novels, did algebra, built elaborate structures with erector sets, and filled in adult-level crossword puzzles at home with his dad, a lieutenant commander for the US Navy. Nick was my inspiration for the smart-kid contract.

His mom and I worked together to get Nick's needs met. I differentiated assignments more appropriate to his brainpower, and the two of us came up with home projects in line with classroom themes. The other students and I had so much fun that year watching him present additional science experiments and neighborhood maps he had meticulously crafted so classmates could find their houses.

At the end of a social studies unit, I asked the kids to choose someone who works in the community (librarian, firefighter, postal carrier) and explain in a few sentences why that person was an important contributor to our neighborhood. Nick seemed stressed about this assignment. He would begin to write, but then get frustrated and crumple the paper. I'd give him a new one and try to talk him through it.

"But I can't write about just one person when we live in a really big world," he said.

"You're right. The world is a big place," I agreed. "Now I want you to think of the impact one person can have. You, me—we're only one person, yet the things we do can affect lots of people."

"But I can't," he shouted, holding his fists against his ears. "You need more than one person for a neighborhood to work!"

I knew when Nick got to this point, he needed space, so I suggested he go to the bathroom and get a drink of water to give his brain time to process.

About 10 minutes later, he returned to the classroom, went straight to his desk, and started writing furiously.

When the bell rang to go home, he looked at me with serious green eyes and asked, "Can I take this with me?" He held up a few papers, covered in writing on both sides. "I want to check out some things."

The next morning, Nick brought a stapled yellow folder to class and handed it to me.

"What's this?" I asked.

"It's yesterday's assignment," he answered and then walked back to his desk.

My jaw dropped when I opened the folder. Nick had written about 20 pages, front and back, of information about Iceland: form of government, customs, population, currency, and economics. He wanted me to know the kind of crowd it took to govern and organize a "neighborhood" and used Iceland for illustration because he reasoned that the country's population was only about 100,000 more people than Chula Vista's, our neighboring city (Bonita, where we lived, was a small, unincorporated area in San Diego County, so he "didn't think comparing our town was appropriate"—his words).

During recess, the two of us discussed what could only be described as his term paper. The information and Nick's arguments would have gone right over the other kids' heads. Iceland didn't have anything to do with the original assignment, but I gave him an A+ anyway.

The next year, Nick's dad got stationed in another part of the country, so the family left when he was in the middle of second grade. That was 20-some years ago. I often wonder where Nick lives and what he's doing now.

FIRST-GRADE CARE AND FEEDING

Many first-graders have a hard time sitting still, and that's normal. Their brains are busy making and strengthening connections between brain hemispheres to coordinate thinking and movement. Both parents and teachers have been guilty of suspecting hyperactivity issues when they would be better off providing kids this age with lots of opportunities for exercise. Physical activity pumps oxygen into the blood, and therefore the brain, giving synapses a workout as well.

Remember, six- and seven-year-olds' fine and gross motor skills are catching up with each other as brain impulses get more in sync between hemispheres. My mom used to tell me she wished she could bottle my extra energy and dab it on her wrists when she needed a pick-me-up most afternoons. This is why doctors generally don't diagnose a child with attention deficit hyperactivity disorder (ADHD) before second grade.

Because your first-grader's body will grow and change so much this year, a healthy diet, plenty of water, regular exercise, and ample sleep are essential for optimal learning. These things also help manage first-grade energy for a happier household.

Z-Time

Is your bedtime ritual still working to ensure adequate sleep, or do you need some modifications? Having to switch up bedtime activities is common. Revisit the list on page 17 to adapt suggestions or try new ones. For example, change the background noise from soothing music to ocean sounds to see if your child's brain will relax more easily into theta waves and then into slower, revitalizing delta waves.

Check to see if you have forgotten a key element in sleep readiness—providing an 8- to 12-ounce glass of water during or after dinner, for instance, so your child's body is in good working order when it's time to fall asleep. Remember, dehydration can keep kids from falling and staying asleep.

Exercise and Playtime

Free time to run around and work off steam, use imagination, and mentally decompress is critical for first-graders. Both you and your child will be happier if you schedule at least an hour every day of physical exercise, the kind that speeds up heart rates and breaks a sweat. Hanging out at the local park or playing in the backyard will give your six- or seven-year-old an opportunity for exercise and pretending at the same time. After-dinner walks or jogs can also be fun workouts, and kids generally love outings like this with parents and caregivers.

If you live in a place where it isn't easy to go outside and play, encourage your child to dance, jump rope, and do other physical activities in the family room. Also consider purchasing a Nintendo Wii or similar product that provides physical video games, such as *High School Musical 3: Senior Year Dance*, where kids groove along with the characters and make up their own moves for a fun, sweaty workout.

In a 2014 study at the University of Tennessee, researchers found that active video games can be a viable alternative for providing the exercise kids need (MacArthur et al., 388). "Our study shows video games [that] wholly engage a child's body can be a source of physical activity," said Hollie Raynor, director of UT's Healthy Eating and Activity Laboratory and associate professor of nutrition.

To find out more about Wii workouts and other electronic jams for kids, type "physical video games for kids" into a search engine for extensive lists and descriptions, often written by involved parents.

5 WAYS TO WORK OUT FIRST-GRADE WIGGLES

1. **"Skip to My Lou."** Try skipping with your child from the parking lot into the grocery store and on other errands. You'll make onlookers smile, get in some giggles of your own, and strengthen connections between the left- and right-brain hemispheres—the same process the brain undergoes during reading. What a fun way to get your child's brain in gear for better learning!

2. **Walk a tightrope.** As you cook dinner, make up a wild story about why your child must get from one side of the room to the other, balancing on the line of grout between tiles, or whatever "tight rope" is available on your kitchen floor (he must save a stranded puppy on the other side of the mountain, for example). Balancing stimulates the vestibular system in the brain, which works in conjunction with visual and audio centers, playing a significant role in language development. Conjure scenarios to have your child walk the balance beam at the park or follow the centerline down the sidewalk. Your child will soon come up with his own creative balancing stories to work out his wiggles—while improving his language skills.

3. **Move to a beat.** Dancing burns off excess energy and blends cognitive thought with muscle memory in the cerebellum, helping kids learn (Bergland 2013).

4. **Bounce balls.** Dribbling a ball back and forth between hands while standing still coordinates brain function between hemispheres, which can improve reading skills.

5. **Jump rope.** Your child won't need a lot of space to work up a sweat and burn off some steam with a jump rope, and the exercise has

added benefits for first-graders. Pat Jones (2016), teacher of more than 35 years, says, "My experience has been that once children begin to jump rope individually with an established beat and a double hop, their reading fluency often . . . improve[s] in two weeks' time."

A Word on First-Graders' Teeth

If your child hasn't already lost a baby tooth or two, ages six and seven are prime times for losing the front four bottom teeth and then the upper ones, resulting in those precious jack-o'-lantern smiles. As permanent teeth grow in, they are extra vulnerable to sugary treats and fruit juices as well as processed carbohydrates, such as bread, crackers, and pasta.

If your child eats those things occasionally, his teeth will be fine provided he brushes them thoroughly in the morning and evening. If you haven't started flossing yet, begin the ritual now to stave off future cavities. And if you've been flossing your child's teeth, bravo! Keep doing it. Permanent teeth come in closer together than baby teeth, and floss reaches the in-between places where brushes can't.

This is also a good time to get dye tablets from the dentist or buy them online to have your first-grader check how well she's cleaning her teeth. Kids usually enjoy the adventure of brushing and flossing, then chewing the tablets, swishing their saliva for 30 seconds, and spitting a red mess into the sink. The gruesome experience of seeing dark patches of missed tarter in the mirror rivals the thrill of dressing up for Halloween, and getting rid of those ugly stains is almost as satisfying.

Nonchalantly checking on your child's brushing about once a month is also a good idea. Give pointers if you notice areas that need improvement, and praise the things your child does well. If the timer has gotten misplaced or broken, be sure to replace it—the two-minute-minimum brushing time is critical to your child's future dental health.

Nutrition

How is your child eating lately? If your first-grader is one of those kids who don't like sugar and happily eat vegetables, I applaud you and must confess I'm a bit jealous. My girls fervently preferred chocolate chip cookies and gummy bears to broccoli and Brussels sprouts.

Kids need plenty of vegetables, though, particularly those high in calcium, such as broccoli, tomatoes, and zucchini, for strong bones and teeth. Veggies are the powerhouse providers of the fiber, vitamins, and micronutrients your child needs for overall health, growth, and brain development. Since edible plants usually aren't high on the list of favorites for first-graders, check out the tips below.

7 WAYS TO GET FIRST-GRADERS TO EAT VEGETABLES

1. **Put your child in charge of produce.** Have your child pick out apples, grapes, mandarin oranges, baby carrots, celery stalks, broccoli bunches, heads of lettuce, and cauliflower for your family. Getting involved in the process will encourage healthy eating.

2. **Have your child choose canned fruits and frozen veggies when fresh favorites are out of season.** If you can't get fresh peaches or green beans, there's no sense in doing without them. You may end up buying the cans or packages with the prettiest pictures, but is it worth paying a few cents more for your child to get the nutrients needed for thinking and growing?

3. **Make up stories.** Your child is a giant who must eat the "trees" (broccoli and cauliflower) to clear the way for Jack to get to the beanstalk. Fair warning: When your first-grader starts making up stories, they may get ridiculous.

4. **Point out that vegetables help kids grow.** Telling six- and seven-year-olds vegetables will make them healthy has little meaning, but first-graders *do* want to get bigger. Reminding your child that veggies will make him taller is a much better motivator.

5. **Drizzle a little rice vinegar on cooked vegetables.** Rice vinegar neutralizes the bitterness kids' keen taste buds detect and gives veggies a sweeter taste.

6. **Serve veggies raw.** Raw vegetables taste sweeter and more palatable to kids. I used to buy bags of precut stir-fry veggies, and my kids and I would eat them in my classroom after school, in the car, on the way to sports, or at the kitchen table while doing homework. Along with being rich in vitamins and fiber, raw veggies provide a satisfying crunch, and they tide kids over without filling them up and spoiling dinner.

7. **Bake veggies with your little sous-chef.** Have your child put foil on a cookie sheet, arrange broccoli and cauliflower florets (or other veggies), and spray them with a thin layer of olive oil. Help your child sprinkle salt, garlic, or other spices over them and bake at 350° for 50 minutes to an hour. Vegetables are delicious this way, and assisting in the preparation may encourage your first-grader to eat them.

Healthy Breakfast—A Must for First-Graders!

Lots of us don't feel hungry in the morning, but it's important to eat anyway. Brains require energy for neurons to fire efficiently. You want your child to be able to think, right? And people who eat breakfast have fewer problems managing body weight, tend to be more physically active, and have more stable blood sugar levels throughout the day (Adolphus et al. 2013). Building good eating habits now can set up your first-grader's nutritional foundation for a healthier life.

Although it seems counterintuitive, make sure breakfast includes some healthy fat. Kids need the slower release of energy until lunchtime to compliment the quick release of carbohydrates. Besides, fat is needed to break down certain nutrients, such as vitamins A, E, D, and K.

If you don't like to eat in the morning, this will create an extra challenge for you. It's difficult to get children to do things the adults in their lives don't model. One of the hardest parts of parenting is how closely our kids watch our every move. On the bright side, both you and your child will benefit from a bit of healthy food before work and school in preparation for a day of thinking. Try some of the quick, easy meals listed below and wash them down with fresh, cool water. Remember, hydration is as important for thinking as fat, fiber, and vitamins.

4 QUICK BREAKFASTS FOR BEST THINKING AND HEALTHY WEIGHT

1. Fresh fruit and an egg—good protein and nutrients. No time to cook? Try making hard-boiled eggs on the weekend. Refrigerated hard-boiled eggs last five days after they are peeled and seven days inside the shell.

2. Fresh fruit and 2 percent milk—protein, nutrients, and a bit of fat to metabolize the vitamins.

3. Fresh fruit and half a frozen burrito heated in the microwave—a quick breakfast with a good balance of fat, protein, nutrients, and fiber.

4. Unsweetened oatmeal with fresh fruit and milk (dairy, pea, almond, oat, coconut, or soy)—a great, filling option packed with protein, fiber, and nutrients.

Note: Did you notice sugary cereals, donuts, yogurt, and breakfast bars didn't make the list? You don't want processed sugar to rob thinking energy after that 20-minute spike.

First-Grade Lunches

The convenience of having your child eat school lunches is tempting, but before giving in, find out what the school serves. Does the menu include healthy choices? Would your child choose those items rather than foods with mostly empty calories? Frankly, if you can spend a little effort to make sure your first-grader's lunch contains the necessary nutrition, his brain will more likely get what it needs to function at its best.

Your child has grown since kindergarten, and this may be his first year attending school for a full day, which means more food needs to go into the lunch box. Since every child is different, you'll have to experiment with preferences and the amount of food your first-grader requires to get through an entire school day. Include protein, fat, and carbohydrates for optimal energy and brainpower.

Whether your child brings lunch from home or eats in the cafeteria, remember to send at least 12 ounces of water. A couple of trips to the bathroom may result at first, but your child's body will soon adjust to waiting for recess and lunch breaks.

HEALTHY LUNCH SUGGESTIONS FOR FIRST-GRADERS

Proteins

- Tuna. Health food stores sell tuna without MSG if that concerns you.

- Lunch meats. Look for brands with less salt and fewer chemicals.

- Hard-boiled eggs or egg salad.

- Milk (dairy, pea, almond, oat, coconut, or soy). Read the labels to compare the nutritional information.

- Cheese. Vary the types and forms: string, cubes, or slices.

- Assorted nuts. Try several kinds to see which your child enjoys—(e.g., cashews, almonds, or pecans). Avoid peanuts—they have less nutrition and can trigger allergic reactions in your child or classmates.

- Nut butter. Often peanut butter has added sugar. Almond, cashew, and other nut butters tend to have better nutrition and are less likely to activate allergies.

- Beans (maybe the other half of the burrito your child ate for breakfast).

Note: Additional items must accompany plant-based proteins to form complete amino acid chains in the body—rice should accompany pinto beans, for example.

Carbohydrates

- Fresh fruit of any kind. You can't beat it for healthy vitamins, minerals, and carbs. Most first-graders eat large fruits best when sliced. *Fun fact:* Bananas are easier to peel from the bottom—like monkeys do— rather than from the top.

- Nut-butter sandwich with 100 percent fruit jelly.

- Dried fruit, such as raisins, dates, cranberries, apricots. Read labels to make sure the product doesn't include added sugar and chemicals. *Note:* Make sure your child has water to drink after eating fruit leather or dried fruit to protect teeth from the concentrated sugar that results in dehydration.

- Whole wheat bread, the kind with nuts and seeds, not the brown bread that looks almost like white bread and metabolizes the same— as a big ball of sugar.

Note: Avoid prepackaged lunches. They're full of chemicals, salt, and sugar. You're better off having your child eat in the school cafeteria. Also, avoid juice drinks, including 100 percent fruit juices. Send your child to school with milk and water. Like candy and cake, flavored drinks are for special occasions.

WHERE DO YOU SEE YOURSELF?

Mr. Gilpatrick talks on a conference call in the den as Mrs. Gilpatrick rushes to grab ketchup and mustard out of the pantry. Jordan, their six-year-old son, is in the formal dining room where the family rarely goes. He knows he's supposed to be setting the table for dinner, but he got home late from soccer practice. If he doesn't squeeze in a game on his mom's laptop now, he won't get a chance to play on the computer at all today. He makes sure to turn off the sound.

Jordan's stomach growls with the smell of hamburger. But he's almost to the next level in the game—he can't stop now.

In the kitchen, Mrs. Gilpatrick dumps ready-made salad into a bowl, tosses the lettuce with blue cheese dressing, and puts it on the table. *Hmm*, she thinks. *No plates or silverware—and Jordan is awfully quiet.* She should call him to set the table, but the spitting frying pan distracts her. She'd better flip those burgers.

Jordan's dad finishes with his conference call and comes into the kitchen. "Hey, honey, are we eating soon? I'm starved, and I have to go notarize some papers for a client after dinner."

"Salad is on the table." Mrs. Gilpatrick pulls a plate from the cupboard, scoops a burger from the pan, and hands it to her husband. "Here. Jordan and I will be there in a minute."

"Where are the glasses and silverware?" Mr. Gilpatrick asks.

"Jordan's around somewhere."

"Jordan!" Mr. Gilpatrick calls.

Jordan hears his dad, but he can't answer now—not when he just got to the next level. He's never made it this far in the game before.

Mr. Gilpatrick sighs. "Forget it." He goes to the cupboard and snags a couple more plates. "It'll be faster if I do it. I have to meet my client by eight thirty." He quickly sets the table and sits down to eat.

"Jordan, dinner!" Mom shouts as she hurries to the table with a plate of burgers in one hand and buns, cheese, and sliced tomato in the other.

Jordan knows he should turn off the computer, but he's almost beat this level, too, for the first time ever. He'll shut down the game as soon as . . . there—he did it!

"Yes!" Jordan says aloud and pumps his fist.

"Jordan James Gilpatrick, get in here right now!"

Uh-oh. His mom doesn't sound happy. Jordan clicks the mouse to save his spot on level five and shuts down the game. Rushing to the kitchen, he slams into Mrs. Gilpatrick in the doorway.

"Oh. Sorry." He scoots around her and skids into his chair at the table.

"Where have you been?" his dad says, his mouth full of burger. "I had to get out the plates."

"I . . . I . . ." Jordan looks from his dad to his mom. If he tells them the truth, they'll take away his computer time. "I was doing my homework."

Mrs. Gilpatrick looks across the table at Mr. Gilpatrick. "I guess we can't be too upset," she says. "Good thinking, Jordan. We got home so late, you'll have to get ready for bed after dinner." She scoops a hamburger onto Jordan's plate and one onto her own.

Oh, boy, so when can I do my homework for real? Jordan thinks.

After dinner, Mr. Gilpatrick takes off for his appointment. Mrs. Gilpatrick barely gives Jordan time to clear the table and brush his teeth before she hurries him off to bed with a quick bedtime story. She still has to get that last load of laundry in the dryer and fold the contents of three other baskets so they'll have clothes to wear in the morning.

Over the next few weeks, Jordan's routine of "doing homework" before dinner morphs into him hardly ever setting the table. His mom silently reprimands herself for not checking the poor little guy's assignments to help him correct mistakes. Between her job, soccer practice, and making dinner, then getting him to bed and doing household chores, she feels so pressed for time.

Jordan's backpack has gotten filthy, so after his soccer game on Saturday, Mrs. Gilpatrick decides to clean it out and throw it in the washing machine with his dirty uniform and practice clothes. She knows Jordan should clean out his own backpack, but it's easier for her to do it.

To Mrs. Gilpatrick's horror, she finds crumpled math pages with sticky notes written by the teacher. For three weeks, she and her husband have been asked to practice adding and subtracting between one and 20 objects with their son. Jordan hasn't been turning in his homework and seems to be having trouble with the concept. Worse, several blank homework papers lay crushed under his lunch box, along with a rumpled sealed envelope with "Mr. and Mrs. Gilpatrick" written on the front in cursive. It looks like they're headed to school for a conference with the teacher.

* * *

(☉☉) Her daughter's high-pitched angry tone catches Mrs. Westerly's ears first as Shandra and her new friend yell at one another in the backyard. *Is that Brenda girl picking on Shandra?* Mrs. Westerly wonders, rushing to poke her head outside the sliding glass door.

"I'm taking another turn," Shandra shouts, then tries to swipe her new best friend's purple four square ball.

"You wouldn't let me when I missed," Brenda counters, turning her body to keep the ball out of reach.

Mrs. Westerly narrows her eyes at the six-year-old with the lopsided mahogany braids. "I thought you brought that ball with you to share," she says.

Brenda winces at the scary adult face. "I did," she says much softer now. "But Shandra isn't playing fair."

"Give me the ball." Mrs. Westerly holds out her hand. "You two can find something else to do."

Brenda's eyes well with tears. "Can I call my mom?" she asks. "I want to go home."

(😇) "You're awfully quiet in there, Jake," Mrs. Landry says as she puts the lid over the fish in the frying pan. "What are you guys doing?" No answer. "Jacob?" She checks the broccoli and cauliflower in the oven. "Where are you? It's time to set the table."

When her son still doesn't answer, Mrs. Landry turns off the burner so the fish won't overcook and walks around the kitchen counter to peek into the family room.

"My turn," Jake whispers on the couch, reaching for Mrs. Landry's e-tablet from his friend Greg. The boys play video games every Monday after martial arts practice and after Mrs. Landry has checked their homework. She'd been busy putting the fish in the frying pan when the timer went off, and the boys took advantage of her distraction to stretch their playtime beyond the agreed-upon half hour.

Knowing Jake, I bet he's justified ignoring the timer because his friend is here. Mrs. Landry crosses her arms, waiting for the boys to notice she's caught them.

"In a minute." Greg yanks the tablet away from Jake, turns his back, and sits on the edge of the couch, tapping away at the screen.

"Hey, what are you doing?" Jake says. "It's my turn!" He reaches over Greg's shoulder for the tablet, but his friend jumps off the couch.

"Keep your pants on," Greg says, his small fingers still scrambling over the screen.

Mrs. Landry smirks. She'd wondered if Greg was the source of that lovely phrase her son had said proudly before she'd explained it was disrespectful to say such things to adults.

She's about to reprimand them for the extra computer time when Jake says, "Fine. Then you can get in trouble for not turning off the tablet. You're already grounded next weekend, so I figure when my mom tells your mom, you won't get to play another game for a month."

That's pretty smart for a kid who just turned seven, thinks Mrs. Landry, and she steps out of sight to let them resolve their problem.

"You gonna tell on me?" Greg's question sounds more like a taunt.

"Nope," Jake says. "My mom thinks I didn't see her spying on us, but she just saw you with the tablet."

"Ah, man," Greg groans.

Mrs. Landry can't help but crack a smile. She peeks around the corner to see Greg hand the tablet to her son. Jake turns it off and puts it on the coffee table.

"Jake?" Mrs. Landry calls out, and both boys jump. "Set the table, please. Dinner's almost ready."

"Okay, Mom." Jake glances at Greg. "Coming."

She's glad Jake worked out the disagreement with his friend. After dinner, she'll talk to the boys about breaking the rules to help them understand the value of keeping your word. By relating the situation to something they'll understand—asking them how they'd feel if she broke her promise to pick them up after martial arts practice, for example—she'll help them see the importance of being trustworthy. Then she'll tell them they can't play on her e-tablet again until they earn back her trust. She commits to checking on them more often, and she'll see in a month if she's ready to let them use her tablet again.

* * *

Do any of these parents seem familiar? Are you the angel who makes sure your child follows through on chores, such as setting the table, or are you too harried to hassle making your first-grader do tasks to contribute to the household? Do you check the homework daily so your child develops solid study habits? (*Hint:* Getting into a routine of having your first-grader clean out his backpack during the weekend can avoid finished pages that don't get turned in and catch blank ones that get past you.) Life can be busy and exhausting, but being consistent in respecting the rules now will make a world of difference once your child hits middle school.

How about disagreements with friends? Are you the angel parent who lets your child work out problems with peers while monitoring to make sure no one gets bullied—or the helicopter parent who intervenes and directs the conversation, often in your child's favor? Sometimes it's hard not to jump into children's arguments, especially when they get heated. But unless kids verbally or physically attack one another, letting them work out issues with friends develops valuable social skills.

First-graders crave the essential order that rules provide and often feel the need to righteously point them out to others. It's funny how they always seem to have a "good reason" for breaking a rule themselves, but they insist that others should follow that same rule without exception.

Relating an infraction to something your six- or seven-year-old has witnessed, or can envision through an experience, gives parents teachable moments. In the example, Mrs. Landry plans to equate her trusting the boys with the e-tablet to their trust in her that she'll pick them up after martial arts. She wants them to understand that we *depend* on each other to keep our promises. Being able to trust the people you care about is a serious thing.

Mrs. Landry could also compare the boys' broken agreement to the unfair behavior of the girl next door who borrowed Jake's basketball the week before and didn't give it back until after Greg had to go home. Now Jake doesn't want to let her play with his ball again. Another example might be to compare the boys' sneakiness to the kid in their class Jake told her about who cut in line during their kickball game at recess and stole Greg's turn to kick the ball. The closer you can relate an infraction to something your child understands, the better the opportunity for him to grasp his own negative behavior and learn how to improve in the future.

An unfavorable consequence is necessary and most effective as a teaching tool if established ahead of time. Your child will also learn best if his fate for breaking a rule directly relates to the infraction. For example, if he sneaks a cookie, he goes without dessert the next day, or if he lies about playing on the computer, he has to wait two days before he can play on the computer again.

Yelling at your child for breaking a rule or saying you're disappointed in him at this age just causes hurt feelings that overpower his ability to learn from the mistake.

CONCLUSION

Your first-grader will grow so much this year: mentally, physically, emotionally, and socially. By the end of the school year, you and your child may write notes to each other. A whole new nighttime ritual and homework routine may have evolved. Hopefully, your child's handwriting has shown up on the whiteboard or family calendar to replace the cryptic pictures.

Your child may be a math whiz because the names for 10 are so ingrained in his neural pathways that adding and subtracting has become automatic. If your child has needed modifications for learning—either to catch up or to branch out to stay interested in learning—you've communicated with the teacher, so interventions for second grade should go much easier.

Have fun over the summer. I can't stress enough the importance of keeping up with your daily reading routine and playing math games when opportunities arise—with marshmallows, buttons, or the contents of the coin jar. When it's time to go back to school, you and your child will be rested and ready—and you'll have a second-grader in the house.

Lucky you.

Second grade expands on what kids learned in first grade with practical application to everyday life, and this age group aims to please. This bunch is sensitive, though, so their feelings can be hurt easily. The next chapter will help your child get the most out of this heartwarming year—socially, emotionally, and intellectually—with lots of great information, stories, and fun games second-graders love to play. Enjoy!

٭ 5 ٭

SECOND GRADE
Eager to Please

You'll be amazed at your second-grader's thoughtful questions, logical pondering, and ability to describe objects and distinguish between them. The tendency for deeper thinking at this age seems to widen their awareness of the outside world as well. Ideas, feelings, and interpretations of social situations will advance so much this year, you'll wonder what happened to your baby. It's always important to spend time talking to your child, but second-graders especially crave a sounding board to help them decipher new thoughts and experiences.

YOUR SECOND-GRADER'S BRAIN

By age seven or eight, a fair number of neurons have been pared away in the brain. That might sound scary, but this trimming defines the person your child will become. In *The Brain with David Eagleman* series on PBS (2015), neuroscientist David Eagleman points out, "The process of becoming someone is about pruning back the possibilities that are already present. You become who you are, not because of what grows in your brain, but because of what is removed."

After the preschool years, when the brain has produced most of its neurons, the maturation process is a sort of precision neural haircut that creates stronger pathways—so connections go from generic to more specific as a result of experiences and environment.

A two-year-old has twice as many neurons as an adult, but by second grade, your child has discovered likes and dislikes as she continually hones neural networks. Experiences that give your seven- or eight-year-old a sense of accomplishment stimulate dopamine in the brain, the pleasure hormone, often making these activities preferred pastimes. Second-graders who discover the joy of sticking with a challenging math problem and solving it, for example, may decide math is their favorite subject.

Having fun finishing a chapter book for the first time may fuel the desire to read many more. An art project during summer camp may have turned out well, and ever since, the best things in life involve holding a paintbrush. Cheers from playmates for kicking a ball into the outfield or jumping rope the most times without missing may spark a love for sports, and so on.

Brain Growth in Second Grade

If unused neurons are getting pared away, how does your child's brain continue to grow? *Glial cells.* Glia divide and multiply to form the "white matter" that supplies blood and nutrients to the brain. The brain's housekeepers, glia also get rid of dead nerve cells and other debris.

Your child's glial cells serve another function as well: coating neurons. Like insulation around hot wires, these cells help form and protect neural pathways that make up the "gray matter," or thinking part of the brain. This coating defines and directs the electrical impulses that send messages and generate responses.

Studies have found that glial cells even participate in the formation and function of synapses, the gaps between dendrites and axons that allow neurons to communicate. Advances in imaging technology show that glia communicate via chemicals rather than electrical impulses, "talking" not only among themselves but also to neurons (Perry 2010).

Your seven- or eight-year-old's brain is likely in a stage of heavy glia growth as new experiences form and solidify existing neural pathways. Periods of rapid change, resulting from behavior shifts to meet new challenges, create greater plasticity in the brain. In short, your child will grow, learn, and mature a lot this year.

This means that healthy eating and plentiful hydration to fuel and cool the brain during its constant state of learning continues to be important. Your child also still requires ample sleep to allow rejuvenating delta waves to reset the brain for each new day—as well as regular exercise to send the brain the high levels of oxygen it needs for development.

Are you sensing a pattern?

But sometimes, in all of the structured sports and other activities, we forget that downtime to relax and pretend are also key ingredients for learning. Veteran teacher Pat Jones (2016) says, "I believe we are overscheduling children. They need to run around and engage in imaginative play, [which] helps with reading and problem-solving."

Due to all that glial action honing and nourishing networks in the brain, your seven- or eight-year-old's attention span may be lengthening. You can give two directions at a time instead of one, and your child will likely be able to follow them if the instructions are clear and concise. Also, now that refined neural pathways allow for more complex thinking, your second-grader may become intrigued by a project requiring focus and determination that just months earlier had caused frustration.

Language skills will take a huge leap this year too. Speaking vocabulary may grow to several thousand words, allowing reading fluency and comprehension to expand dramatically.

Hooked on Video Games

As mentioned in chapter 2 (page 25), dopamine plays a role in how children get drawn to electronic games. The constant rewards cause the brain to release this pleasure hormone. Kids quickly forget failures by starting a fresh game with lots more readily available points and magic tools. When the timer goes off, parents often hear, "I can't stop now. I'm almost to the next level!"

But take heart. Remember, according to scientists, kids' brains seem to be fine when electronic devices are used cumulatively for no more than two hours a day (see page 26). That limit may get severely tested, but if you stay firm, your child will learn that the rule is the rule and argue less often.

You may want to reevaluate your parental control software to determine if it's still meeting your family's needs. If you decide to upgrade or change your system, see *PC Magazine*'s latest list online.

THE REAL DEAL
Electronic Games and My Friend's Son

A friend of mine was a single mom who tried to limit time on video games, but she kept track by glancing at the clock rather than setting a timer. When she got busy, which happened a lot, she'd forget about her two boys playing on the computer in another room. The games kept them occupied so she could get dinner made and do other chores without interruption, a welcome reprieve after a busy day at work.

Both sons are now college graduates, and her older son hasn't noticed difficulties resulting from spending a lot of time playing video games. Her younger son, however, attributes too much screen time to his ongoing struggle with focusing and fuzzy memory. He often has to double- and triple-check his reports at work for completeness and accuracy before turning in a project.

SECOND-GRADE SOCIAL TRAITS

This year, children transform into social creatures and become more involved in their school lives. They tend to withdraw from adults, favoring their friends. It's an exciting time, but with their ever-growing awareness of others, second-graders also experience some stress.

Second-Grade Perfectionists

Kids in this age group want to appear that they know what they're doing. Many become highly self-critical at this stage and worry—about school assignments, scuffles on the playground, and the way the teacher and their classmates view them. You may hear complaints when others don't comply with how your child views the world. Occasional outbursts may occur when feelings of inadequacy become overwhelming.

Your Relationship

A word of caution: Be gentle in your discipline and mindful of your sense of humor. Second-graders tend to be extremely sensitive. Doing something as innocent as chuckling at an art project that is insufferably cute because of a few slightly askew pieces, could cause your child to decide he is terrible at art for decades. This may sound dramatic, but I bet you can come up with some equally silly reasons for some of the decisions you've made about yourself along the way. Ask what your child learned while making the project, rather than commenting on the lopsidedness of his Picasso-like sea-animal mobile.

Clarify the Rules

Seven or eight is also the age when kids start to feel guilt and shame. Include your child in reestablishing household rules and reasonable consequences for breaking them. (Remember to phrase the rules as positive statements and avoid negative words like "wrong" and "don't.") You may have to dial back your child's suggestions because second-graders' self-righteousness—the belief that *they* would never break said rule—can lead to ridiculous ideas for punishments—at least until they make an inevitable mistake. Participating in setting family boundaries will help your child accept responsibility for missteps rather than seeing discipline as a personal affront or disapproval of his character.

Family

At this sensitive stage, lasting hurt feelings can result from siblings' teasing. Listen carefully to your kids' banter. Most often, they will work out their issues, but if one of your children gets cruel, step in to talk about respecting one another.

If your second-grader is the one who lashes out, you may be tempted to give harsh corrections, but keep in mind that she's learning how to process her feelings. You don't want her to shut down and go silent when hurt. Patience and open communication will be your most valuable tools along this parenting journey.

On the bright side, seven- and eight-year-olds often do well when trusted with new family duties, especially if they receive frequent encouragement and positive feedback for their efforts. For example, if setting the table was your child's chore in first grade, add clearing the table and taking out the trash after dinner. Think of other jobs, such as feeding the family dog or cat and checking the mailbox daily. The actual tasks don't matter as much as your child's regular contribution to the family.

New responsibilities—thus increased trust and respect for their abilities—can be exciting for second-graders at first, like cleaning up after a new puppy. It can be trickier to make sure the chores get done after the novelty wears off. Remember that creating a habit takes lots of repetition, so remain calm and consistent. Your follow-through now will create a more enjoyable household during the middle and high school years.

★THE REAL DEAL★

What's a Virgo?

My big sister left her *Teen* magazine on the coffee table, open to the horoscope section. I tiptoed to the hallway, glanced up the stairwell, and smirked at my good fortune. With stealthy seven-year-old fingers, I turned the page, hoping to solve the "Virgo mystery."

I'd barely found my zodiac sign when I heard, "Who said you could look at my magazine?"

I jumped at my sister's voice. Face hot, heart pounding, I spun to face her. "If you don't want me touching it, then tell me what a Virgo is."

"I told you, you don't want to know." She reached for the magazine.

I grabbed it off the table and shouted, "Tell me!"

She tried to wrench it from my hand. Zzzt went a few pages. "Great. Now it's ripped."

I sprinted with the magazine to the other side of the table. "You can have it back when you tell me," I said.

"Fine." She crossed her arms. "A Virgo is a *butt*."

My jaw dropped. That couldn't be true—could it?

"See?" she said. "I knew you'd be upset."

She marched over, snatched the magazine from my hand, and left the room.

The idea seemed ridiculous, but my older sister knew everything—and she'd tried to warn me. I stared into the mirror on the wall above the television, wondering how I could have been born in such an awful month. My nose tingled, and soon I choked on sobs. My eyes and cheeks swelled, all red and puffy—maybe like a big ol' fat butt!

The door squeaked as my mom came in from the garage with a full laundry basket. "What's the matter, honey?" she asked.

"I'm a butt!" I screamed.

"What?" Mom put the clothes on the couch and tried to hide a smile.

"It's not funny!" I shouted. "Why did you have to have me in September?"

"What does September have to do with . . .?" Mom's eyes lit with understanding, and she turned toward the stairs. "Jan, get down here!"

"What?" came Jan's voice from the behind the wall, followed by peals of laughter.

"Did you tell your sister she's a butt?"

"Not exactly." Jan sauntered into the room with a crooked grin.

"What did you tell her?" Mom picked up some jeans from the basket and started folding.

"She asked me what a Virgo was, so I told her."

"A Virgo is a maiden." Mom dropped the jeans to her side and looked at me. "A young woman."

"Well . . ." My sister shrugged. "I was close."

"Really? How do you figure that was close?" Mom said and started laughing.

Jan joined her, and I began to giggle through my tears. While it's true that laughter is contagious, I was relieved to be born in the month of the maiden and not the butt.

Friends

Unlike first-graders who pick a friend of the week, children this age maintain friendships longer and move toward choosing friends who share their interests and traits. They generally treat others with respect during outdoor games or class projects, and with guidance—sometimes from adults, other times from peers—this group can see things from another person's point of view. As with first-graders, you'll want to wait to see if your child can work out issues with playmates before getting involved.

Be prepared for times that your child may snap at you in response to something you say. Before you scold her, understand that such a reaction may stem from a situation at school that day. Take a deep breath, and try asking a question, something like this: "Hey, did you mean to talk to me like that, or are you upset about something else?"

By getting your second-grader to stop and think, you can help her apply her recently increased ability to mentally process relationships to realize when she's responded inappropriately. Give her an opportunity to practice repairing the relationship by apologizing. You'll also be able to figure out the root of the snarky behavior and give your child strategies to deal with social and emotional challenges.

Remember, brains must feel safe to do their best thinking. If an event or circumstance threatens your child's emotional safety, consciously or subconsciously, mental energy will be spent on perceived peril rather than on learning. Model patience, asking questions, and attentive listening to show your child how to work through problems, an important life skill.

SECOND-GRADE ACADEMICS

Second grade teaches kids how to use all those math and language ideas they were exposed to in first grade and delves deeper into concepts. Your child will continue to develop reading and writing skills, moving forward on the road from learning to read toward reading to learn by fourth grade. Math applications will focus on skills for practical use, such as measuring, telling time, and using numbers in everyday life.

See the general list of second-grade academic skills to understand the purpose of the games you'll play together this year. Choose activities in this chapter not only to have fun but also to build confidence and skills and to increase your child's enthusiasm for learning.

SECOND-GRADE ACADEMIC SKILLS

Language Arts

- Talk about the *who, what, where, when, why,* and *how* of a story.

- Retell stories, fables, and folktales and understand their lessons or morals.

- Explain how words and phrases create rhythm and meaning in a story, poem, or song.

- Understand the beginning of a story introduces characters and the central conflict, the middle reacts to the conflict, and the end concludes the story, usually solving the conflict.

- Recognize characters' different points of view and their individual voices.

- Use pictures and text to talk about the characters, setting, and plot in a story.

- Compare versions of the same story by different authors or from diverse cultures.

- By the end of the year, understand stories and poetry leveled for early third grade.

- Use correct English grammar in writing and speaking, including irregular plural nouns (e.g., children, people), reflexive pronouns (e.g., himself, myself), past tense irregular verbs (e.g., took, found), adjectives and adverbs, and simple and compound sentences.

- Use writing conventions (e.g., use capital letters to begin proper nouns, an apostrophe for contractions and possessives, commas to open and close a letter).

- Understand second-grade spelling patterns and use a dictionary to look up words.

- Determine meanings of unfamiliar words via context in a story, by interpreting prefix, suffix, and root word clues and by consulting a glossary or dictionary.

- Write opinion and informational paragraphs using examples to support the topic, and write narratives recounting an event or events with a beginning, middle, and end.

Mathematics

- Use addition and subtraction within 100 to solve one- and two-step word problems.

- Know all fact families from 1 to 20 (if your child mastered the Names for 10 game in first grade, this progression will be a snap).

- Understand odd and even by grouping objects from 1 to 20 and counting by 2s.

- Add objects in rows and columns up to five (preparation for multiplication).

- Count to 1,000 by 1s, 5s, 10s, and 100s.

- Add up to four two-digit numbers.

- Mentally add or subtract 10s or 100s from a number.

- Understand the place value of 1s, 10s, and 100s (a fast, clear, fun way to do this is by using physical objects, such as Popsicle sticks and rubber bands, as described on page 98).

- Explain why addition or subtraction should be used to solve a problem.

- Find the length of objects using tools, such as rulers, yardsticks, or measuring tapes.

- Measure objects in both the English and metric systems (e.g., inches and centimeters).

- Estimate measurement in both the English and metric systems (e.g., yards and meters).

- Measure to determine the difference in length between objects.

- Tell and write the time to the nearest five minutes, noting a.m./p.m.

- Count money with a variety of coins and bills, and write values using $ and ¢ symbols.

- Solve simple problems using data from bar and picture graphs.

- Name, describe, and draw shapes up to six sides, including the cube.

- Divide a rectangle into equal rows and columns of squares to count them (a precursor to finding area using multiplication).

- Divide circles and rectangles into equal halves, thirds, and quarters using the fractional terms, and understand that two halves, three thirds, and four quarters are equal to one whole.

To find out what your child will be expected to master in your area, type into a search engine the name of your state and "education standards K–12." Skills may appear in a different grade in your state's standards.

WHO'S HIDING? A HIGH-FREQUENCY WORD GAME

Your child's reading vocabulary will increase by several hundred words this year. You can make reading and writing easier by doing this fun activity to learn and spell these words we use all the time.

Used by lots of kids for schoolwork, e-tablets have a highlighting function for stories, assignments, and e-books. Have your second-grader choose a color to highlight the words on the list. Because the words are often used, every page will light up with blocks of color.

Ask your child if she can find a mystery object—an elephant's head or a train engine—similar to looking for shapes in the clouds. Make up a story together about the object she "sees" in the pattern of her highlights.

If your child doesn't use an e-tablet, pull up stories on the internet and highlight high-frequency words by clicking the mouse. Kids seem to enjoy doing this at the library, even if you have a computer at home. Go figure.

50 High-Frequency Words—Second Grade

above	air	always	around	because
been	before	below	best	both
buy	call	change	cold	does
don't	fast	first	five	found
gave	goes	green	its	laugh
made	many	off	people	pull
read	right	sing	sit	sleep
tell	their	these	those	upon
us	very	wash	which	why
wish	work	would	write	your

11 FUN GAMES THAT IMPROVE FOCUS, COORDINATION, AND MATH AND LANGUAGE ARTS SKILLS

1. **We Got the Beat!** Come up with a sequence of fast and slow claps for your child to copy while waiting at red lights or in line at the DMV—for example: fast, fast, slow, fast, fast. And ask your child to

repeat the rhythm. Then it's your child's turn to clap a rhythm for you to repeat. Try tapping two fingers into your palm for quieter clapping. Repeating rhythms gets several parts of the brain to communicate between hemispheres, which helps kids learn to focus and sharpens short-term memory.

2. **Add a Move.** Make a move, like clapping your hands or snapping your fingers. Have your child copy the move and add one of her own. Repeat your move and hers, and then add another one. Keep going until one of you "misses" by skipping a move in the sequence. The person who wins starts the next round. Kids love to "out remember" their parents.

3. **Add a Verse.** "The Other Day I Met a Bear," "B-I-N-G-O," and "There Was an Old Lady Who Swallowed a Fly" are the classic add-on songs, where you sing a song over and over and add a line of lyrics with each repetition. This is great for exercising short-term memory. But any music strengthens multiple areas of the brain responsible for memory, movement, planning, and attention. That's why putting vocabulary words to a familiar tune is such an effective way to remember them.

4. **Walk or Jump on the Wild Side.** Have your child count steps as he walks or count hops as he jumps rope, from 1 to 100. Then skip count by 2s to 100. If he's enjoying himself, skip count by 5s and 10s as far as he can go. Coach him up to 1,000. If he wants to keep going, skip count by 25s to 1,000. The physical action and rhythm while counting requires the use of multiple senses and solidifies those important number relationships. The stronger your child's foundation, the easier math will be—forever.

5. **Count the Change.** In kindergarten, your child stacked like coins and could count the pennies. In first grade, she could skip count the dimes by 10s and the nickels by 5s. Now in second grade, she

can skip count quarters by 25s and assemble a variety of coins into groups valuing 100¢. Once she discovers there are 4 quarters, 10 dimes, 20 nickels, and 100 pennies in a dollar, she can count the change in the family coin jar or in your wallet. Second-graders love counting change, especially if they get to take a trip to the ice cream truck with a handful of coins they've assembled for a treat.

6. **ABC Scavenger Hunt.** Participants point out things in the environment that begin with each letter of the alphabet, in order—e.g., apple, book, clock, dog, elbow. You can take turns or just blurt out words. Both ways are fun. *Note:* Unless there's a xylophone nearby, you may want to do a couple of jumping jacks and say "exercise" because there aren't many nouns that begin with the letter *x*.

7. **ABC Road Signs.** Similar to ABC Scavenger Hunt. Lots of kids love finding words in alphabetical order on street signs, posters, billboards, or any other printed material seen on a walk or from the car window. Some of the words they come up with are hilarious.

8. **Five W Super Clues.** Use the question words "who, what, where, when, and why" for a clue about the noun of your choice (person, place, thing, or animal) and add an action (verb). Have your child guess the noun, and then give him a turn. Examples:

   a. *What* starts with *b* and *chews* on wood? (Beaver)

   b. *Who* helps Santa make toys and *wears* tiny clothes? (Elves)

   c. *Why* does your nose *tickle* after a good night's sleep? (The dog licks my face)

9. **Opposites.** While you're getting gas, cooking dinner, or matching socks, blurt out a word and have your child give you the opposite. You say, "Up." She says, "Down." She says, "Tall." You say, "Short." The easy, obvious ones go fast. Then move on to less obvious ones: for example, deep and shallow, smile and frown, squishy and hard.

10. **Same-Same.** This game is similar to the antonym game, except someone starts with a word, and you take turns saying synonyms: Big—large, gigantic, huge. Keep going until you can't think of any more. Count as you go to beat your "record" for the most synonyms.

11. **Love Letters.** Write notes to your child as often as possible. There's no better motivation to read and write than to find a note from a loved one. I used to write quick notes a couple of times a week and put them in my kids' lunch boxes or stick a Post-it note on a binder for them to find when they took it out of their backpacks. Leave notes on the dining room table, or surprise your child with a note on his bed or pillow. It won't be long before you start getting notes from him too.

TREASURE HUNT: THE HILARIOUS, FUN GAME
THAT DEVELOPS LOTS OF SKILLS

You can play this game anytime, anywhere. Take your child on a descriptive mental tour in whatever setting seems appealing: a museum, a forest, or another planet. Pretend to find money throughout your journey, listing the coins and bills for your second-grader to calculate. At the end of your trip, ask your child the amount of treasure you've collected.

If the two of you come up with a different answer, retrace your "steps" aloud and recount the money. Once you complete your tour by determining the correct amount of money, your child gets to make up a story about where he finds money, giving you a similar treasure hunt to compute in your head. Start simple with something like this:

I cleaned the living room and found two one-dollar bills stuck between the couch cushions and a quarter in the dog's bed. Then the

vacuum started pinging, and when I turned it off, a nickel, a dime,
and three pennies tumbled onto the carpet. I think I struck it rich.
How much treasure did I find? (Answer: $2.43)

Adapt the game to suit your second-grader's growing skills throughout the year. You'll be amazed by the complexity of your mental adventures. All kinds of silly characters will come to visit—for example, bank robbers, invisible aliens, and talking animals.

When your child gets good at adding in her head, practice subtraction by having some of the money you found spill from your pockets, or use a portion of your treasure to pay for food and gas to get home. If you think your second-grader is ready for another layer, replace your losses by "earning the cash back," pretending to wash cars or do other odd jobs.

The possibilities are endless. And the bonus? Your mental math and description skills will improve along with your second-grader's.

Tear-Free Homework in Second Grade

This year's homework may entail more time and thought than in first grade. Your child is no longer considered a "little kid" now that he has a couple of years' experience in school. It will take more brainpower to complete assignments designed to solidify concepts introduced in class as well as to build your child's sense of responsibility.

Education has been moving in the direction of making kids think to accomplish tasks, rather than learning through repetitive practice. Depending on the teacher, your second-grader may still be expected to write vocabulary words on the blanks in a sentence and answer math problems lined up on a page, but likely, projects will come home that require your child to apply a concept learned in class. Application demands a higher level of thinking than rote learning.

The problem for parents comes in when your child had been distracted in class and doesn't understand what to do to complete a project. Reading the directions on a worksheet and giving some guidance is seldom an issue. But when your child comes home with a paper displaying five rows of six mysterious segmented vertical bars with no explanation, the afternoon can get tricky.

Generic graphs like this are provided by publishers for multiple experiments. This assignment could be, for example: Label the bars, one through six, in each row. Then roll a dice 20 times, and color the boxes in the vertical bars on the number where the dice lands. Do five trials (hence the five rows of segmented bars). Write a conclusion about throwing dice using the data. This lesson in probability will probably be fun for the children who paid attention in class. The kids who stared out the window or fiddled with stuff in their pencil boxes may be lost and frustrated.

Here are a few things you can do at the beginning of the school year to minimize, if not eliminate, homework problems in your household:

1. **Routine.** A routine can be challenging to maintain when there are extracurricular activities and parents' work obligations. Reestablish your child's homework routine from last year, or have your second-grader choose a new location and time after school that fits into your family life. Making homework a habitual event makes all the difference in having a pleasant afternoon or evening.

2. **Downtime.** Remember, your child's brain needs some downtime to do its best thinking. You can avoid a lot of miserable afternoons by allowing your second-grader to recharge with a bit of free play before she dives into homework. Watching TV or playing video games doesn't count. Screen time is like eating cookies—enjoyable and fine in moderation. Remember, unlike the alpha waves generated during free play, the theta brain waves produced while playing electronic games don't rejuvenate cells for thinking. (For a refresher on brain waves, see chapter 2.)

3. **Support system.** At the beginning of the school year, have your second-grader exchange phone numbers with at least two or three other

kids in her class, and post the information on the family calendar or bulletin board. That way, a brain vacation while the teacher explains an assignment won't cause a panic. Your child can take responsibility by calling a few friends in case one was absent and another took that moment to zone out too. Talking with classmates about homework will also help build a sense of community. Businesses and educators have found that networking and collaborative efforts produce the best results. Second grade is an optimal developmental stage to encourage reaching out to others—seven- and eight-year-olds like to feel empowered by solving their own problems.

4. **Timer.** Don't hesitate to revisit the timer to help your child complete homework that takes too long (you can expect 20 to 30 minutes of homework a night in second grade). Start by setting the timer in short increments to accomplish small tasks so your second-grader can enjoy little victories. As your child builds confidence and focus, increase the amount of time and the portion of the assignment to be completed when the bell rings.

5. **Homework check.** Review homework for completeness and correctness to the extent possible. Showing you believe education is important will reinforce a positive attitude toward school.

Concepts of Space and Time

Supported by glial cells, neural pathways will become more specific, and concepts of space and time will begin to solidify this year. The material your child learns in school will reflect this developing organization in the brain. For example, second-graders begin to understand and use fractions, mostly halves, thirds, and quarters. When talking to friends, a second-grader might say, "There are three of us, so let's divide the gummy bears into thirds."

Your seven- or eight-year-old may want to measure to find the lengths of objects in inches or centimeters, so have a ruler handy. Another fun measuring device is a metal measuring tape. This age group likes the idea of using an adult tool, especially one that magically re-tracts, slipping from their fingers and making them giggle.

Most of us have digital clocks, but second grade is a good time to purchase a clock with hands if you don't already have one so your child can see what "clockwise" and "counterclockwise" mean. An analog clock in a prominent place—the kitchen, for instance—also provides orientation.

Children learn the passage of time with the physical movement and position of the hands throughout the day: where the hands are when they leave for school, arrive back home, do their homework, set the table, eat dinner, and go to bed. Clocks with hands present opportuni-ties to experiment with going forward and backward in time, and they provide a practical reason to count by fives.

You can ask questions like this: "We have to leave by 7:30. How many minutes do I have to get everything into the Crock-Pot?"

Don't be surprised if your child stops rounding off to the nearest five (also a good skill) and gives an answer like this: "You have 23 min-utes." Second-graders enjoy being precise, not because they're sticklers for detail necessarily, but because they want their answers to be cor-rect—part of that need to feel competent.

Your second-grader should know the months of the year and days of the week in order. If these concepts are still fuzzy, search on YouTube with your child and explore the songs and raps that will help cement this common chronology in the hippocampus for long-term memory.

A particularly fun thing about seven- and eight-year-olds is their realization that language isn't always literal, although they still view the world in a black-and-white way. In fact, you'll probably see a de-veloping sense of humor. They love to hear and tell silly jokes:

Q: "Why do fish live in saltwater?"
A: "Because pepper makes them sneeze."

Joke books are good gifts at this age, especially if you have a reluc-tant reader, because the potential for a good laugh is a powerful motivator. Also try playing together with words by making up silly rhymes and puns. Not only do homemade jokes spark ridiculous groans and giggles, but this kind of creativity also involves the same neural pathways required for scientific, literary, and artistic activities (SickKids Hospital Staff 2011).

Reading Independence

Second-graders delight in making their own decisions. If you haven't gotten your child a library card yet, second grade is the perfect time. Browsing bookshelves spurs new interests, and kids this age love to choose and check out their own books. Although kids' reading comprehension on electronic devices is getting better and better, studies indicate they still enjoy holding a book and the physical act of turning pages (Myrberg and Wiberg 2015).

Give your child a little more responsibility by making it his job to mark the library due dates on the family calendar. Borrowing books means you don't have to buy and store as many, and your child will always have fresh or favorite stories to read.

Library visits are particularly important during the summer months and other vacation breaks. You don't want your child's hard work in forming and strengthening neural networks during the school year to get pared away from lack of use. Kids this age still thrive on routines, so if you can establish a regular monthly or biweekly trip to the library—the first Friday of the month, for example—you'll pay fewer fines for overdue books, and taking adventures together through stories will become an integral part of your lives. The key here is to treat reading as recreation—the fun thing we *get to do* daily—as enjoyable as using our imaginations in free play.

Your second-grader's desire to prove his personal competence, both to you and to himself, may motivate him to read his first chapter book independently. That's something to celebrate! Make a big deal over the accomplishment. Maybe start a family tradition, a rite of passage that includes a favorite dinner or dessert in his honor. If your child has younger siblings or cousins, this victory may ignite motivation for them too.

Don't make the mistake of not reading with your child anymore because of his achievement, though. The snuggle time with you creates a sense of safety and warmth toward reading—and brains learn best in safety, right? If you haven't been taking turns reading aloud, try it out. Some kids this age don't like the interruption of switching readers, but others love it. If your second-grader enjoys taking turns, her reading fluency and comprehension will take a big leap.

Talking over how characters react to the conflicts in stories increases vocabulary and develops thinking skills. Often stories illustrate concepts of right and wrong, something second-graders are sorting out for themselves, and a discussion with you can give your child tools for handling a difficult situation in the future. This time together in the early years makes learning easier and more fun—forever.

THE REAL DEAL
Continuing to Read with Mom and Dad

Our older daughter read her first chapter book in second grade and continued reading with her little sister and me through fourth grade. By fifth grade, she most often read on her own because her eyes moved much faster over the print than I could possibly read aloud, and she didn't have the patience to allow a story to unfold at our limited verbal pace.

Our younger daughter also read her first chapter book in second grade, and after the family celebrated, I started rereading the Harry Potter series aloud. She had been in kindergarten our first time through the series, but the mean Dursley family had scared her, so I read separately with the girls. God bless J. K. Rowling.

Though our older daughter was reading the fourth book in the series to herself, *Harry Potter and the Goblet of Fire*, she often drifted into the bedroom and snuggled with her sister and me as I read the first book, *Harry Potter and the Sorcerer's Stone*. We had the most amazing conversations about Harry, the humble hero, and his similarities to the villain, Voldemort. We had deep discussions about right and wrong and about the power people have to choose their attitudes and actions.

Second-graders often experience what Maria Montessori called a "sensitive period" for analyzing moral issues. Their brains seem primed to ponder how people might feel in various circumstances. That year, we all learned as much from our youngest family member's interpretation of the way people behave as she did from us, maybe more.

Our older daughter went back to reading independently, but our younger daughter and I read books aloud together for several years after that, particularly when we were on the road to her tennis matches. We always prized those hours of literary adventure together, discussing characters, plots, and settings, and relating them to real life.

Motivating Reluctant Readers

Sometimes kids are plenty smart, but they would rather rake the leaves in the yard after a windstorm than pick up a book. However, with the boost in technology in the last couple of decades, it has become increasingly difficult to find a place in the world as an adult without being a proficient reader. Luckily, these three quick tips can get kids fired up about books:

1. Find something in print that excites your second-grader.
2. Read aloud regularly with your child.
3. Make sure your child sees you reading.

Simple, right? Try taking turns reading aloud, but don't force it. If your child enjoys participating in your story time together, the practice will be a big help in kick-starting independent reading. Some kids hate slowing down the story, though, or giving up the relaxation after a long day. The idea is to do what works for your child. If you haven't started reading chapter books yet, second grade is generally a good time.

Experiment with titles and authors. Some kids go crazy for pony stories. Some discover fun facts in nonfiction, and they can't get enough. Some howl with laughter over stories about farting and nose picking. This is a job for the library. Between knowing your child and trial and error, you'll find something to strike his fancy.

To help you get started, refer to the lists of motivating book series for second-graders. Kids this age start to mingle with the opposite sex, but they're still fairly gender specific, so there are separate lists of titles for boys and girls, although both genders have been known to enjoy books from either list. If your second-grader gets excited about the first book in a series, there's a good chance he'll want to read the next one—and the next. Of course, this is a jumping-off point. You'll find many more titles available.

8 FAVORITE SERIES OF SECOND-GRADE BOYS (AND GIRLS TOO)

1. Matt Christopher Sports Classics (50+ books)—a collection of many stories about sporty kids.

2. Dog Man series (5 books) by Dav Pilkey—his latest silly series that has kids clamoring for more.

3. Stink series (11 books) by Megan McDonald—Judy Moody's second-grade brother gets into all kinds of fun predicaments with the best of intentions.

4. Stink-O-Pedia series (2 books) also by Megan McDonald—a pair of books of gross facts little boys love.

5. Super Smart Science series (10 books) for kids by April Chloe Terrazas—complex science concepts explained in a way kids understand.

6. Nate the Great mystery series (25+ books) by Marjorie Weinman Sharmat—for kids who need practice to get to grade-level reading and like a good whodunit.

7. Magic Tree House series (50+ books) by Mary Pope Osborne—for various reading levels; brings history to life and promotes conversations about historical events.

8. Magic School Bus series (12 books) mostly by Joanna Cole—also various reading levels; entertaining read-along books about science concepts learned through adventure.

8 FAVORITE SERIES OF SECOND-GRADE GIRLS (AND BOYS TOO)

1. Mercy Watson to the Rescue series (6 books) by Kate DiCamillo—the Watsons' pet pig gets into all kinds of ridiculous trouble trying to save the day.

2. Junie B. Jones series (28 books) by Barbara Park—hilarious, charming character kids love.

3. Gooney Bird Greene series (6 books) by Lois Lowry—second-grade girl tells "true stories" to her classmates that are outlandish and fun.

4. Toys series by Emily Jenkins (3 books)—little girls' toys and their zany adventures together.

5. Ivy and Bean series (11 books) by Annie Barrows—two unlikely girls become friends and engage in hilarious antics together.

6. Super Smart Science series (10 books) by April Chloe Terrazas—complicated science concepts explained in an understandable way for the younger set.

7. Judy Moody series (14 books) by Megan McDonald—feisty, socially awkward third-grader who usually learns lessons the hard way; great early chapter books with fun illustrations.

8. Amelia Bedelia chapter book series (11 books) by Herman Perish (nephew of Peggy Perish, author of the picture book series)—entertaining stories that misinterpret idioms and homophones.

Extracurricular Activities in Second Grade

By age seven or eight, children often exhibit certain talents—in art, music, or sports, for example—and organizations abound to nurture any propensity imaginable. If your son or daughter hasn't joined the Scouts yet, second grade is the perfect time. Troops get into full swing trying new things, contributing to the community, and setting and reaching goals. Since second-graders mentally process on a deeper level, this is also a good time to consider enrolling your child in some form of spiritual education.

Parents commonly sign up second-graders for sports teams so their kids can get the physical activity they need to grow up healthy and learn to work toward a common goal. Regular exercise is crucial for supplying developing brains with oxygen and nutrients for defining neural pathways, coordinating signals between hemispheres, and developing glial cells for process and function.

Life becomes a buffet of opportunities for after-school and weekend activities.

But choose wisely.

Overscheduling cuts into sleep, causes junk food eating on the run, and mounts emotional stress. Kids and parents find themselves exhausted and crabby. Remember, daily downtime periods allow children's brains to assimilate what they learned in school as well as wander into creative thought.

It's all about balance.

Start with one extracurricular endeavor and ask yourself these four questions to see how well your child adjusts to a tighter schedule:

1. Does homework still get done with ease?
2. Is there an hour or more each day when your child can relax and pretend?
3. Can you read together without shortening your story time or feeling rushed?
4. Is there room for your bedtime ritual so your child can wind down and get to sleep?

If a weekly scouting meeting, for example, comfortably fits into your family life, consider adding another activity—maybe dance lessons or a sport's team. But keep the four questions in mind before making the commitment.

More than two activities outside of school in second grade can get overwhelming quickly. If your child has a burning desire to do something that would add another obligation to the weekly schedule, but you believe the family couldn't adjust without compromising on sleep, exercise, or downtime, say no. Tell your seven- or eight-year-old to wait until spring to talk about taking art lessons or joining a science club during the summer break. Should you decide to add something to the schedule, make sure you can pull the plug on the third activity if your week becomes too hectic.

Family Organization Checkup

Have you found a way for everyone in the family to communicate events, activities, and appointments—a communal calendar, a whiteboard, or another device that works for you? Is whatever tool you're using working to keep things from getting missed or forgotten? Has your child become an integral participant in the system? Is your second-grader still using pictures to let you know about events, or have words replaced symbols—or maybe a little of both?

Instilling the value that every member is responsible for keeping the family informed will save a myriad of headaches, literal and figurative. Not only can elementary school kids be a big help in keeping track of your busy lives, but getting into the habit now also means better communication in the middle and high school years, an endeavor that requires focused intention.

If maintaining some form of centralized exchange of information has waned or fallen apart in your household, give it another try. Maybe the whiteboard didn't work because someone kept walking away with the dry-erase markers, or a calendar hanging on the wall was too hard to write on. Try tying the dry-erase marker to the whiteboard with a string. Leave the calendar flat on the kitchen counter, or put sticky notes on it. The benefits will far outweigh the extra effort needed to consistently remind your kids and partner to write down their plans for the next few months.

Are life's essentials getting their due in your family members' lives? Let's review the four ingredients for raising smart, confident kids:

1. Adequate sleep
2. Healthy food and plenty of water
3. Regular exercise
4. A lot of time talking and having fun with you

If any of these are lacking, do what you can to strengthen your foundation. Revise or reestablish the bedtime ritual, and be conscious of your child's need for 8 to 10 hours of sleep. Read labels and experiment with a variety of snacks and food items (revisit "Nutrition" on pages 117–120 for ideas), especially vegetables (page 117), to ensure your child gets enough fuel as well as all the building blocks for a healthy mind and body. Come up with creative ways for your second-grader to break a sweat three to five days a week (see page 11). No matter how busy life becomes, do your best to listen and respond when your child talks to you. Ask questions, and be a confidant, a catalyst for learning, and a playmate who enforces boundaries.

Most important, be patient with yourself. You don't have to be perfect. In fact, when you make mistakes, admit how you messed up and apologize. That's the best possible modeling you can do for your child.

SECOND-GRADE OUTSIDE THE NORM

What is "normal" anyway? Children have strengths and weaknesses in all kinds of combinations. Some kids pop out answers to math problems and never show their work because they do the work instantly in their heads, but their artwork looks like a two-year-old's finger painting. Others count on their fingers and hate math, yet they read above grade level and write engaging stories. Still others appear to struggle in every academic subject, but they're great at sports, dance, or another activity.

Parents can encourage their kids to become balanced human beings by nurturing their gifts and interests while helping them strengthen their weaknesses. That sounds logical, right? The games in this book are designed to capture your child's interest and painlessly become more challenging as your second-grader's skills improve.

The Tortoise: When Games and Reading Aren't Enough

Suppose you're reading to your child every day and playing games on car rides and in the grocery store, but your second-grader's language or math skills still seem to lag compared to the other kids. Interventions vary in private schools, but public schools generally follow the parameters outlined in the federal Individuals with Disabilities Education Act (IDEA).

If your child goes to a public school, his first-grade teacher likely brought the discrepancy to your attention, and the staff has probably already met to discuss interventions in the classroom. You may have also met with the teacher, school psychologist, and speech specialist to discuss activities you can do at home to bolster your child's academic development.

The next step is to meet with this year's teacher and the rest of the team to discuss the effectiveness of the interventions. You'll decide together if your child's best interest would be served by scheduling the school psychologist to do a battery of tests to determine if a learning disability is the culprit. Once the results come back, the psychologist will explain your child's strengths and weaknesses and, if warranted, discuss special education options with you.

Maybe the second-grade teacher contacted you for the first time about learning concerns. The good news: In most school districts, second grade is the first year your child would be eligible for formal interventions that provide extra individual and small group help. As mentioned, students need to be at least two years behind peers to receive special education services in an Individualized Education Plan, or IEP. For this reason, unless your child was diagnosed with a disability in preschool, schools seldom test kids before second grade.

Try not to worry. If your child is getting help as early as second grade, that's something to celebrate.

Children's author Patricia Polacco says, "I wasn't a very good student in elementary school and had a hard time with reading and writing. I didn't learn to read until I was almost fourteen years old. Reading out loud for me was a nightmare because I would mispronounce words or reconstruct things that weren't even there. That's when one of my teachers discovered I had a learning disability called dyslexia. Once I got help, I read very well!" (Scholastic, n.d.).

What if your child struggles academically, but the teacher hasn't contacted you? Discuss your questions and concerns with the teacher at the fall conference, usually six to eight weeks after the school year begins. If the situation is urgent or the school doesn't have a formal conference period, call the school or email the teacher to schedule a meeting.

Jot down a list of your questions and concerns before the discussion. You don't want to be smacking your forehead on the way home, realizing you forgot to ask or mention something important. If after talking to the teacher, you believe a formal evaluation to diagnose possible learning issues would best serve your child, request an assessment in writing.

IDEA requires public schools to comply with your appeal for testing and have results within 60 days. The staff has another 30 days to assemble a team to discuss further action. You should have the information you need to further assist your child in developing the skills needed to be successful in school within 90 days.

If your child goes to a private school, you can either hire a licensed educational psychologist (LEP) to conduct the testing or go to the public school district office in your area and request that your child be assessed for possible learning disabilities. The district will assign a psychologist on staff to evaluate your child, and the 90-day deadline still applies.

Evaluations include the following:

- Observation of classroom behavior
- Vision and hearing tests
- Evaluation of motor skills
- Oral language patterns
- Self-help skills
- Academic progress
- Social and emotional health

Remember, unless your child shows a two-year delay in one or more of the areas listed above, the public schools are not required to offer special education services, and many private schools don't provide formal interventions for struggling students. However, children with "other health impairments" that affect learning, as specified in the Special Education Guide (Degree Prospects, n.d.), such as attention issues, bipolar disorder, and Tourette syndrome, don't have to be two years behind to receive services. Sometimes this rule gets confused in schools, though, so it's helpful for parents to know.

LEP Susan Cradduck (2016) says, "I wouldn't recommend special education unless your child really needs it because it's not a magical fix. Parents should work with the teacher and see what they can do at home [to] minimize the internal labeling that affects children's self-confidence."

If you want to explore options to help your child—or your second-grader doesn't qualify for services—consider hiring an LEP to interpret the data from the school's test results. The LEP will likely give you lots of suggestions and resources to help improve your second-grader's academic performance. In addition, LEPs usually have a list of learning centers in the area, and they know which ones will best suit your child's needs.

Often a few months of concentrated effort to develop lagging skills will be all that's needed to get your child caught up and happier at school. The LEP can also do an Independent Educational Evaluation (IEE) if you want more information about your child's learning or you're unhappy with the school's assessment.

"If your child doesn't qualify for services, [parents can also] consider a 504 Plan," Cradduck adds. "The student study team assembles accommodations within the classroom, such as extended time to complete tests or audiobooks for kids with dyslexia, until they learn to compensate."

Keep in mind that a 504 Plan isn't legally binding like an IEP. For a 504 Plan to help your child, the degree of buy-in from your child's teacher will be the most important factor. The teacher will be included in setting up procedures for supporting your child's learning, but when put into practice, the additional responsibilities can sometimes get overwhelming in a classroom of 20 to 35 other seven- and eight-year-olds. If your child's teacher struggles to meet 504 Plan interventions, talk to an LEP, check out tutoring services, and search online for activities to meet your child's specific needs.

Note: Visit understood.org to find out more about learning and attention issues. You can also find more resources in the next chapter on pages 199–201.

THE REAL DEAL
Kids Told Her She Was Stupid

Lily tried as hard as she could in second grade, but when the teacher wrote on the board, Lily's eyes couldn't focus fast enough when she turned her attention back to her paper, and she'd forget what to write. The teacher gave the prescribed 20 minutes of daily homework, but it took lots of time to keep track of the letters as they jumped and twitched on the page. Lily needed at least an hour and sometimes more to finish the assignments. Still, Lily soldiered on, determined to be a good student, having no idea letters stood still for the other kids.

Mrs. Hansen watched Lily get off the school bus one day and her heart sank. The light had gone out of her little girl's bright-blue eyes. "What's the matter, honey?" she asked.

"Raymond called me stupid in front of the whole class." Lily's lip quivered, and her eyes filled with tears. "Everyone laughed."

Mrs. Hansen kneeled on the sidewalk, wrapped her arms around Lily, and held her close. "You are not stupid, young lady. Not only do you remember everything you learn, you always know what to say to make people feel better." She released the hug enough to look at her daughter. "That's a special gift."

"But Raymond's right. I sound all jerky when I read out loud, and I'm always the last one done with everything." "That boy is *not* right. You're smart." Mrs. Hansen gave Lily's shoulders a gentle squeeze. "What did your teacher say?"

"She yelled at the class, especially Raymond, and we missed part of recess." Lily started to cry. "Mom, I don't want to get everyone in trouble."

"We'll figure this out, honey." Mrs. Hansen held Lily close again. "I promise."

Mrs. Hansen had regularly witnessed Lily lending emotional support to family and friends, demonstrating wisdom well beyond her seven years. This trouble with schoolwork didn't make sense, so she set out to find a solution.

Sometimes Lily's eyes jerked from side to side and seemed out of alignment when she tried to focus. *Maybe an eye doctor would be able to help her*, thought Mrs. Hansen. She searched online and found a pediatric optometrist who looked interesting. Shortly after reading about the optometrist, she ran into an acquaintance who mentioned the same doctor and took it as a sign to make an appointment.

The pediatric optometrist found that Lily's eyes didn't focus as a team, so the world looked flatter than normal. Her brain also delayed the transition between looking at objects from far to close. It was no wonder Lily had trouble tracking print or lining up math problems.

The optometrist offered vision therapy to help Lily strengthen her eye muscles and train her brain to work in sync with sensory input so she could immediately process what she saw. Mrs. Hansen and her husband discussed the treatment at length, mostly about how they would pay for it because their insurance wouldn't cover any portion of the cost. They worked out a payment plan with the doctor and embarked on a 14-week program.

Once a week, the doctor worked directly with Lily in a therapy session and then gave her tools and games to practice at home. Lily had fun with her "flipper glasses," which had lenses that flipped up or down to transition her focus from far to near and back again. And one of her favorite games consisted of nothing more than a marble and a table.

"Okay, Lily." Mrs. Hansen tipped the coffee table slightly. "Follow the marble with both eyes, and see if you can catch it."

The marble plopped into Lily's hand on the sixth try, and her eyes went wide. "I did it!"

"You did!" Mrs. Hansen clapped. "Let's try it again."

Lily tracked the marble and caught it several more times, laughing and squealing with each victory.

"I gotta tell you, Trish," Mrs. Hansen said when I interviewed her. "More than once, my eyes got teary when Lily mastered a new game. We played games for an hour a day, and by the end of the 14 weeks, Lily went from a kindergarten reading level to fifth grade. I'd known she was smart, but I had no idea how smart."

(As of this writing, Lily has earned an associate of arts degree from community college with a 3.78 grade point average. She's currently attending Oregon State University and doing very well.)

Is Your Child Gifted?

Most schools begin to test kids for advanced ability at the end of second grade or in third grade. According to the National Association for Gifted Children (2010), "gifted and talented" students

> demonstrate outstanding levels of aptitude (defined as an exceptional ability to reason and learn) or competence (documented performance or achievement in top 10 percent or rarer) in one or more domains. Domains include any structured area of activity with its own symbol system (e.g., mathematics, music, language) and/or set of sensorimotor skills (e.g., painting, dance, sports).

Specialized programs are generally available to students in the third or fourth grade, after the school receives test scores and compiles a list of those who meet the state and district parameters for gifted instruction. Districts encourage teachers to include differentiated instruction in their curriculum by providing modifications within lessons to meet the educational needs of various learning capacities. But depending on class size and circumstance, the degree to which lessons are altered to meet gifted students' needs varies widely.

A common misconception about these kids is that because they're smart, they'll be fine. The truth is that many gifted students struggle with challenges commonly seen in this age group, including perfection-istic tendencies, difficulties with social skills, a feeling of not belonging, a heightened or disproportionate sense of justice, and over-empathizing with the plight of others. In addition, gifted students who aren't taught material that suits their intellectual or artistic abilities can get bored or feel marginalized, leading to behavioral problems. The idea is to help gifted kids develop socially and emotionally (often weak areas) as well as to support their artistic or academic talents.

Just as struggling students can get additional help through special education services, gifted students are offered opportunities to nurture aptitudes through the use of in-class projects, pull-out programs, or both, depending on the district and individual school, usually in third or fourth grade.

What can you do in the meantime if your second-grader finishes work quickly and needs to be challenged to stay interested in school? Ask the teacher what activities are available for bright students in the classroom, and check in with the teacher occasionally to support your child's learning. If the teacher gives your child busy work—an extra math paper with the same kind of problems assigned to the rest of the class—rather than enriched assignments, set up a conference.

Ask about current classroom material, and brainstorm ways to incorporate concepts in an activity that requires deeper thinking and more advanced problem-solving skills. Some schools and districts are better than others at training teachers how to optimize learning for gifted kids. Being an advocate for the teacher as well as for your child will benefit many gifted students for years to come.

Find out about classroom themes. Surf the internet with your sec-ond-grader to come up with fun projects and books that go with the curriculum. Share your discoveries. Think of yourself as a partner in your child's education, and remember that you and the teacher are on the same side.

Ultimately, your greatest influence will come from modeling and helping your second-grader develop a work ethic and complete tasks, even boring ones. Building character now will create tolerance and tenacity for adulthood. Intelligence and talent mean nothing unless people can apply themselves in something productive.

When our older daughter used to flake on completing "boring" assignments or zone out during class and miss the directions, we used to tell her: "The world won't care that you're smart—it will only care what you do with your intelligence."

Learning shouldn't be drudgery though. Playing games like Treasure Hunt (see page 143) will keep your relationship with your second-grader fun and spark all those neurons that specialize in curiosity, creativity, and logic, giving both the right- and left-brain hemispheres a workout. You'll find your seven- or eight-year-old coming up with progressively complicated treasure hunt settings and stories. Figuring out the amount of treasure you accumulate by the end of your adventure will require more operations to calculate. The same kind of evolution is true for the rhythm, math, and language activities on pages 139–143.

Research confirms that brains are malleable, and practice through play is the most effective path to enrichment—at your child's pace.

COMMON TRAITS OF GIFTED CHILDREN

If some of these sound familiar, your child could be gifted:

- Unusually active and alert

- Learns quickly and has excellent recall

- Uses advanced vocabulary, engages in wordplay and storytelling

- Enjoys solving puzzles with numbers, words, and images

- Improvises ways to solve problems

- Exhibits abstract, complex, insightful, and creative thinking

- Responds to and demonstrates strengths in the arts

- Focuses intensely on single or varied interests at the same time

- Is highly inquisitive and asks probing questions

- Insists on doing things her way, yet can be loyal and modest

- Has deep, intense feelings and emotional reactions

- Is concerned with truth, equity, and justice

- Displays a keen sense of humor, at times better understood by adults

- Daydreams—lives in her own world

- Has a vivid and precise imagination

(List adapted from http://www.nagc.org/.)

Orchids Versus Dandelions: An Empowering Way to Look at Kids with Special Needs

A philosophy gaining traction in the last several years compares mainstream children to those with special needs using the orchids and dandelions metaphor. The idea is that mainstream children are like dandelions: they're hardy, able to grow anywhere with a little rain and sunshine, including in the cracks in the pavement. Kids with disabilities or other significant challenges require more specialized care, similar to the orchid that needs porous soil and a specific range of humidity, light, and nutrition to grow, but the results can be stunningly beautiful.

Clinical psychologist Bruce Steven Dolin (2009a) points out, "The key to understanding orchids, dandelions, and parents might be in . . . moving away from the notion of stand-alone gifted or troubled children toward an emphasis on trusting and nourishing versus troubled and destructive relationships."

In fact, more often than people realize, children with disabilities—such as dyslexia, attention deficits, or bipolar disorder—are also gifted. These kids are termed "twice exceptional," or 2E children. Education psychologist David Palmer (2011) notes the following:

Children who score in the gifted range on an IQ test can also be identified as learning disabled. . . . Some of these children get their needs met through flexible and creative programming in the general education setting, while others may receive formal support from a special education teacher.

When educators and parents view these kids as orchids, individuals who need more nurturing than the hardy dandelions but who are well worth the extra effort, these children are more likely to flourish.

4 TIPS FOR TALKING TO TEACHERS THAT GET RESULTS

Whether you're concerned about your second-grader's focus, motivation, academic progress, or social scrapes on the playground, these tips will team up you and your child's teacher for great results.

1. **Be appreciative and understanding.** Few teachers can get the job done within contract hours, so they're already working unpaid overtime before you walk into the classroom. Start a conference with gratitude, saying something like "Thanks for your time. I know you're busy, but I could really use your expertise."

2. **Share your concerns and what you're doing at home.** This conveys that you realize your child's education is a partnership between home and school. The teacher will likely tell you what she's currently doing as well as things she's willing to add to further support your child's learning in the classroom.

3. **Ask for additional ideas to try at home.** It may amaze you how much the simplest adjustments to schedules or homework habits can help.

4. **Find out how you can support the teacher.** For instance, create a behavior or gifted contract (see pages 49 and 64) that will set up a partnership and quick communication to help make the curriculum more effective without sapping everyone's resources.

SECOND-GRADE CARE AND FEEDING

Second-graders may gain muscle coordination, and their vocabularies may soar to new heights, but this is also a period when vision problems become apparent. By now, your child is also flashing precious jack-o'-lantern smiles because her four front teeth are probably in various stages of replacement. Here is a heads-up on what to look for and how to handle your child's eyes and teeth.

Second-Graders' Eyesight

Your child may be nearsighted (can see close but not far) if she complains about how often the teacher writes on the board or uses the big screen. Kids usually don't realize that the blurry blobs they see are crisp letters, words, and images to their classmates.

Your child could be farsighted (can see the whiteboard, but words in a book or on an e-tablet are hard to see) if she gets watery or red eyes, complains of "burning" eyes, squints to see the words on a page, or suffers from occasional headaches.

Most schools have students identify letters on an eye chart, and pediatricians give similar exams at annual checkups, but children's eyes can change quickly at this stage. Tests for close vision, for tasks such as reading, usually must be requested by parents because farsightedness is less common and generally not routinely checked. Watch and listen for clues that your child may be having trouble seeing clearly.

★THE REAL DEAL★

Second Grade Was a Blur

I probably needed glasses in second grade, but like most seven- and eight-year-olds, I wanted to give the "right" answers to the person conducting my eye exam. When my turn came to read the eye chart, I said the same letters as the kid had before me. At that point, the letters were fuzzy, but not indecipherable.

My older sisters read with the "Eagles," whereas I struggled to keep up with the "Doves" and sometimes ended up in the "Buzzards" reading group (the teachers didn't call them that, but we knew where we stood).

Four years later, in the sixth grade, as my dad and I playfully teased one another, I put on his glasses that had been sitting on the dining room table—and my jaw dropped.

"Oh, my gosh! Dad, I can see leaves on the trees outside!" I shouted.

Shortly afterwards, I got my first pair of glasses. Funny how my grades improved in every subject, and school became more interesting. I hadn't realized what I'd been missing.

A Word About Second-Graders' Teeth

By the end of second grade, the four front permanent teeth, top and bottom, have usually finished coming in. Your second-grader is probably becoming a pro at brushing his teeth in the mornings and evenings and flossing daily. Encourage gentle brushing on teeth only partially grown in to avoid bloody gums and sensitivity.

If you've helped create healthy oral hygiene habits up to now, when your child reaches the upper grades, you will likely dodge the horror of multiple cavities, painful fillings, and repairs that will remain for a lifetime. This parenting thing is a big job, though. If making sure your child learns how to take care of his teeth hasn't been one of your best areas, second grade is the optimal time to spruce up and solidify your child's dental routine.

Find the two-minute timer stuffed in the back of a drawer or buy a new one. Remind your child how to brush his teeth by doing it for him a few evenings, and spend two or three weeks supervising, making sure he's brushing effectively for the full two minutes. Remember to floss his teeth daily for him until he's eight or nine, when his hands and fingers will be strong and flexible enough to do it on his own. Try brushing your teeth along with your child and model the behavior you want to see. As mentioned, second-graders tend to want to do things well to prove their competence, so this is a great opportunity to teach oral hygiene.

The key here, and probably the most difficult part, is to be consistent for at least a month. Your child needs time to develop good brushing and flossing habits. Give yourself reminders—sticky notes on your

bathroom mirror, alerts on your phone, whatever it takes to ensure
that your efforts now will pay off in helping your child learn how to
take care of his teeth.

WHERE DO YOU SEE YOURSELF?

😁 Mrs. Sanders pulls into the driveway that leads to the Washington Elementary School parking lot. The place is mobbed, and the cars
barely move. She knew she needed to get there before the rush if she
had any hope of getting to the dentist on time, but her last client took
longer than expected.

Wait. Is that her pudgy little boy on the sidewalk across the parking lot? She can't believe her luck. They won't be so late if Jared hops
into the car near the entrance. She can make a U-turn and avoid that
mess in the parking lot. She puts down the window in her black SUV
and yells over the gridlocked cars, "Jared! Over here!"

"But you told me I'm supposed to wait until you get to the sidewalk," Jared shouts back before he stuffs the last bite of something
into his mouth.

Mrs. Sanders would bet money that whatever he ate filled his molars with something sugary, perfect for going to the dentist. She opens
the car door and steps out of the SUV. The cars start to move, and she
waves at the drivers behind her to go around. "Run down the sidewalk
and meet me over here, Jared. We have an appointment."

"We always have to go somewhere," he whines, shuffling toward
the SUV. "I want to go home."

A man in a small car honks at Mrs. Sanders and narrows his eyes
as he inches past the SUV to get into the parking lot.

"Get your butt over here!" she shouts at her son. Can't Jared see
the SUV is in the way of the other cars?

Jared stops and twists at the waist to look at his backside.

Sometimes she forgets he's self-conscious about his bubble butt. She
thinks it's cute, and he'll probably grow out of it. "Come on, hurry
up!" she yells.

His eyes fill with tears, but he starts to run. She feels bad for hurting his feelings, but he's so darn sensitive lately. Her seven-year-old looks both ways, as she taught him, and she smiles.

Jared waits for the oncoming car to stop. His face turns red when the driver impatiently waves at him to jaywalk across the driveway to the SUV. He jumps into the backseat and slams the door so hard the impact shakes the chassis.

"Hey, not so hard," Mrs. Sanders scolds.

"Where are we going?" Jared asks, his voice shaky, on the brink of full-blown sobs.

She hears his seat belt click into place. He's such a good boy. "To the dentist, remember?"

"Not the dentist," her son shrills in the closed car, and she winces.

"You like Dr. Cadwell," she reminds him as she makes a U-turn, proud of herself for slipping between other exiting cars.

"I know, but I just ate a cookie that Alex gave me."

"You can brush your teeth when we get there." She turns right onto the main street and glances at the clock. They have only 5 minutes to make a 15-minute drive, but Jared's shortcut to the car means they won't be late enough to miss the appointment that she's already had to reschedule twice.

"Mom, you didn't tell me," Jared whimpers. "I want to go home."

"I wrote 'Dr. Cadwell' on the calendar."

"Nuh-uh," Jared whines.

"You must have forgotten to check," Mrs. Sanders says, but doubt creeps in. Did she put the appointment in her cell phone but forget to write it on the calendar again?

"Today had the only blank square all week." Jared's voice cracks.

She glances in the mirror to see him wipe a tear on his sleeve, and her chest deflates. "I'm sorry, honey." She tries so hard to be a good mom. "I could have sworn I wrote it on the calendar."

"I hate the weeks with lots of writing." Jared's voice sounds muffled, like he's talking with his face in his hands. "I'm too tired to go to the dentist."

Better to break the news now, thinks Mrs. Sanders. "We're also going to your sister's basketball game this afternoon." Her mouth tugs into a grimace. "I guess I forgot to write that on the calendar too."

Jared dissolves into sobs. "Nooo . . ." He gulps for air. "Mommy . . . I can't."

"But you love eating hotdogs and getting candy from the snack bar." It occurs to her that their crazy schedule could have something to do with how chubby Jared's gotten this year.

"I don't want to go. Please don't make me."

"I'll look at the calendar for next week and see if we can skip a few things, okay?" Between soccer, Spanish lessons, choir practice, basketball, and her husband's softball games on Sunday evenings, she has no idea what to cut without upsetting someone in the family. "I need you to be strong and get through the rest of today. Can you do that for me, Jared?"

They pull into the parking lot at the dentist office, and she looks over her shoulder at her weepy son.

The poor little guy's swollen eyes gaze at her and he nods. "Okay."

"Thanks, buddy." They both get out of the car, and she puts an arm around him as they walk into the waiting room. "You're such a good boy."

Jared gives her his jack-o'-lantern smile with his front teeth still coming in, and her heart swells with pride. She so loves this kid.

The office manager at Washington Elementary School shuffles papers at a desk as Mrs. Torino stands at the counter reading a flyer about head lice while she waits for her daughter, Valerie, to take her to the dentist. She smirks at the flyer, sure that *her* daughter would never get lice. Mrs. Torino brushes and braids her second-grader's hair every morning and has explained why sharing hats is a bad idea.

Every day this week, she's volunteered in Valerie's classroom and helped with the PTA's cookie dough fund-raiser. But are her efforts appreciated? She'd thought so, but today Mr. Santorin, Valerie's teacher, suggested she only come in to correct papers and lead a small group once a week rather than three or four days.

"Give Valerie a chance to do more on her own," he'd said. She rolls her eyes at the thought.

At least Mrs. Torino had the forethought to make her daughter's dentist appointment 10 minutes before school let out. Avoiding the mess of cars inching along in the parking lot after school is a welcome reward for an exhausting, thankless week.

When Valerie gets to the office with her green slip that lets her out of class, Mrs. Torino's jaw drops. Her seven-year-old is munching on what looks like a chocolate chip cookie, and the bulge in her jeans pocket suggests she has more sugary treats than the one in her hand. Mr. Santorin knows better than to let her daughter eat empty calories without her permission. Is this what he means by letting her little girl make her own decisions?

"What do you think you're doing?" says Mrs. Torino, hands on hips. "You know we don't eat junk food, Valerie, especially not on the way to the dentist to get your teeth cleaned."

Her second-grader stops munching, mid-chew. "But it's Alex's birthday," Valerie garbles and looks up at her mom with those big brown eyes.

"Come on." Mrs. Torino sighs. "I brought your toothbrush. We can clean your teeth when we get there."

Valerie's eyebrows lift. "Does that mean I can have the cookie in my pocket too?"

"Sure, if you don't fight me about brushing your teeth at the dentist's office. I want to make sure we get all that sugar out of your molars." Mrs. Torino can't help smiling at the gaps in her daughter's grin. She's taken so many pictures, but she's not sure she'll ever have enough photos to document the tiny white dots poking through her little girl's gums.

Valerie's brows scrunch. "Mom, I can do it myself. I'll get them really clean, I swear."

"There's a reason you've never gotten a cavity. Going to the dentist isn't the time to change what we've been doing up to now."

The office manager, who has been quietly working beyond the counter, says, "Maybe this is the perfect time for Valerie to brush her teeth.

Ask the dentist to give her those tablets that show where she's missed, and you can give her hints on how to get them cleaner."

This is the second person today to question Mrs. Torino's parenting, and she's had it. She is itching to say that if she wants people's opinions, she'll ask for them. Instead, she grabs Valerie's hand. "Let's go, sweetie," she says, practically dragging her little girl out the door.

Mother and daughter power walk to their small car in the parking lot in silence. Valerie gets into the backseat and rushes to buckle her seat belt before Mrs. Torino can do it for her. "Good job," she tells her daughter, feeling both proud and slightly sad. Her baby is growing up.

"Can I brush my teeth and try those tablets Mrs. Jackson told us about?" Valerie asks as Mrs. Torino drives out of the parking lot.

Mrs. Torino glances into the rearview mirror to see her daughter's hopeful eyes. "Let's ask the dentist what's in those tablets first. My guess is they don't use plants to make the dye."

"Mom, please? Then you'll know I'm doing a good enough job."

Maybe Mrs. Torino can relinquish brushing duties to her seven-year-old—if she's satisfied that her daughter is getting her teeth clean. "We'll see," she says.

😇 Mrs. Cohen waits at the curb in her minivan in front of the office at Washington Elementary School. She glances at the digital clock on the dashboard. The bell will ring in six minutes. Last week, she got permission from her boss to leave work early and sent a reminder email that morning. She made her son's dentist appointment several months earlier so she could get a time after school lets out. That way, Zach won't have to miss part of class.

Usually, parents are required to park in the lot, but she called the school on her cell phone as she left work to ask if she could wait out front to pick up Zach and take him to the dentist. The administration is aware of the after-school traffic and is generally accommodating if informed ahead.

A minute after the bell rings, she sees her second-grader trotting toward the van with his backpack slung over his shoulder. She cracks a smile, remembering Zach looking at the whiteboard on the wall in the kitchen at breakfast, like he always does.

"Hey, Mom, I'm going to see Dr. Cadwell at 3:30 today," he said. "Wait till he sees all the teeth I lost since last time. He won't even recognize me!"

Her baby is growing up so fast.

Zach slides open the side door, sits on the seat kitty-corner to his mom, and buckles his seat belt. "I came out as soon as I could," he says.

"You did great. What did you do in school today?" Mrs. Cohen pulls away from the curb to drive to the dentist office.

"We read about Dr. Martin Luther King Jr.," he says. "Let's go on a treasure hunt to Alabama. You start, okay?"

"You got it." Mrs. Cohen tries to remember as much as she can about the Civil Rights Movement. "We're African Americans standing in the rain in 1955," she says, setting the stage. "We're waiting at the bus stop to get across town to go to work."

"Do we have umbrellas?"

"No. We're holding newspapers over our heads, and the ink is getting on our hands."

"Like grandpa told us about when he was young."

"Exactly," Mrs. Cohen says. "I see something shiny in the weeds growing through cracks in the sidewalk."

"I follow your eyes and bend down to grab it," Zach says, proud of himself. "It's a dime, which Mr. Santorin told us could buy a whole milkshake in those days."

Mrs. Cohen chuckles at her son's enthusiasm. "I'm about to ask if anyone lost a dime when the bus drives up and splashes everyone with dirty rainwater. We choke on the exhaust because gas contained lead back then, and it was really stinky."

"How many people are standing there?" Zach asks.

"You tell me."

There's a pause before Zach answers, "Six." Another pause. "Yeah, six of us. The doors open—pueeeshshsh." He pushes air between his lips to make the sound.

She glances over her shoulder to see him separate his hands like doors opening.

"We climb into the bus, one at a time," he says, "and drop coins in the bus driver's change thingy to pay for the ride."

Mrs. Cohen knows there is probably a more precise term than "change thingy" but since she has no idea what it's called, she asks, "How much does it cost?"

"I don't know. We could look it up online."

"Sounds like a good idea. Do you have to use the dime you found?"

"No. I had bus money with me."

Mrs. Cohen cracks a smile at how Zach gets so absorbed in these games. "The money you pay for transportation is called a fare," she says. "You know: bus fare, plane fare, train fare."

"That means I brought bus fare, and now I have an extra dime in my pocket," Zach clarifies with a smile in his voice. "But we have to sit in the back of the bus."

His tone has turned somber, and he leans forward to tap her seat with the tip of his tennis shoe. "We have to sit in the back because we have dark skin. Can you believe that, Mom?"

"Sad, huh?" She sighs and shakes her head.

"I'm glad people get to sit anywhere now. Otherwise, me and James wouldn't get to sit together on field trips."

"Me, too, but we still have a long way to go." She's tempted to correct his grammar, but this isn't the time.

Zach gets quiet. She thinks the conversation will take a deeper turn until he says, "I see two quarters and a nickel on an empty seat in the front of the bus and scoop them up before we walk down the aisle."

Mrs. Cohen is tempted to talk more about civil rights, but they're out of time, which is just as well. The topic will come up again at the dinner table when Zach's dad and big sister can participate. "We're here," she says, pulling into a parking space. "How much money did you find?"

"Sixty-five cents?" Zach pushes the button to open the sliding door.

"That's what I got," Mrs. Cohen says. "What should we do with it?"

"Get milkshakes." He laughs. Then his eyes go wide. "They were so cheap back then. We could get one for Dad and Jeanne too—and still have money left over!"

As they walk from the car to the glass doors, Mrs. Cohen asks, "If milkshakes were only 10 cents each and we bought four of them, how much would we have left?"

Zach goes quiet. She can almost see the neurons firing in his head. They enter the office, and Zach sits in the waiting area while she checks in with the receptionist. When she relaxes in the chair next to him, he says, "The milkshakes would cost 40 cents, so we'd still have 25 cents left, five cents more than we would need to buy two more milkshakes."

"What would you do with the extra nickel?"

"My teacher said candy bars cost only a nickel in those days." Zach chuckles and crosses his arms. "But I don't think we should tell Dr. Cadwell about all that sugar."

Mrs. Cohen laughs. "Good thinking."

"Zachary Cohen?" The dental assistant stands at an open door next to the receptionist's desk.

"Do you want me to come with you?" Mrs. Cohen asks.

Zach stands and walks toward the dental assistant. "No thanks," he says over his shoulder before disappearing behind the door.

Mrs. Cohen knows the staff well. Her son will be safe. Zach's growing confidence and competence is rewarding, but she feels a little wistful about the days when she got to be the center of her little boy's universe.

(*Note:* Mrs. Cohen and Zach played the Treasure Hunt game on page 143 during the car ride to the dentist office.)

* * *

Do you recognize the feeling of being happy, even grateful, that your child is maturing and developing independence? But do you miss the earlier years? Do you recognize that stressed feeling of trying to fit in all your obligations and unintentionally hurting feelings?

I did my best to be the "angel parent" as much as possible, but I fell into "harried parent" more often than I'd like to admit. And my older daughter had attention issues, so I've been accused of being a "helicopter mom." There's a fine line between hovering and being an advocate for a child with special needs, and sometimes it takes a while to figure out a balance.

In other words, most of us will be harried, helicopter, and angel parents depending on circumstances, the amount of sleep we've had, and many other factors. All that anyone, including ourselves, can expect is that we give our best effort. If we appreciate and respect our kids, set clear consistent boundaries, and have lots of conversations with them, they'll grow up to be confident, competent, and generally happy human beings.

CONCLUSION

Second-graders' brains further define neural pathways while generating more glial cells to insulate neural pathways and help process information. Seven and eight-year-olds undergo serious mental, emotional, social, and physical growth, from losing baby teeth and making space for permanent ones to reading chapter books and using math to make sense of their world.

Second grade largely builds on concepts learned in first grade, putting them to practical use. This age group begins to make lasting friendships with kids who share their interests, and they learn how to be a responsible member of a group. This can be a sensitive time when feelings bruise easily, and second-graders may lash out or, alternatively, go silent when someone hurts them.

All in all, second-graders are a lovely bunch—wide-eyed, eager to learn, and keen to do things for themselves. Your child will go through many changes this year. Here's to a wonderful journey!

And if you think your baby will mature a lot in second grade, just wait until your primary schooler hits what I call the "transition year" in the third grade. You can relax, though. The next chapter will give you plenty of insider information and fun stuff to do with your child for a smooth, successful transition to the upper grades.

* 6 *

THIRD GRADE
Starting to Get the Joke

Third grade is one of my favorite grades to teach. No longer in the primary grades, yet not quite considered upper, eight- and nine-year-olds transition from learning to read to reading to learn, and take on this big change with a blossoming sense of humor. Second-graders crack up over silly jokes and puns and begin to infer things, like when they hear a friend's stomach growling during math, they figure it's time to clean up and go to lunch. In third grade, in addition to inference and wordplay, kids become more aware of cause and effect and begin to use deductive reasoning, making this age group even more fun.

YOUR THIRD-GRADER'S BRAIN

Many of the jokes that flew over your child's head before will make him laugh now. In fact, you may find your third-grader quips along with you, especially if your family often banters and plays around with language twists and multiple meanings. These kids' neural pathways seem to click into a critical connection for humor, relating to language on a whole new level.

Swiss developmental psychologist Jean Piaget termed ages 8 to 10 the "concrete operational period," or the stage when children begin applying logic and reason to events. This means they recognize when logic gets tipped in a surprising way, making them laugh.

Neural pathways have become more defined, so information travels faster now. Glial cells have insulated a greater number of electrical highways that reach in every direction, and the development of myelin coating begins to allow signals to transmit with more efficiency. Unnecessary neurons are being swept away in favor of more direct routes and smoother sailing (Stiles and Jernigan 2010).

In effect, communication between the left hemisphere (largely responsible for language) and the right hemisphere (in charge of creativity) becomes more adept, hence your third-grader's increased ability to process figurative phrases intended for humor.

The left brain handles a person's primary language, but functional magnetic resonance image tests (fMRIs) show that additional languages light up various areas in both hemispheres. Because brain hemispheres are getting more in sync, if your child speaks two or more languages, you may notice an improvement in her ability to mentally process in the secondary languages. Third and fourth grades are often the years when language learners catch up with peers who have been learning only in their primary tongue (Klein et al. 2014).

On the other hand, achieving fluency in an additional language after age 9 or 10 becomes more challenging because of the number of neurons that have been pared away by this time, along with the number of pathways that have been coated with myelin for better conduction. That is, children who begin to learn a new language after third grade will usually keep a bit of an accent and have more difficulty mentally processing in that language.

Improved Memory

"Working memory," the executive function that temporarily stores and manages information until we need to use it, improves in third grade and continues to advance through the middle-grade years due to the brain's speedier, more effective transmission of input (Lightfoot et al. 2009, 404–10). The memory jump and more efficient neural connections enable kids to not only solve multistep problems in math and language more easily, but also become more independent in everyday life.

What does that mean on a practical level? Third-graders are quite capable of getting out their own clothes to wear to school if they haven't been doing so already (although some outfits may turn out kind of funny—take a picture for giggles in later years). Eight- and nine-year-olds can make their own beds and pick up their dirty clothes too. Remember, our job as parents is to work ourselves out of a job—to help our kids grow into capable adults.

But this is key: Although a third-grader's memory improves relative to that of a second-grader, eight- and nine-year-olds can remember only half the number of items that an adult can (Kharitonova et al. 2010).

You may have to remind your child that he has the mental tools to figure out a problem—walk him through the process to determine how long it will take to earn the money to go to Six Flags, for instance. Your third-grader may also be motivated to practice athletic, musical, and academic skills—improvement will come faster than ever, with more striking results.

Since your eight- or nine-year-old's attention span will likely continue to lengthen, following instructions with multiple steps should become easier this year. Your third-grader may collaborate with classmates to come up with and carry out detailed school projects. At home, you may hear schemes hatch with friends to accomplish small goals— like a plan to wash your car to earn a couple of bucks so they can dash to the street corner to buy a Bomb Pop.

As neural connections increase and become more efficient, your child will develop a more sophisticated understanding of cause and effect, prompting him to slant situations in his favor. You may hear something like "I read so long over the weekend to finish my library book—I shouldn't have to read after school this week," or "—I should be able to spend more time playing video games," or "—I should be able to watch TV instead." In other words, due to quicker, less-linear thinking, your eight- or nine-year-old may challenge family rules and your decisions more often.

You may be tempted to relax the rules when your child delivers a salient point, and it is good to reward thoughtful negotiation with a successful outcome, but it's a careful balance. In the example, because the child read for several hours already, you might be inclined to give in. But the daily reading ritual is critical in third grade, so you shouldn't relax the requirement. Remember, this is the year children make the shift from learning to read to reading for information.

Rewards and the Brain

Remember that due to brain development, eight- and nine-year-old children process positive feedback in a way that motivates them to do better. So if you say to a third-grader "Well done! Now let's give you the secret to fixing the part you missed," you will go a long way toward reaching a desired behavior. On the other hand, if you say "You didn't do that right. You have to do it this way," your child will likely tune you out.

This isn't just "you'll catch more flies with honey than vinegar" mentality. Using fMRI testing, researchers can observe the difference in neural reactions in the cerebral cortex between adults' and kids' brains given positive and negative feedback. It turns out that third-graders' brains fire a bunch of neurons when they receive positive feedback, and their brains hardly respond at all to negative feedback—physical evidence that looking on the bright side gets better results with kids this age (Van Duijvenvoorde et al. 2008).

Scientists think children may do better with reward than punishment because understanding that they didn't do something well requires a more intricate process in the brain than acknowledging something that they did well and moving on to the next step.

THIRD-GRADE SOCIAL TRAITS

Third-graders can see beyond themselves better than they could in second grade, making their conversations more give-and-take. This is the ideal time to teach them how to listen, an essential skill in creating or enhancing a relationship. Helping your child develop healthy friendships while you still have a fair amount of influence may be one of the most important things you can do this year.

Your Relationship

You may think your eight- or nine-year-old can handle more teasing now that she laughs at jokes she didn't catch before. She may use idioms, such as telling you how she's going to "kill two birds with one stone" by reading a book for school that will also get her a badge in her Brownie troop. But beware. Your third-grader may be able to process language in more depth, but peers, teachers, and family members still appear in black and white. Kids this age take teasing personally, especially jabs by their parents or caregivers whom they trust.

One act can color your child's view of whether someone is mean or nice. For instance, you might tell your third-grader she can have a friend over *after* she does a chore or finishes her homework, and she'll think you're mean. Then you'll do something she perceives as nice, maybe give her a cookie to munch on while you help her with her homework, and she'll change her mind about you entirely. The main thing to remember is to keep communication as upbeat as possible.

Your third-grader may want to spend progressively less time with you in favor of developing independence, but she will need you nearby to answer questions or help solve problems. Consider providing a private place for reading or doing homework—a small table tucked behind the couch, a tree house, a large closet, a section of the garage, or the attic. Occasionally stop by and ask a question or share a funny comment or story, rather than asking if everything is okay. This age group enjoys personal space, and giving them their own spot implies trust and respect.

Kids this age can draw on personal experience to predict outcomes, respond to questions, and feel empathy for others. In effect, they get better at making inferences about what people say. For example, if you mention, "I sure have a lot of presents to wrap," your child may glean that you need help and ask you to teach her how to wrap gifts so you don't have to do all the work by yourself.

When your third-grader offers you a chance to teach a new skill, do your best to drop everything and seize the opportunity—even when you're busy. You may not get another chance. The dinner that gets to the table late will be long forgotten.

As my husband likes to say, "Don't confuse the urgent with the important."

Friends

Third-graders often narrow friendships to just a few regular buddies they like to play with, but sometimes they change groups to try out new people to see if they can find a better fit for their interests. These social experiments can turn out great—or cause drama and anxiety. Although your child will seek even more independence from you this year, your support, encouragement, and opinions regarding what happens among his friends will be more important than ever before. You are home base, the safety zone, so your child can venture out and try on new opinions, pastimes, and personalities.

The Social Magic Bullet

Model asking questions for your third-grader, along with listening to the answers and providing feedback. Specifically instruct him on how to make inquiries about friends and family members and respond to people's answers. Being an excellent listener will enhance your child's relationships all the way through school—and even into adulthood as someone's partner, coworker, boss, or friend. The ability to engage in real conversations, which means focusing on what the *other* person has to say rather than interrupting or thinking about what to say next, will open doors for your child for the rest of his life.

Attentive listening makes people feel respected and appreciated and helps avoid miscommunication. Learning to listen in third grade, when neural pathways are freshly equipped to empathize with others, will make the skill second nature.

This year, you may find the stories coming home from school are told in much greater detail and are more persuasive and engaging. In fact, before getting upset with another child or the teacher for something that supposedly happened at school, get the other side of the story. Kids this age are notorious for relating situations in a way that puts them in the best light and places most, if not all, of the blame on others.

Cell Phones and Your Third-Grader

The marketing company Influence Central did a survey of 500 moms and their children in February 2016, a follow-up to their 2012 study of 1,000 moms and kids, to find out to what degree children use cell phones. Predictably, the latest numbers reveal a sharp increase in use and influence. Kids typically get their first phone at age 10, but children carry minicomputers in their pockets as early as age 8.

Psychotherapist Michael Rubino (2016), who specializes in working with children and teens, says, "In my opinion, [children don't] need a cell phone until they enter middle school, and at that point, all they need is a basic cell phone . . . so they can check in with you if their plans change, or if they feel they are in need of help."

If your family has special circumstances and your child already has a cell phone, or if you intend to supply one soon, think about setting ground rules. For example, face-to-face communication is imperative for kids to learn to decipher body language and social cues in a safe environment. Banning phones from the dinner table, including parents' phones, will encourage traditional conversations during the evening meal, helping you stay connected and up-to-date with one another's lives.

Note: For more information and tips on kids and their cell phones, see pages 230 and 283 in the fourth- and fifth-grade chapters.

THIRD-GRADE ACADEMICS

By the end of third grade, your child will be expected to read fluently with few pauses to decode unfamiliar words. You should notice your eight- or nine-year-old reading a variety of fiction and nonfiction material and catching words he's misinterpreted when they don't make sense in context. This year's reading will make huge strides in comprehension and take a big leap in vocabulary—between three and six thousand words!

This drastic jump will be due to brain development as well as independent reading, so it's crucial to keep up with regular reading at home. You can be a big help by continuing to read chapter books aloud together that are slightly above your child's reading level. Talk about the characters and plots, along with the actions your third-grader might take if he were in the protagonist's shoes.

As reading vocabulary grows, so too will your child's speech and writing. This is a good thing since third-graders are expected to speak and write using adjectives, adverbs, and compound sentences to provide clearer pictures of what they want to say. They learn more about how to include proper punctuation and to write narratives describing something that happened in their lives, along with opinion pieces and persuasive paragraphs. As these kids transition to reading for information, they get introduced to doing research about science and social studies topics both online and at the school library.

If you've been using a whiteboard, or some other form of family communication, you may notice more descriptive notations. If you've been writing notes to each other, you may see sentences and punctuation becoming more accurate. If not, encourage your child to use capitals, commas, and ending punctuation, making the point that whatever we practice tends to become habit.

Third grade is also an intense year for growth in math. All that repeated addition in first and second grade will pay off when your child learns about multiplication. Helping your eight- or nine-year-old memorize the multiplication tables, 1 through 10, as soon as possible will give her a huge leg up for learning all kinds of other required third-grade skills.

Multiplication facts are merely a tool for solving multiple-step word problems that can include geometry, projected and elapsed time, and measurement of distance, area, and volume. Then, before you know it, division facts come on the scene. Fractions go from simple halves, thirds, and quarters to fifths, sixths, sevenths, and so on. Your child will learn long division, be introduced to ratios, and lots more (see the list of mathematics skills in "Third-Grade Academic Skills" on page 186).

Becoming proficient at multiplication right away makes division easy. In fact, most of the other concepts will make more sense too. If your child doesn't have to stop to figure out the answer to 6 x 7 while trying to solve a multiple-step problem, he'll get to enjoy the exciting intrigue of learning how math can be used to figure out so many practical things: when he has to leave for soccer practice to get there on time, how much cardboard he'll need to make his Halloween costume, or how many hours he has to pull weeds and rake leaves to earn enough money for that skateboard he wants to buy.

Third grade is a huge year for building a sturdy math foundation for the rest of your child's life, so have fun with numbers at the store, in the kitchen, or out in the world. If math isn't your best subject, you'll find playing some of the games in this chapter will hone your skills sharper than ever. If you're good at math, strap yourself in. You and your child are headed for a great adventure.

THIRD-GRADE ACADEMIC SKILLS

Language Arts

- Retell fictional stories and cite evidence of the central message; determine the main idea in nonfiction by pointing out proof in the text.

- Refer to the text to ask and answer questions.

- Describe fictional characters' traits and motivations, and tell how their actions affect subsequent events; explain cause and effect in nonfiction.

- Figure out the meaning of words and phrases in context.

- Understand the meanings of common prefixes and suffixes, decode multisyllabic words, and know third-grade irregular verbs.

- Understand literal versus nonliteral language.

- Describe how events build on earlier sections or stanzas in a story, article, or poem.

- Determine who is telling the story—the point of view (e.g., a narrator or character).

- Compare stories written from different points of view.

- Explain how illustrations and photos contribute to fiction and nonfiction material.

- Use text features and search tools to locate information relevant to a given topic.

- Compare themes, settings, and plots of stories on the same topic; compare details in nonfiction texts on the same topic.

- Read third-grade material independently with comprehension and fluency.

- Write opinion pieces, informative essays, and narratives, and do short research projects.

- Write pieces that include an introduction, a body that supports and builds on the introduction, and a conclusion. Provide supporting facts and events.

- Begin to edit their own writing using feedback from adults and peers.

- Be an active, productive member of a group, participate in oral presentations using notes, and speak in complete sentences.

Mathematics

- Understand multiplication as the product of a number of rows of repeated addition—for example, 4 rows of 3 pennies each illustrates the meaning of 4 x 3 = 12.

- Know multiplication facts from 0 x 0 = 0 through 10 x 10 = 100.

- Understand multiplication and division fact families (e.g., 3 x 4 = 12, 4 x 3 = 12, 12 ÷ 4 = 3, 12 ÷ 3 = 4).

- Use place value concepts to round whole numbers to the nearest 10 or 100.

- Use multiplication and division within 100 to solve word problems.

- Decide whether answers make sense by mental computation, estimation, and rounding.

- Add and subtract within 1,000 using trading and regrouping (carrying and borrowing).

- Multiply 1-digit numbers by multiples of 10 (e.g., 9 x 80 = 720).

- Understand the numerator in a fraction is the number of parts and the denominator represents the whole (e.g., 7/8 means seven equal pieces out of a possible eight).

- Understand and create models to show simple equal fractions, like 2/4 = 1/2 and 4/6 = 2/3.

- Recognize that fraction denominators must be the same to compare.

- Tell, write, and measure time intervals to the nearest minute. Solve word problems involving addition and subtraction of time periods to the minute.

- Measure volume and weight using metric units (gram, kilogram, liters), and add or subtract like units to solve word problems.

- Use picture and bar graphs to display or interpret data.

- Measure objects with rulers showing half and quarter inches.

- Recognize rhombuses, rectangles, and squares as quadrilaterals, and draw examples of quadrilaterals that do not belong to these subcategories.

- Understand the area of plane figures, and why and how area is calculated in square units.

- Solve real-world mathematical problems involving perimeters of polygons.

To find out what your child will be expected to master in your area, type into a search engine the name of your state and "education standards K–12." Skills may appear in a different grade in your state's standards.

THIRD-GRADE HIGH-FREQUENCY WORDS

To build fluency and comprehension, it's important for your child to know how to read and spell the high-frequency words that make up 50 percent of all text. Imagine how much more your child will enjoy reading without getting tripped up on these common words.

Make flash cards, play the Who's Hiding? game on page 139, and post the lists on the family bulletin board until your children know all the words and don't need the lists anymore.

50 High-Frequency Words—Third Grade

about	afraid	almost	also	asked
become	believe	build	carry	caught
clean	clothes	done	draw	drink
eight	fall	far	full	getting
grow	hold	hot	hurt	I'm
journal	kind	knew	laugh	light
long	much	myself	never	only
own	pick	show	small	something
start	sure	today	together	try
warm	weather	whole	year	you're

THIRD-GRADE GAMES TO STAY SHARP, CATCH UP, OR KEEP INTEREST IN SCHOOL

1. **Ratchet up the Treasure Hunt game.** Remember the Treasure Hunt game (page 143), where you and your child make up adventures that include finding, earning, spending, and losing money? If you haven't played the game in a while, third-graders tend to love this game even more than second-graders. Your child's growing vocabulary will

add spice, and new multiplication and geometry skills, among others, will create a whole new dimension for your imaginary exploits. For added fun:

    a. Record your treasure hunts on your cell phone. You won't believe the giggles you'll share while listening to your imaginary journeys together.

    b. If your child doesn't come up with the idea first, say something like this: "You know what would be cool? Why don't you type the story on the computer?" Third-graders' writing is expected to take a big leap this year, so encourage your child to type out one of your adventures as a fun way to boost that skill. But it isn't necessary to listen to the recording to write the story. In fact, sometimes writing from memory invites exciting, new twists. More ways to enjoy the story after it's written:

        • Suggest drawing pictures to go with the text.

        • Encourage your child to read the story to family members and friends.

        • Have your child ask for permission to read the story to her class.

2. **Revisit the second-grade games.** Make up new silly songs together to sing to familiar tunes. Clap patterns with added moves to make the rhythm trickier for third grade. Have your child jump rope and count by 3s, 6s, 7s, 8s, and 9s, rather than 2s, 5s, and 10s.

3. **Bounce a ball back and forth.** Each time you bounce the ball, use a synonym—then switch to antonyms—then try homophones, which will be covered this year. In his book *Teaching with the Brain in Mind*, Eric Jensen, PhD (2005, 61), says, "The evidence has become a groundswell . . . most neuroscientists agree that movement and cognition are powerfully connected." Since movement and thought are

both processed first through the cerebellum, the organ in the back of the brain (under the occipital lobe), thinking in conjunction with physical activity seems a magical combination.

4. **Sing songs on the radio with your child.** By third grade, most kids prefer Top 40 music to children's songs. If you listen to the radio together in the car, you'll be familiar with societal influences and be able to address them. Enhance reading and writing skills by keeping a steady beat and pointing out language discrepancies, such as "near-rhymes," and comparing verses to stanzas in a poem.

5. **Keep a joke book in the car.** Encourage your child to read jokes to you, and invent new puns and silly wordplay together.

6. **Play Story Starter.** When you see an interesting person on the street, give pretend reasons why they dress the way they do and tell how they got there and why they're in a hurry (or not in a hurry, whichever the case may be). If your child doesn't contribute to the story on his own, ask him the person's name and whom the person might meet. Not only is this a fun pastime, but conjuring random explanations for things will also help develop skills for creative writing.

A FUN, SUREFIRE WAY TO MASTER MULTIPLICATION FACTS

Third grade is a big year for picking up new math skills. Learning the multiplication tables from 0 to 10, without hesitation, will give your third-grader an advantage in grasping other concepts, such as two-place multiplication, division, long division, fractions, area, and volume.

1. If your child isn't intrinsically motivated, common for eight- and nine-year-olds, agree upon a reward for each set of facts mastered, preferably something healthy, such as a family picnic at the park—but a carpet picnic of takeout pizza in front of the TV works too.

2. For the first set of facts, show your child she already knows 0s, 1s, 2s, 5s, and 10s. Challenge her to make flash cards for all of those facts and master them in one or two days. This is a doable goal that will motivate her to learn the harder 3s, 4s, 6s, 7s, 8s, and 9s.

   Note: Remind your third-grader that any number x 0 is 0, any number x 1 is the same number (identity property), and any number x 2 is a double. She knows the 5s from learning to tell time and counting nickels and the 10s from learning base 10 and counting dimes.

3. When your third-grader is ready for the next set of multiplication tables, ask her to make flash cards for the 3s, from 0 to 10.

   a. When she's finished, have her set out the cards and collect the facts she already knows (3 x 0, 3 x 1, 3 x 2, 3 x 5, 3 x 10).

   b. To reinforce the vocabulary she's learning at school, coach her in telling you the reason she knows these products is because of the *commutative property* (0 x 3 = 3 x 0, 1 x 3 = 3 x 1).

   c. Then ask her to count the number of cards with facts that she still has to learn (3 x 3, 3 x 4, 3 x 6, 3 x 7, 3 x 8, and 3 x 9).

   d. Give her a week to go through the 3s, first alone for a day or two, and then have her mix the 3s with the bigger pile of facts she knows.

   e. Come up with another reward for when she knows the entire stack of multiplication facts (0s, 1s, 2s, 3s, 5s, and 10s) without having to pause to think.

4. When your child has mastered the 3s, ask her to make cards for the 4s, from 0 to 10.

   a. Point out that your child knows 4 x 3 because of the commutative property.

b. Ask her to count the new facts (4 x 4, 4 x 6, 4 x 7, 4 x 8, 4 x 9).

c. Repeat the additional steps above—including a new reward!

5. After mastering the 4s, continue the same process with the 6s, 7s, 8s, and 9s. Your child will be thrilled that when she gets to 9s, she has only one new fact to learn! *Note:* Before giving your child a reward, make sure she mixes the new flash cards with the entire stack and can answer them all without pausing to think.

4 GAMES TO MAKE THIRD-GRADE MATH FUN AND EASY

1. **Spending money.** Start with your child adding the change in the family jar or the coins in your wallet and then try the games below to help him learn the value of money.

   a. Make up prices for hypothetical items, things your child would enjoy—a box of colored pencils, an ice cream cone, a trip to the movies—and ask your third-grader to show you a combination of coins that would pay for each thing.

   b. Have him add up the amounts for the objects on your list and give you a total.

   c. Bring out some paper money: $1, $5, and $10 bills. Choose an item to buy with a paper bill, and walk him through how to count out change for one of the bills using the coins.

   d. Ask him to choose an item and show you how much change the cashier should give him for a $5, $10, or $20 bill.

   e. Once your child gets the hang of this, consider getting some play money and a toy cash register. When friends come over, it will keep them busy for hours.

2. **Family timeline.** Understanding number lines and directionality is a big help in learning several third-grade skills, so make it fun and personal by creating a family timeline. You won't believe how long your third-grader will remember everyone's birthday and how much he'll learn about his extended family!

   a. Have your child draw a long line of chalk on the sidewalk or in your driveway.

   b. Using his foot to measure equal distances, have him put a short vertical perpendicular mark at the beginning of the chalk line at his heel and another one at his toe, from left to right. Then, have him put his heel on the toe perpendicular mark, draw another mark at his toe, and continue until he gets to the end of the line of chalk.

   c. Label the vertical marks, beginning the decade before the earliest birthday in the family, including grandparents, aunts, uncles, and cousins.

   d. Ask him to mark all the family members' birthdays—month, day, and year—in chronological order (he'll need help from you with the dates, of course).

   e. If this project excites your third-grader, after all the mistakes have been made in chalk on the pavement, have him make a more permanent birthday timeline by taping together construction paper or using a roll of butcher paper.

3. **Sudoku.** This is a strategic game that clarifies number relationships. Pick up a book of puzzles you can do together in the car or waiting for an appointment (this is great for gifted kids and high achievers).

4. **Yahtzee.** Five dice, strategy, number patterns, probability, physical movement—what more could you ask for? If your child hasn't begun to play this game already, third grade is the perfect time!

5. Jenga. This tactical puzzle of wooden pieces requires thinking, employs rudimentary engineering and physics, and involves physical manipulation. Kids love to beat their parents—and eventually they do (this is another great game for gifted kids and high achievers).

Homework in Third Grade

As your child gets older, you'll find the homework becomes less familiar. The material hasn't changed since you went through elementary school as much as education has made a shift. For example, kids used to learn math by rote: doing multiple problems of the same kind of operation to cement that concept in the brain. Nowadays, experiential learning is encouraged: children grasp concepts by using them to solve problems in everyday situations. Many educators have found that both kinds of learning have merit and take an eclectic approach, using drill as well as practical application.

In any case, the way kids are taught in schools these days has changed, and reading the directions on a homework paper may not be enough for you to help your third-grader when she gets stuck. It will be crucial to get phone numbers from at least three classmates this year—and every year through college! Calling other kids to get homework information rather than depending on parents encourages personal responsibility as well as responsibility to the classroom community. Also, when multiple students tell the teacher that the directions are unclear, she can adjust future projects accordingly.

This year, your child will build on the distinction between nonfiction and fiction, becoming aware of the difference between fact and opinion—"facts" can be proven through repeated experiments, whereas "opinions" are interpretations of facts or situations. Fair warning: You may disagree with a "fact" presented at school—and your third-grader will take the teacher's side. After all, the teacher is your child's academic authority (unless you homeschool). If you find yourself frustrated about a "fact" your third-grader learns in class, email or talk to the teacher and ask for clarification. Kids sometimes construe things differently than intended.

THE REAL DEAL
Math in the Classroom Next Door

When our younger daughter was in third grade, in the classroom next to mine, she came home one afternoon frustrated with a page of word problems that required her to figure out the amount of elapsed time between two events. While she sat at the kitchen table, I got up from my chair and modeled how to find the answers on the analog clock on the wall.

And our eight-year-old blew up at me.

"That's not how my teacher does it, Mom!" she yelled.

I silently counted to 10, wondering how she could think I didn't know what I was doing. But for years, parents had told me stories of similar arguments—my students had treated their moms and dads as if they knew nothing and I, the mighty teacher, knew all.

"I'll do it myself," she said, propping her elbow on the table and her head on her hand.

"I just taught—" I flinched as her fist slammed the table and her pencil tumbled to the floor.

"Forget it. I'll ask Mrs. MacMillan tomorrow."

I wanted to yell at her to chill out or go to her room, but knowing that telling agitated kids to calm down usually has the opposite effect, I forced myself to say instead, "We don't have to use the kitchen clock. Let me show you how to do the problems with the paper clock you made in school today."

She picked up her pencil and tilted her head in confusion. "How'd you know I made a clock?"

"Because I taught this same lesson to my class today." I have to admit there was a certain amount of edge to my voice at this point.

"Well, you don't do it right," she said, shoving her mostly blank math paper into her backpack. "And anyway, I left my clock on my desk."

"You're willing to miss recess rather than trust me to know what I'm talking about?"

"Yes." My little girl threw her backpack over her shoulder, ran up the stairs, and closed her bedroom door.

As was our custom, we took turns talking about our days at the dinner table that night. My husband had been sure our youngest would bring up the homework drama, but she didn't say a word about it.

The next day after school, she came into my classroom and stopped at the table in the front of the room where I sat working on my lesson plans for the following week. She stood next to me, looking at her feet and said, "Um . . . Mom?"

"Yes, honey," I answered, still scribbling in my plan book.

"Mrs. MacMillan showed us how to do the math problems with the real clock above the whiteboard today."

"She did?" I put down my pencil and looked at her, fairly sure I knew what was coming.

"Aw, come here." I rolled my chair out from the table and pulled her onto my lap. Kids this age are sensitive and emotional, our little girl maybe more than most.

"I was so mad I couldn't do it." She buried her face in my blouse and started to sob.

"I know," I said. "You usually catch on quickly, so you get impatient when something takes time for you to learn." I kissed her hair and gave her a gentle squeeze. "But I'm proud of you for hanging in there with Mrs. MacMillan today to figure it out."

"Really?" She gazed up at me and wiped her cheeks with the back of her hand.

"Yeah. The better you get at pushing through when things get hard, the cooler the stuff you'll get to learn."

That experience seemed to be a turning point for her. From then on, she jumped into challenges and didn't let up until she was satisfied with the results. Who knew? It's amazing how such a small circumstance can become a life-changing event.

Family Reading

The best way to ensure your child does well throughout school, including college, is to maintain your family reading habit throughout elementary school. Competition from television, computers, e-tablets, and cell phones will increase as your child grows older. Watching rather than reading can be fun, and some shows and games offer excellent education opportunities. Still, there's no substitute for regular reading for your child's brain to evolve into an efficient reading, comprehending organ that, frankly, generates better pictures.

13 AUTHORS TO KEEP THIRD-GRADERS READING

As kids grow up, they get busier with school, homework, friends, sports, and other activities. Still, regular reading is important for success in school, and the best way to keep children reading is to supply great books. You'll recognize many of them. Some titles may be too difficult for your third-grader to read independently, which makes them perfect for you to enjoy together.

1. Horrid Henry series (27 books) by Francesca Simon—chapter books (around 100 pages) about a boy who often gets into trouble but has a perfect brother. Snappy dialogue, lots of laughs. If your child likes the first one, there are plenty more!

2. Wayside School series (5 books) by Louis Sachar—100 to 150 pages of outlandish stories that third-grade boys (and many girls too) find hilarious.

3. *The One and Only Ivan* by Katherine Applegate—inspired by a true story of an ape who spent 30 years in an indoor cage at the zoo. Presents the power of unexpected friendships.

4. Melonhead series (5 books) by Katy Kelly—clever, inventive boy goes from one hilarious adventure (sometimes calamity) to the next, a big hit even with reluctant readers.

5. Captain Underpants series (14 books) by Dav Pilkey—a wacky series that has gotten many kids reading.

6. *The Giraffe and the Pelly and Me, Fantastic Mr. Fox*, and *George's Marvelous Medicine* by Roald Dahl—quirky characters solve problems in surprising ways.

7. *The Lucky Baseball Bat* by Matt Christopher—author of many books about sporty kids.

8. *Because of Winn-Dixie* by Kate DiCamillo—a child adopts a dog that helps her make friends and come to terms with family issues.

9. *Ramona Quimby, Age 8* by Beverly Cleary—Cleary has a series of Ramona books, but this title is third-grade reading level.

10. Judy Moody series (14 books) by Megan McDonald—feisty third-grader learns lessons the hard way.

11. Cam Jansen mystery series (30+ books) by David Adler—child sleuth with a photographic memory.

12. Arthur chapter book series (30+ books) by Marc Brown—familiar lovable characters learn lessons.

13. *Harry Potter and the Sorcerer's Stone*—first in the series by J. K. Rowling, leveled at mid–fifth grade, but third-graders love to read with an adult or challenge themselves.

THIRD-GRADE OUTSIDE THE NORM

Warning: If your child still lags behind peers in reading or math, and you haven't gotten help, do it now! The common belief is that some kids mature slower and will eventually catch up to their classmates. While brain development varies and children learn at different rates, studies have shown for decades that kids who struggle with reading by third grade don't catch up without intervention.

Your Tortoise May Not Win the Race Without Help

Some children have learning gaps that can be filled in to build understanding, whereas others have brains that function differently than those
in the mainstream. These kids require special strategies to become proficient readers. If your child still struggles to decode words, has trouble
with comprehension, or can't seem to grasp number patterns, values,
and operations, it's time to act.

According to the American Federation of Teachers (2004), three
long-term studies conclude that "late bloomers are rare; skill deficits
are almost always what prevent children from blooming as readers."

Remember, by the end of the year, your third-grader should be putting mental energy into absorbing information rather than deciphering
words and the meaning of phrases. Success in science, social studies,
literature, and even math in the upper elementary grades depends on it.

If the school hasn't begun the process to determine why your eight-
or nine-year-old still wrestles with one or more subjects, make an appointment as soon as possible and request an assessment. Remember,
legally, the school has 90 days to provide test results and recommenda-
tions to help your child become a proficient reader and problem solver
(see page 157).

A learning disability may be the culprit for reading or math trouble. In that case, the sooner your child has strategies for developing
skills within the framework of how his brain processes information,
the better.

The Conscientious Parent's Dilemma

Often moms and dads spend a lot of time assisting their struggling
children with homework and reteaching failed classroom assignments
in hopes of keeping their "tortoises" from falling behind. For some
kids, though, the extra work isn't enough. Testing may reveal that
your child needs specific techniques to help her learn to read and understand math concepts.

But here's the problem: In many districts across the country, kids
who haven't fallen two years behind standardized expectations can't

get special education services. Note, however, this yardstick doesn't apply to children diagnosed with a chemical imbalance, such as attention deficits, anxiety, bipolar, or similar disorders. These children qualify under "Other Health Impairments" in the Special Education Guide (Degree Prospects, n.d.).

The Individuals with Disabilities Education Act, or IDEA, allows states to determine the criteria for kids' eligibility. To qualify in most states and districts, students must show the following:

- Evidence of a learning disability specified in IDEA
- A discrepancy between their IQ score and achievement level
- A lag of two years or more in reading and math

That's right. If your third-grader is dyslexic or has an auditory processing problem but isn't far enough behind, the school staff won't be allowed to offer services. Many parents feel they're punished for helping their kids, and their children are penalized for the extra effort spent on homework and school projects.

Has Mom's or Dad's diligence become a detriment to their child's education? No! Parental help models the importance of education for kids. If your child isn't far enough behind to receive special education services, don't worry. Your third-grader can still grow into a well-adjusted, well-educated adult.

Remember, brains are imminently malleable. Try the following four ideas to help your child fill in the gaps and achieve academic success:

1. **Get as clear a diagnosis as possible.** Have the school psychologist explain your child's learning patterns and challenges gleaned from the testing and observations to determine eligibility for services. A diagnosis, such as "dyslexic tendencies," will help in finding avenues for support.

   If you feel you need more information, consider consulting a private licensed educational psychologist (LEP) to do another assessment or to analyze the test results you receive from the school.

LEP Susan Cradduck (2016) says, "The LEP should be able to provide a list of organizations in the area to meet a child's needs, and lots of great stuff is available online."

2. **Visit Understood: For Learning and Attention Issues.** Understood is a website dedicated to helping kids with special needs and their parents. The site provides great information, professional advice, and a "Tech Finder" that pulls up links to apps and online games specific to children's learning challenges. These games help kids train their brains to absorb math and reading in a way that works for them.

3. **Type your child's disability into a search engine.** Here are three examples: "dyslexia," "dysgraphia," or "attention deficit hyperactivity disorder." You won't believe all the fabulous games, activities, and other helpful resources available to people with learning issues these days.

4. **Remember the physical connection to learning.** Make sure your child gets plenty of exercise—jumping rope, running, skipping, bouncing and kicking balls—to create those neural connections that sharpen thinking (see page 11).

You may resent school personnel for disqualifying your third-grader from special education services. But your attention has kept your child from getting too far behind. Playing online games specific to your child's needs, along with continued regular reading practice and exercise, will likely prepare your third-grader for the rigors of fourth grade and beyond.

Gifted and Talented Education

Studies indicate that when sharp kids are given projects suited to their intelligence, they tend to remain interested in school, pursue higher education, and become successful adults (Kell et al. 2013). If your child hasn't taken a test in second grade to determine giftedness, an assessment will likely be given in third grade, usually by the reading specialist or school psychologist.

The tests usually require kids to solve problems through logic, applying what they learn from previous questions to work out progressively difficult puzzles. A score between 95 and 100 percent generally qualifies children for gifted and talented education (GATE), though parameters vary. High scores on annual state tests, advanced skills in music or drawing, and teacher observations are commonly considered as well.

According to the National Association for Gifted Children (2013), "Program criteria is left to the district or individual school. Parents and administrators should work together in a positive and collaborative spirit to . . . develop an appropriate educational strategy for gifted students."

In most schools, gifted programs begin in second, third, or fourth grade. Instruction may include projects within the regular education classroom that require less repetition and higher-level thinking skills than those assigned to the rest of the students. Your child's school may have a pull-out program that allows students to leave the classroom to work on projects with other kids of similar abilities.

Sometimes schools group these kids in a gifted cluster within the same classroom to receive specialized instruction. Many districts have magnet schools that specialize in science and math or literature and the arts. Magnet programs can be great for keeping gifted students stimulated and engaged in learning. Truthfully, though, some studies indicate that schools and teachers often have a hard time getting smart kids' needs met due to time and material constraints (Bui et al. 2012). So if your child is designated gifted, check out what programs are available in your area.

Here are five ways you can assist the teacher in keeping your gifted child engaged in school, learning to his full potential:

1. **Expand on the theme.** As you have likely done in the primary grades, find out what themes will be covered in science and social

studies in third grade, and take a look at the grade-level academic expectations. Explore online with your child to find fun projects that capitalize on those themes and provide opportunities for using third-grade skills in depth.

2. **Dig deeper.** Encourage your third-grader to look for books at the public and school libraries that incorporate those themes.

3. **Create a contract.** Ask your child's teacher about setting up a contract with thematic projects, due dates, and scheduled times for your child to share finished activities with the class (see page 64).

4. **Offer your materials and resources to the teacher.** She may want to assign the project to other students so your child will have buddies to work with. *Note:* Your child's teacher has the right to decline to participate in activities not included in the general curriculum or the district (or private school) employee job description. Please don't give the teacher a hard time if she can't squeeze in a contract or allow your child to share home projects in class.

5. **Engage with other parents.** Regardless of the teacher's participation, consider inviting other parents of gifted kids or high achievers to look up thematic projects and books with their children. Assembling a small group to share enrichment activities can be less work and more fun, for both parents and kids. Ask the administration if your group can meet weekly or monthly at the school to share ideas and projects.

Gifted Students Versus High Achievers

Kids who ace the intelligence test and meet other district or school requirements are designated "gifted." Conscientious workers who do well in school but don't score as high on the tests are termed "high achievers."

If your child falls into the high-achiever category, there's no need to stress. Kids who want to participate—and are willing to do the extra work—are often welcome to engage in GATE projects at school. Keep in mind that although some gifted students don't perform in school to their potential, largely due to boredom from revisiting material they've already mastered and social immaturity that hasn't caught up with their intellect (Page 2010), high achievers have developed a work ethic that will serve them well throughout their lives.

THIRD-GRADE CARE AND FEEDING

Here are the things your third-grader needs for a healthy developing brain, a strong body, and a happy outlook for the best social, emotional, and academic growth. If you've already read other chapters in this book, the ingredients for optimal health and thinking—sleep, nutrition, water, and exercise—will be familiar. The details vary from year to year, though, so be sure to refresh your knowledge and renew your commitment.

Sleep

The National Sleep Foundation recommends that children 6 to 13 years old get 9 to 11 hours in dreamland every night. Your child may be an outlier who seems to function well on seven or eight hours, but if you notice random snooze fests—naps in the car on short trips, occasional marathon siestas, or 12-hour nights—she's not getting enough regular rest.

Your third-grader is growing and needs ample sleep to rejuvenate cells and make new ones, clean out impurities, and generate refreshing delta brainwaves for clear thinking. Adjust your family schedule if bedtimes have become rushed or have crept later and later. For help with a kid who has a hard time falling or staying asleep, revisit page 17 for possible solutions.

On the other end of the spectrum, if your child often sleeps more than 12 hours, talk to your pediatrician. You'll want to rule out a sleep disorder, vitamin deficiency, or other problem.

Nutrition: An Absolute Must for Growing Brains and Bones

Newspaper columnist Doug Larsen had a point when he said, "Life expectancy would grow by leaps and bounds if green vegetables smelled as good as bacon."

If you've been consistent with a good balance of vegetables, fruit, protein, and fats, bravo! Remember, fats are required for metabolizing vitamins A, E, D, and K. Your child is getting the building blocks for a strong mind and body, and will likely practice good eating habits through adulthood.

Sadly, most kids prefer pasta, breads, and fried foods, and they leave the salad and broccoli on their plates. Then later those kids eat dessert! Or the adult in charge says, "You can't have dessert because you didn't finish your dinner" but then allows a snack a short while after dinner—something that isn't green.

By eight or nine years old, kids' brains are fully equipped to learn to eat vegetables and lean proteins regularly. Without these essentials, children are robbed of the nutrients their brains and bodies desperately need for healthy growth and development. It's like running your car on the dregs in the gas tank with the engine low on oil.

Worse, unless children are overweight, parents may not notice the effects of poor eating habits. Children suffering from lack of nutrition may struggle with paying attention, get irritable easily, lack patience, resist trying new things, have asthma, appear sad, or become easily overwhelmed (Birch et al. 2009).

Providing healthy foods, along with being consistent about the expectation that your child will eat them, is one of the greatest gifts you can give him for a healthy life. Include salads, raw and cooked vegetables, and lean proteins, making sure not to overload his plate. Eating past being comfortably full starts young and contributes to obesity later. Little kids may require a bit of indulgence in food choices, but by eight or nine years old, children can understand the rule: You get to choose whether to finish your dinner, but remember that leaving the healthy food behind means you're done eating for the day.

Make this rule a rite of passage for your third-grader—the transition from little kid to big kid in your house. You may endure whining, even screaming and crying, the first time your child tests you—hysterical reports of hunger pangs after he chooses not to finish a modest portion of zucchini—but force yourself to be strong.

A human being can go six weeks without a morsel of food before dying of starvation. One night without snacks after an unfinished dinner won't hurt your child—at all—no matter how pathetic the wailing and begging gets. By the next morning, he will understand that not finishing vegetables and salad truly means no other food will be allowed for the rest of the evening.

Once your child knows you're going to be consistent, you'll likely never need to argue about food again. You may get occasional hopeful probes like "If I don't eat my green beans, can I still have a cookie after dinner?"

You'll smile, maybe give a kiss on the cheek, and say, "Good try. You know the rule."

Sometimes parents worry their kids will starve before eating vegetables or other foods they claim to hate. Although it's a good idea to find vegetables and other nutritious items your child enjoys, realize that if you don't give in with snacks and alternative favorites, he will eventually eat what's on the family dinner menu. Honest. If your eight- or nine-year-old doesn't have an eating disorder, give consistency a try for seven solid days and see what happens.

Explain the rule ahead of time, and then keep it light. No cajoling into tasting this or taking one more bite of that. You don't want to create a battle of wills. In fact, ignore your child's eating except to take note of whether food gets consumed. Those who finish dinner get a small dessert, and those who don't must wait until the next morning to eat again. In the beginning, this transition may be tough, but this could be one of the best things you ever do for your child.

The aim is for moderation—eat healthy most of the time, but enjoy celebrations with family and friends. Declare parties, visitors, and outings "special occasions" when your child can leave a few bites of salad and have more dessert than usual. When you and your kids socialize, go ahead and add extra whipped cream, and declare it a special treat.

Water

Our bodies may be able to go for six weeks without food, but we'd barely live a week without water. Your third-grader needs to drink five to seven cups of water every day, including the liquid absorbed from fruits, vegetables, and milk. No kidding. Maybe more if you live in a dry climate or your child exercises regularly and sweats a lot.

Not only does water comprise an average of 60 percent of our body weight, we need it for just about every bodily function: keeping our brains cool for better thinking, regulating blood volume, getting oxygen and nutrients to cells, removing waste, lubricating our eyes, noses, and mouths, and lots more.

Please, please, send your child to school with a container of water and possibly milk for hydration throughout the day. Forget the soda and fruit drinks, with real fruit or otherwise. The sugar spikes give energy at first, but the crash 20 minutes later causes sleepiness and brain fog that can last a couple of hours. Further, an analysis of 88 studies revealed that soda intake directly correlates to diminished calcium and protein consumption and largely contributes to obesity (Vartanian et al. 2007). Water is accessible, inexpensive, and healthy—hands down, the best liquid your child can drink. Why mess with perfection?

Note: Send water to school in a reusable container. Disposable water bottles begin to break down after a couple of uses and can emit harmful chemicals.

Exercise and Free Play

Yours may be one of those families whose kids get in so much physical activity that keeping them fed and hydrated is more of a challenge than making sure they get their hearts pumping at least one cumulative hour every day. They may exercise active imaginations while racing around too—you feel like this is one area your third-grader is in great shape.

By the time kids reach eight or nine years old, though, school has gotten more demanding, and outside activities may eat up more time. Many parents find physical activity and free playtime have dropped close to the bottom in importance. Their third-graders may become irritable, often attributed to hormone changes rather than good old-fashioned stress. Interestingly, hormones in elementary school children are seldom the offenders when it comes to unpleasant behavior.

Exercise and downtime allow the brain to recharge, specifically to receive an abundance of fresh oxygen and give glial cells a chance to clean up after busy neurons. When we let our minds wander, scattered neurons light up on an fMRI scan in synchronized patterns, what scientists call a default mode network. This is the mechanism for mulling over what we wish we had said in a conversation and reaching epiphanies in the shower or bathtub (Smith 2013).

It turns out that space for mental zoning is as important to our brains for processing, cleaning up, and nourishing networks as physical exercise is for maintaining a healthy heart, weight, and outlook. Do yourself and your family a favor. If your schedule is too full, move things around or delete activities entirely to make sure you all get a chance to do a little daydreaming.

Third-Graders' Teeth

If you haven't been taking your child to the dentist twice a year for regular cleanings already, third grade is a good time to start. Most eight- and nine-year-olds have lost several of their primary teeth, and their new incisors, or front teeth, grow in with bumps on the top edges. The enamel will grow thicker in the next couple of years, so teeth will become whiter and the edges smoother. Until then, bumps can easily break off, so permanent teeth are particularly vulnerable. If your child plays sports, consider purchasing an inexpensive commercial mouth guard to protect those fragile bumps as well as the rest of your third-grader's mouth.

Third grade is also the age to ask the dentist or dental hygienist to give detailed instructions while flossing your child's teeth the next time you go for a cleaning. Before you go home, get some flossers with handles—kids usually find them easier to maneuver than a long strand of floss. When your child gets ready for bed, stand next to each other in the bathroom mirror and floss your teeth together.

Start with the front teeth, making sure to use up and down motions to gently scrape the tarter and debris from both sides of the teeth. If your child does a good job with the front, move to the back teeth. Sealants will protect the grooves in the molars on the chewing surface, but cavities often form between teeth. In fact, most dental professionals contend that flossing is as important as brushing.

My dentist likes to point out that when we brush, we only clean the front and back surfaces of our teeth. We have to floss to get the sides that the brush can't reach. You wouldn't take a shower and only wash one side of your body, right?

Although you want to introduce your child to flossing independently in third grade, First Choice Dental in Wisconsin recommends stepping in to make sure nooks and crannies are truly clean until your child is 11 years old. By the end of fifth or beginning of sixth grade, your son or daughter will have great flossing habits and be a veritable flossing expert.

WHERE DO YOU SEE YOURSELF?

Mrs. Harris looks at her watch. Dang. She has a list as long as her arm of things to get done before bedtime—in less than three hours. If she doesn't get them done now, how will she find time before the party on the weekend?

She races around the kitchen to combine the ingredients for cookie dough. Once the sugar cookies go into the oven, she tosses the dirty utensils into the dishwasher and hits the start button. On her dash to the den to wrap presents for the winter holiday, she bumps into her third-grader in the hallway.

"Ouch!" Rebecca stumbles backward. "Mom!"

"Oh. Sorry, honey. I should have been watching. I just have so much to do!"

Rebecca looks up at her mom with earnest brown eyes. "I can help you."

Mrs. Harris starts down the hallway. "Oh, sweet pea, thanks," she says over her shoulder, "but I have a lot of presents to wrap and—"

"I got a good idea." Rebecca follows her mom to the den. "You can show me how to do it, and then you won't have to wrap them all yourself."

Mrs. Harris sighs. She has such a time crunch, and showing her daughter how to measure the paper around the gift, fold the paper, pull it tight, and tape it would take longer than wrapping most of the presents herself. "Thanks for offering." She puts a hand on Rebecca's shoulder. "We'll have to do that another time."

"But—"

"Sorry," Mrs. Harris says, shaking her head. "Not now." She grabs five bulging plastic bags from behind the easy chair and pulls out articles of clothing, toys, and collapsed boxes, setting them on the hardwood floor. "Why don't you go read that Harry Potter book we got at the library, and then I'll read a chapter to you before you go to bed." *If I have time*, she thinks.

"My teacher said I'm not a good enough reader for that book, and anyway, you said you would read to me last night, but you didn't."

Ding! goes the timer.

"Oh shoot." Mrs. Harris rushes back down the hall to rescue the cookies from the oven when her daughter's reply dawns on her. "What do you mean your teacher said you aren't a good enough reader?" she shouts toward the den.

"She said I'll flunk the comprehension test," Rebecca yells back.

Mrs. Harris can't believe the nerve of that teacher. *I'll have a talk with the principal, see what he has to say about telling students they aren't good enough, that they'll flunk the test.* Mrs. Harris is so incensed that she opens the oven and almost grabs the cookie sheet with her bare hand. An inch from searing her fingers, she pulls up and snags a pot holder from the drawer next to the stove.

Rebecca wanders into the kitchen. "I don't have to read today anyway because I read all day Saturday after soccer so I could turn in my overdue Junie B. Jones book to the library."

"That doesn't mean you don't have to read," Mrs. Harris says, setting the metal sheet on top of the stove. She grabs the slotted turner from the stand on the counter, moves the cookies to the cooling rack, and puts fresh dough on the cookie sheets to bake the next batch.

"I figured it out." Rebecca leans against the breakfast table. "Since I read for five hours, I don't have to read for homework for the next two weeks."

"Yes, you do. Just because you got behind and had to read a lot doesn't mean you can get out of the habit of reading before bed."

Mrs. Harris catches Rebecca's smirk out of the corner of her eye before her daughter slinks out of the kitchen. That crooked smile means Rebecca has no intention of reading unless Mrs. Harris takes the time to get her started on the new book.

But it's all she can do to get the next batch of cookies in the oven and wrap a present or two before the timer goes off again. Who's she kidding? She won't have time to talk to the principal about that insensitive teacher either.

👀 Mrs. Hover had been incensed when her eight-year-old came home yesterday saying his teacher said he wasn't a good enough reader to tackle the book they got at the public library. Mr. Perry told Sammy he'd flunk the comprehension test, for cryin' out loud. Sure, the book is a little more difficult than the ones Sam usually reads, but he'd been so excited to read it. She'd thought Mr. Perry was a reasonable man, but apparently not.

The bell rings. Outside Sammy's classroom, she waits on the bench for the children to leave before she goes inside to confront the teacher. She took time off work to speak with the principal, but the woman had to reschedule for something that came up at the district office.

Sammy's friend Jake comes out the door and shouts, "Hey, Sam, your mom's here!"

Mrs. Hover's son bursts out the door with his backpack over his shoulder and a huge smile. "Hi, Mom. Are you taking me for ice cream?"

"Ice cream!" yells Jake. "Can I come?"

"We're not going for ice cream." Mrs. Hover stands up from the bench and adjusts her blouse. "I came to talk to Mr. Perry."

Jake's eyes go wide. "Oh, man. What'd you do, Sam?"

"I . . . I don't know." Sam looks up at his mom with panic in his eyes.

"*You* didn't do anything, Samuel." She grabs her son's hand. "Let's go talk to your teacher."

Sam shrugs in Jake's direction. "See you tomorrow."

Jake waves and takes off in a hurry as if he's afraid he'll be in trouble next if he sticks around.

When she opens the classroom door, Mrs. Hover is greeted by classical music as Mr. Perry rearranges teachers' guides and his lesson plan book on the table in front of the room. He glances up at them and grins. "Hey, Mrs. Hover. Did Sam tell you the big news?"

Mrs. Hover stops and looks at her son. "What news?"

The worry on her little boy's face vanishes, replaced with a grin so wide, his front teeth in their various stages of growth all gleam at her at once, and she can't help but smile back.

"I got a 100 percent on the comprehension test for *Harry Potter and the Sorcerer's Stone* today and got 12 points!"

Her smile sags. She read that book to Sammy at the beginning of the school year, and she's not sure what to say.

Sam must understand her concern because he says, "Oh, don't worry, Mom. Mr. Perry told me if I read the book again by myself, it would be fair for me to take a test on it."

"But I never saw you . . ." Her voice trails off as it occurs to her that she may not want to call her son a cheat in front of the teacher.

Mr. Perry puts a hand on Sam's shoulder. "He wanted to surprise you. Sam read the book in class and in after-school day care." The teacher raises his brows. "And a few times under the covers with a flashlight, I understand."

"Mr. Perry," Sam says, glancing at his mom, "you weren't supposed to tell her that," he says out of the corner of his mouth.

She can't help but laugh. If reading under the covers is the worst thing Sam does growing up, she'll take it. "You mean you read the whole book, and I never knew?"

"Yep. All by myself." His smile falters, and he looks at his teacher. "But Mr. Perry told me that the next book, *Chamber of Secrets*, is a lot harder." He glances at Mrs. Hover. "So I should read it with you first and then wait until fourth or fifth grade to read it by myself and take the test."

"Well, the book is almost sixth-grade reading level." Mr. Perry crosses his arms. "If you try to read it now, without your mom, you may not do as well on the test. You don't want to give up 14 points, right?"

"It'd be more fun to read with my mom anyway." Sammy cracks another adorable lopsided smile that warms his mother's heart. "Then we can talk about the story in the car and at dinner, like we did with *Sorcerer's Stone*."

Mrs. Hover feels so relieved that the principal had to reschedule their meeting. She would have felt like a fool if she'd complained about Mr. Perry, who sounds like he never said Sammy wasn't a good reader. He merely wants her son to be okay with being a third-grader and take some other steps before reading such a high-level book to himself.

Besides, she could kiss Mr. Perry for getting Sam excited to read with her again. Lately, Sam had complained about their nightly chapters of the current book they were reading. Frankly, she wasn't too interested in it either. In fact, she couldn't remember the title offhand.

😇 Ms. Solis finishes stacking the ingredients to make three kinds of cookies on the kitchen counter for the family party this weekend and glances at the couch in the family room, piled with plastic bags full of gifts to wrap. She rolls her eyes. In her glance at the ceiling, she notices a spot of grease and grabs a chair at the table to reach the smudge.

What am I doing? she thinks. *Cleaning random stuff won't get me to bed any earlier tonight.*

The timer dings, and she exhales her relief.

"Hey, Juanito, time's up," she calls into the hallway. "And I need your help."

"Ah, Mamá! Five more minutes!" comes her son's voice from his bedroom. "I'm almost to the next level!"

"Save the game and stop now, or that five extra minutes will cost you tomorrow's computer time," she reminds him, shaking her head.

Seconds later, Juan wanders into the kitchen. "What do you need help with?"

"Three batches of cookies." She hands him the recipe for Mexican wedding cookies, a family favorite. "We have to get them all baked tonight because of your soccer game in the morning." She points a playful finger at him. "But no snitching dough. We can lick the bowls after the cookies are made."

He laughs. "Okay, but if I don't get to, you don't either."

She raises a brow, then shrugs. "I guess fair is fair," she says, and her eight-year-old laughs some more.

Ms. Solis gets ingredients for the chocolate chip cookies and the snickerdoodles mixed in separate bowls by the time Juan makes the dough for the Mexican wedding cookies. She's so glad her third-grader has become such a good reader and has had enough practice cooking with her that she doesn't have to supervise as closely.

Luckily, she's collected four cookie sheets over the years. After she and her son fill the first two with dollops of chocolate chip cookie dough and she puts them in the oven, she checks on Juan, who's putting snickerdoodle dough on the next sheet.

"Wait. We need to make these smaller, or we won't have enough for everyone." She picks up a raw cookie and pinches off the excess.

Juan takes dough from the cookie next to her modified snickerdoodle and reshapes it. "Like this?"

"Perfecto. Can you finish loading the other two cookie sheets while I start wrapping presents?"

Her son smirks. "How 'bout I bake the rest of them if you let me eat a raw cookie?"

That's Juan, she thinks. *Always bargaining. But he did eat his broccoli and salad at dinner . . .*

"Okay." Ms. Solis puts up her pointer finger. "One raw cookie. And when they're all done, we each get to pick two baked ones to have with a glass of milk. Deal?"

He puts out his sticky hand to shake on it. "Deal."

She washes her hands and gets busy folding clothes and putting them into garment boxes for her sisters and brothers-in-law, and wrapping toys for nieces and nephews. Occasionally, she reminds Juan to set the timer, and she still takes the cookie sheets out of the oven, but their system has worked quite well. She may get to bed before midnight after all.

She and her son already talked about their days during dinner, so while Ms. Solis measures paper for the next gift, she asks, "How's the book you checked out at the library?"

Juan looks up from the cookie sheet he's been filling. "My teacher said I'm not a good enough reader for that book."

"*¿En serio?*" She can't believe Mr. Perry said that. "You're a great reader."

"Nuh-uh." Juan scoops another glob of dough onto his teaspoon. "He said I'd probably bomb the test."

She loses her grip on the wrapping paper. "He did not say that."

Juan shrugs. "Ask him."

"Maybe I will."

I feel like marching into the office and lodging a complaint with the principal—but at parents' night at the beginning of the year, Mr. Perry asked us to talk to him first.

She grabs her cell phone from the end table and emails Mr. Perry with Juan's story to ask what's going on. Hopefully, the teacher will answer soon. Frankly, she doesn't know where she'll fit in the time to go to the school until after the winter break.

The timer dings, and Ms. Solis gets up to take out the hot cookie sheets. "Hey, these cookies look even better than the last ones."

"Does that mean I get an extra cookie?" Juan gives her an awkward smile with his front permanent teeth in various stages of growing in.

She chuckles. "Well, you have done a great job."

"And these two cookie sheets are the last ones." He points at the dough on the counter, ready to go into the oven. "Come on, *Mami*. If you let me have another one, that's only four cookies, counting the dough you said I could eat and the ones we're having with milk."

"Sure. Go ahead and eat an extra cookie." Ms. Solis's shoulders drop, and her eyes go to the pile of unwrapped gifts still on the couch. "At the rate I'm going, you'll be eating the other cookies without me too. I still have seven presents to wrap."

"I'll help you." Juan's sincere dark eyes gaze up at her.

"That's really nice, son, but . . ." *I'd have to show him how to do it—which may take even longer. And who knows what his wrapping will look like?*

"Don't worry." Juan slides the last sheets into the oven and sets the timer for 15 minutes. We'll finish the presents after these are baked. Then we can eat cookies together."

How can she turn him down? "Okay. Thanks. You're the best."

In the end, the presents Juan wrapped looked less than perfect, but Ms. Solis figured his aunts might enjoy the slightly askew paper. He conked out as soon as they finished reading a chapter in the latest Adventurers Wanted book. She'd have to email a thank-you note to M. L. Forman for writing such an exciting series that she and her son have enjoyed so much together.

The next morning an email comes from Juan's teacher:

Dear Ms. Solis,

Thanks for asking about your conversation with Juan. Ha! It's amazing how kids interpret things sometimes. I told him he'd have fun reading Harry Potter and the Chamber of Secrets *with you this year and then reading it on his own in the next year or two because the book is leveled close to sixth grade.*

I also told him the test is a little tricky, and he'll want to earn all 14 points for reading the book. We all want Juan to succeed,

and taking a test on a 5.9 book doesn't seem like a winning play.
I hope that helps.
Regards,
Mr. Perry

Ms. Solis is glad she didn't complain to the office and sent an email to Juan's teacher instead.

* * *

We hope these parent scenarios bring some points to the surface that will help you create the best possible balance in your family.

When my older daughter was in the third grade, she asked me to teach her how to wrap gifts so she could help me. I declined her offer and wrapped all the presents myself, deciding that overseeing her would take more time, not less. I later taught her how to wrap presents at my convenience, and she wrapped the gifts she bought or made for other people, but she never offered or agreed to help me with the chore again. This was one of many lessons I learned the hard way.

It's funny. We make decisions as parents that seem innocuous, having no idea of the consequences. I learned that if I wanted my daughters to contribute in the future, unless the sky was falling, I had to drop everything and accept an offer of help with appreciation. Hopefully, you'll learn from my mistake.

Both our girls were expert negotiators, a good skill they use as professional adults now. My husband and I took their points into careful consideration before accepting or rejecting reasons for more cookies or permission to watch a TV special during the week. Sometimes kids make salient points, and other times they can be little manipulators with arguments like these:

"I got a lot of sleep last night, and I promise not to stay up late at the sleepover."

"But I really want to watch this show. I'll read twice as long tomorrow. I promise."

After having to reestablish homework rules several times, especially with our oldest, by third grade, we decided not to bend when it came to reading and other assignments from school. My husband and I often relaxed other rules in special circumstances, though. The key is to keep a unified front. If you disagree with your partner, talk about it behind closed doors where little ears can't hear. And if you get upset about a story your child tells you happened at school, keep it to yourself until you have a chance to communicate with the teacher.

Once a third-grade student of mine told her mother she wet her pants because I wouldn't let her go to the bathroom during class—which I found out from the principal! My younger daughter had occasional accidents. I never would tell children they weren't allowed to relieve themselves. I simply reminded my students as they left for recess to take a trip to the restroom, drink some water, and run around a lot, so they would be ready for whatever cool thing we were going to do next.

I ended up in a conference with the parent, my student, and the principal to deal with the potty issue. After a half hour of talking to the child, we discovered my routine reminders had turned into "My teacher won't let me go to the bathroom" when, in fact, the little girl neglected to visit the restroom at recess, didn't want to miss what we were doing in class, and was embarrassed that she had to go to the office to get a change of clothes. Had the parent come to see me instead of the principal, or even called me, the problem could have been cleared up almost instantly rather than causing all kinds of upset and taking everyone's valuable time.

Open communication works the best in most situations, and flexibility is good. Also, remember that when you mess up with your child, take responsibility, learn from it, and move on. You don't have to be a superhero. You're only human: perfectly imperfect and a wonderful parent.

CONCLUSION

Your third-grader will grow so much this year: mentally, physically, and socially. Neural connections will have sharpened memory and expanded thought to a growing grasp of multiple meanings. Ridiculous jokes will fly, and you won't get away with flippant remarks to another adult like you used to. With a fledgling understanding of fact and opinion, you may find your comments challenged more often—especially if what you say conflicts with your child's teacher.

If reading remains a struggle, third grade is the year to make sure your child gets help and you have a plan of support in place, if needed, for the upper elementary grades, where the students are expected to read for information. At the same time, a child who reads well still needs daily practice at this age so skills don't get rusty. Remember, your child's brain continually plucks or reassigns seldom used neurons. Fewer neural pathways to recreate means a smoother transition to learning state history and internalizing science concepts in greater depth next year in fourth grade.

Multiplication facts from 0 to 10 as well as how to apply them will have been a main topic in math this year. Do your child (and yourself) a favor and review the flash cards a few times during the summer break. With multiplication facts (and thus division facts) in place, learning harder concepts—to add and subtract fractions with uncommon denominators, for example—will be a snap. Without those facts, fourth-grade math can be a painful experience.

Collect your child's writing pieces, if you haven't begun to save them already, and keep them in a special place. Your third-grader's personal narratives and earnest persuasive essays will provide great entertainment when you read them together in a few years.

In the meantime, let's get ready for fourth grade, a year of higher academic demands, a later lunch recess, and a longer school day. Nine- and 10-year-olds' enthusiasm, increasingly important peer relationships, and quick emotional shifts (that have nothing to do with hormones in most cases) make fourth grade an endearing, pivotal year.

* 7 *

FOURTH GRADE
From Comfort Zones to Social Cliques

Strap yourself in and get ready for ups and downs. By fourth grade, most kids' brains have made enough neural connections to allow them to truly see outside themselves to empathize and sympathize with others. They feel deeply as they start to make their own way in a social world that often causes emotional turmoil.

YOUR FOURTH-GRADER'S BRAIN

As pointed out in chapter 2 (page 9), the neurons in the brains of 8- to 10-year-olds don't fire in the prefrontal cortex in response to negative feedback. If you've ever said to your child something like "You shouldn't have done it that way" and gotten a blank stare, that's because most kids' brains can't fully process such a comment until 11 or 12 years old. Older children are better able to use negative feedback to learn from their mistakes.

On the other hand, the prefrontal cortex lights up like a neon sign in younger children when someone makes positive comments like this: "Good job! Now let's see if you can . . ." (Leiden University 2008).

Neural connections have been getting stronger and more consistent, but fourth-graders are still developing pathways for forward thinking. If your child does something stupid and you ask "Why did you do that?" you'll often get the honest response "I don't know." Nine- and 10-year-olds are still learning to apply cause and effect to their own lives. Ask gentle, open-ended questions to help your fourth-grader process how he landed in trouble. Remember, the frontal cortex responds best to positive inquiry.

When you remind your child to do something you've already been working on for a while, rather than saying "How many times have we gone over this?" try giving her a smile, along with a question like "Whoops, what did you forget?"

Maintaining positive communication also means designating household and moral rules with clearly defined consequences for crossing the line. Lots of parents struggle with being consistent, especially after an exhausting day or in the midst of life crises, such as divorce or grief over a death. If you're someone who waffles on rules, remember that your child's brain is getting "programmed" via experiences.

The more your child can depend on you to honor the boundaries you set, the more secure he will be. This means less cortisol production in the brain, ergo less stress—your consistent parenting frees up your child's brain for learning (El Nokali et al. 2010).

The Gender Split

At this age, myelination accelerates; that is, neural pathways continue to get coated with glial cells to make communication more efficient between areas of the brain. But be aware: During fourth grade, girls' frontal lobes begin to grow at a faster rate than boys' do. This means that motor function, problem-solving, spontaneity, memory, language, initiation, judgment, impulse control, and social behavior mature faster in girls than in boys at this stage (Lenroot et al. 2007). Outward physical changes will be less apparent, but developmental brain disparities between genders often cause misinterpreted social interactions and hurt feelings.

Brain Boosters

In addition to heart-to-heart talks, you can help your child this year by keeping your fourth-grader physically active for 60 cumulative minutes a day. Heart-pumping, oxygen-infusing exercise stimulates new brain cell growth and boosts memory centers in the brain to apply three-dimensional thinking—like cause and effect. Technically speaking, a study from the University of Illinois concludes, "Consistent with predictions, higher-fit [9- and 10-year-old] children showed greater bilateral hippocampal volumes and superior relational memory task performance compared to lower-fit children" (Chaddock et al. 2010). Regular exercise will help your child work off emotional and social stress too.

Music is another big booster for neural and hippocampal growth at this age. A Swiss study found that "children who undergo musical training have better verbal memory, second language pronunciation accuracy, reading ability, and executive functions. Learning to play an instrument as a child may even predict academic performance and IQ in young adulthood" (Miendlarzewska and Trost 2013).

Researchers agree, however, that kids have to enjoy musical engagement to reap the benefits. If your child dreads piano lessons, find an instrument that excites and motivates him, rather than hoping he'll "grow into" appreciating manipulating keys.

Although vocabulary and sense of humor continue to grow with maturing neural pathways, these kids' brains still haven't made enough connections to see much beyond black and white. When children learn by doing (hands-on science experiments, for example) and use math in real life (like adding fractions to double a recipe), they grasp concepts more easily and find learning fun.

FOURTH-GRADE SOCIAL TRAITS

As their awareness increases, fourth-graders relate to both parents and peers with more depth. Occasionally, an astute perception will pop out of your child's mouth that will drop your jaw, and you'll wonder where such wisdom came from. Be assured that much of your child's mental processing has grown from listening to you over the years and witnessing your ideals in action.

Fourth-graders tend to be high-energy, happy folks, eager to try something new, yet they burn out quickly. Downtime, even a short walk to grab something from another room, can be helpful in getting them to refocus. After a break, these kids pick up speed again, followed by the need for another breather. Fits and starts seem to define fourth-graders as they take on more academic responsibility, stress over friends, and begin to define how they see themselves in the big wide world. Maintaining a consistent schedule and set of rules in your household to reduce these pressures is critical to your child's happiness this year.

Nine- and 10-year-olds also begin to notice how people's values may differ from their own, recognizing that not everyone views right and wrong the same way. They challenge others' ideals, keep score academically and socially, and tend to tattle on kids who they think aren't behaving properly. The common fourth-grade outcry is "That's not fair!"

Your Relationship

This is a great time for philosophical conversations with your child to help him form empowering realizations that inspire self-confidence. When our kids used to complain that something "wasn't fair," for example, my husband used to say, "Funny, you never complain about the things that are unfair in your favor."

He'd proceed to list two or three of their personal talents, and their chests would puff with pride. On occasion, he also reminded them of the basics: how lucky they were to have a comfortable place to live, parents who loved them, and plenty of food to eat.

Fourth-graders generally gain perspective quickly. And if someone they respect acknowledges their positive attributes, it stings less when they lose at four square or when a good friend partners with another classmate on a school project.

Friends

This age group's evolved ability to relate to others makes friends even more important than before, so family members may take a backseat on the list of priorities. This continued shift toward peers worries a lot of parents but is completely normal. The good news is that your less frequent input will carry more weight.

Seemingly random tears and snippy remarks at home may stem

from competition for popularity at school and on sports teams—verbal battles won and lost. For kids experiencing prepuberty, hormones may affect them, but for most fourth-graders, what you're observing is more likely due to their struggle to find their place in the social order and learn how to relate with others.

As explained, because the lobes and organs in male and female brains begin to grow at surprisingly different rates at this time, the genders often clash in the upper elementary grades—and some continue to have trouble relating to the opposite sex through high school. Fourth-graders say or do hurtful things to those they "like," often without a clue they made a mistake.

After trying to have a tea party with her grandsons, a woman who'd raised two girls told me, "Forget *Men Are from Mars, Women Are from Venus*. Girls and boys are from different universes!"

How You Can Help

Conventional wisdom used to be that parents should let their children work out issues with other kids on their own. Trial and error. Learn by muddling through. Collecting a few emotional bruises builds character.

Nothing could be further from the truth.

Don't misunderstand—parents shouldn't fight their children's social battles. In fact, adults should let kids talk out issues independently unless someone is getting bullied and needs protection from abuse. But kids need coaching on how to eat well, get enough sleep and exercise, practice good hygiene, follow rules, read, write, gather facts, form opinions—so why would it make sense to leave children alone to learn something as important as how to relate to others? Researchers at the University of Pittsburgh found that parental guidance in social behaviors had more of a positive impact on children's social skills than parental involvement in academics had on academic skills (El Nokali et al. 2010).

The truth is this: Helping your child wade through and learn from prickly social situations will be a big part of your parenting in the upper elementary grades.

Who said what and who did what at school may come up a lot at home as your fourth-grader jockeys for position in the social pecking order. Jealousies and residual hurt feelings may arrive at your dinner table in the form of crankiness or silence. Try to be patient and ask gentle questions. If your child doesn't feel like talking yet, share the events of your day first. Go around the table and offer a second chance to share once everyone else has spoken.

This daily forum for personal updates during the evening meal will be critical from now through high school. It not only helps kids process their emotions but also develops trust and empowering habits for when more sensitive subjects arise in adolescence. For example, this year will be a good time for your child to internalize Stephen Covey's fifth habit: "Seek first to understand, then to be understood." Kids who learn how to listen and assert confidence without aggression will be miles ahead in the social game.

11 WAYS TO HELP FOURTH-GRADERS NAVIGATE SOCIAL CIRCLES

1. **Establish a daily sharing tradition.** Set up a consistent time in your schedule for family members to talk about their days. This regular forum will be a key factor in maintaining a good relationship with your child into adulthood. Share your day-to-day experiences and encourage your child to do the same. Give-and-take conversations (without interruption) model how effective adults handle social situations.

2. **Define the qualities of a good friend.** While driving or grocery shopping, talk about what you think makes a good friend, and ask your child for her thoughts. Then ask her which qualities her friends at school have. A lot of heartache may be avoided by understanding how to be a good friend and what to look for in others.

3. **Assure your child that it's okay to let go.** Sometimes children feel stuck in miserable relationships, especially with friends they've had for a year or more. If your child has problems with a "friend" lying,

gossiping, or doing any number of hurtful things, explain that they may have grown apart and don't have to spend time together anymore. Suggest your child go play a different game at recess and talk to some different kids.

4. **Role-play how to deal with social situations.** Practice makes competence and, therefore, confidence. If your fourth-grader comes home with hurt feelings, listen carefully, and then offer to role-play the offending person. Coach him on what to say without belittling the child who hurt your baby's feelings (I know it'll be hard to do, but force yourself to be respectful). If your child struggles with friends in general, try role-playing other scenarios too, like asking a group to join an activity, striking up a conversation, or responding to a kid who tries to kick him out of a game.

5. **Foster good friendships.** If your child starts hanging out with a classmate you like, provide opportunities for them to get together outside school. Invite the classmate along on a trip to the public library or while you run errands to keep your child company.

6. **Ask open-ended questions, and be patient with unsatisfying answers.** "I don't know" is probably an honest response in fourth grade. Your questions may help your child mentally process, though, and you may hear about whatever was bothering her in the next day or two.

7. **Point out that situations may appear "unfair" until we understand them better.** For example, after losing an aerodynamics contest, your child says, "It's not fair! I worked all day after school yesterday on my paper airplane." Then you gently point out that his glider looked the coolest, but the challenge was to throw something that would fly the farthest—which is why the kid who threw a baseball won. But hard work is never wasted. He had fun making the airplane, and the experience will apply to another project someday.

THE REAL DEAL: When I was in fourth grade, my dad gave my friend a piggyback ride, something he no longer did for me because he said he had a bad back. I was crushed when he said I couldn't have a turn after her. When she went to the bathroom a little later, he took me aside and said, "Trishie, she lost her dad a while ago. You get to have me every day." Talk about perspective!

8. **Volunteer in community projects as a family.** Spend time at the local food bank or homeless shelter to teach the importance of contributing to our world and appreciating things we take for granted. Getting outside of our own heads and doing for others also helps kids (well, all of us) stop sweating the small stuff.

9. **Pay attention to mood changes.** If your child gets unusually quiet, tired, short-tempered, or teary but can't yet articulate what's wrong, be patient. Snuggle on the couch together with a book, or do another calm activity that will engender a sense of safety. Remember, safe brains are active ones. Hopefully, she'll bring up what's bothering her by bedtime, but if she doesn't, gently ask her again. You might be able to offer advice or role-play to help her work it out.

    If your child's mood doesn't improve within the next couple of days, talk to the teacher or other parents whom you trust and might know more about what's going on that's upsetting your child. Fourth grade is a year of labeling, giving classmates titles like "loser," "brain," or "sporty," and competing for popularity. Sometimes kids do mean things, hoping to gain a few strides in the race for the most BFFs. Also, check social media because if your child is getting bullied at school or online, the evidence is bound to show up.

10. **Encourage eye contact.** When your child talks to you, remind him to focus on your eyes. Model the same behavior by returning eye contact and ignoring your cell phone until the conversation has ended.

Eye contact conveys respect for the speaker, and at times, your child's attitude may prove more important in an interaction than the words exchanged.

11. **Demonstrate how to shake hands with confidence.** First impressions matter. A good one takes a while to ruin and a bad one takes even longer to disprove. Fourth grade is the perfect time to begin practicing a firm, but not crushing, handshake that exudes friendliness and self-assurance.

5 SILLY SOCIAL GAMES FOR HELPING KIDS GET ALONG

1. **Emotion Charades.** Take turns making facial expressions and changing positions of arms, legs, and shoulders to express emotions for players to guess. This game gives kids insights into body language so they can interpret how someone might be feeling, enables them to glean other nonverbal information, and helps them decide how to respond in social situations. It also helps them describe emotions in their writing.

2. **Staring Contest.** Staring into another's eyes until someone blinks or glances away keeps kids busy on long car rides and builds confidence in maintaining eye contact in conversations. Adrian Furnham (2014), psychology professor at University College London, says, "Where, when, and how we look at others [is] . . . one of our most important and primitive means of communication."

3. **Backstory Body Language.** This game is great for building awareness of unspoken language, understanding subtext in reading, and improving descriptive skills in writing. While you and your child are waiting in line in a crowd, point out how various people hold

themselves, and make up a story about what happened prior to that moment to cause their facial expressions and body positions.

4. **The Greetings Game.** Help your child understand that social situations require different kinds of greetings by giving examples of situations and having your fourth-grader give a firm handshake, offer a formal hello, or give a high-five. Examples: you meet a friend's parent or caregiver, you're introduced to a great aunt, you run into a friend shopping for Halloween costumes, and so on.

5. **Dialogue Drama.** Take turns reading dialogue between characters in the books you read together, experimenting with changing inflection. Your fourth-grader will probably get silly on you, which is part of the fun. You can talk about how volume, pitch, and tone of voice can change communication. This kind of practice helps kids pick up on tonal cues in real life.

The Cell Phone: A Great Tool if You Set Boundaries

If fourth-graders want to communicate with their parents during the school day, a trek to the office to make a phone call is no longer needed for many of them, since the average age for a first cell phone is slightly over 10 years (Influence Central 2016). E-tablets are still more popular than phones for keeping kids occupied in the car, but phone entertainment is on the rise. (*Note:* We hope you'll talk to one another in the car and play verbal games to nurture your relationship and stimulate your child's brain whenever possible.)

Kids also text their parents and siblings, even at home. Many of them visit random sites online and fill out accounts to join social media, such as Snapchat, Instagram, and Twitter. Psychotherapist Michael Rubino (2016), tween and teen specialist for more than two decades, advises parents that if they believe a cell phone is necessary for family communication due to their circumstances, to purchase a basic cell phone, without internet capability.

Often, though, kids inherit the use of their parents' old smartphones. In that case, Dr. Rubino encourages parents to set guidelines so children's access to a smartphone keeps problems associated with surfing online and social media to a minimum.

5 WAYS TO MAKE CELL PHONES A HELP, NOT A HEADACHE

1. **Decide if a cell phone is necessary.** Keeping track of a device at age 9 or 10 can be stressful for kids and expensive for parents. It's easy to break or lose phones—or get them stolen.

2. **Make sure your child understands you own the phone.** And you can ask for it back at any time.

3. **Set ground rules before getting the phone.** For example, no cell phones at the dinner table, the phone is turned off during homework, and your child must move the screen away from his line of sight when he talks with a grownup. Dr. Rubino (2016) points out, "[Children] have forgotten cell phones are privileges . . . [and] . . . accuse parents of child abuse if they . . . set limits. You are not being abusive—you are being a responsible parent."

4. **Type up a contract for you and your child to sign.** Getting agreements in writing makes boundaries and commitments clear for a much more peaceful home life. *Note:* Check out Dr. Rubino's sample contract on the Pleasant Hill Patch website (see "References and Further Reading").

5. **Consider getting an app to protect your child.** MMGuardian Parental Control (mmguardian.com) is an example of an app you can download to block inappropriate websites, keep track of your child's location (and pinpoint the phone when it gets misplaced), set time limits, know your child's activity, shut down the phone at night, and much more.

THE REAL DEAL

Cell Phone Pajama Dash

Mrs. Glow's daughter, Chloe, checked the picture window in the living room for the umpteenth time. Erica, her best friend at school, would arrive any minute to sleep over. Pepperoni pizza awaited the preheated oven, and Netflix was set to play a family movie. Mrs. Glow watched her 10-year-old peeking through the glass pane yet again, almost vibrating with anticipation.

Soon the familiar black pickup crackled over the icy gravel, and Chloe flew out the door to greet her friend. Mrs. Glow waved at Erica's parents from the window as the truck reversed back down the driveway. The girls ran past her, their excited chattering fading deeper inside the house.

Curious as to what could be so exciting, she put the pizza in the oven, set the timer, and walked to her daughter's room where both girls laid on their stomachs on Chloe's bed, propped on their elbows, staring at a smartphone.

Mrs. Glow stood in the doorway. "So, *that's* what all the commotion is about."

"Yeah, my dad gave me his old smartphone because he got a new one," said Erica without looking up. Chloe laughed at something on the screen.

"The pizza will be ready in 15 minutes," Mrs. Glow said, but they continued staring at the phone. "Ladies, dinner's in 15 minutes." Still no response. "Girls!" she said, louder than she'd meant to.

"Jeez, Mom," Chloe said, her eyes still glued to the small screen. "You don't have to yell."

The cell phone arrived at the dinner table where the girls texted friends from school, giggling in their own world as Mr. and Mrs. Glow glanced at each other. When the girls left the kitchen, still engrossed in Erica's cell phone, Mr. Glow threw out the take-and-bake pizza box and said, "Do we call the girls in here to set cell phone rules now, or talk to Chloe after Erica leaves?"

Mrs. Glow collected the plates and began putting them in the dishwasher, a job Chloe usually did without being asked. "First, let's think about what rules to set."

"Good point." Her husband chuckled as he put the milk carton back in the fridge.

The girls didn't come out of Chloe's room all evening—not for the movie, not even to make ice cream sundaes for dessert. At 11, Mrs. Glow asked Erica to power down the cell phone for the night, and she turned out the light for the girls to go to sleep.

After putting on her flannel nightgown and climbing into bed with her husband, she said, "We are definitely having a talk with Chloe after Erica goes home. Those girls spent all evening messing with that phone. I doubt they said 20 words to each other."

"Not to mention they ignored us at dinner," Mr. Glow added.

At about 11:30, as Mrs. Glow was about to doze off, she heard an engine that sounded weirdly close to the house. She rolled over to glance out the window and saw a sedan in the driveway with a small silhouette trotting toward it.

Oh no. Mrs. Glow jumped out of bed. *That looks like Erica!* She flew through the house and out the front door.

"Erica!" she yelled, opening the passenger door of the strange vehicle, determined to save her daughter's friend from who knows what?

"Gwen?" Erica's mom widened her eyes from the driver's seat. "What are you doing out here in the cold?"

"Sherrie? When did you get this car? And what are you doing here?" Suddenly, Mrs. Glow felt the snow stinging her bare feet and the breeze biting through her nightgown.

"Erica texted me to come pick her up because she couldn't sleep."

"And neither of you thought to tell me?" She wrapped her arms tightly around her waist.

Erica turned away from Mrs. Glow and looked at her mom.

"I . . . texted you," said Erica's mom.

"Really? I didn't hear an alert that I got a text." A shiver racked Mrs. Glow's shoulders. "Now that I know Jack the Ripper didn't come to steal your daughter, I'm going to get out of the cold before my toes fall off from frostbite." She closed the passenger door and started toward the house.

"Uh, sorry for the mix-up," shouted Erica's mom out her window.

Mrs. Glow's teeth chattered too hard to acknowledge the weak apology. When she got back inside, she snuggled under the covers to thaw out and picked up her phone from the nightstand. There wasn't a recent text.

Erica's mom must have been too embarrassed to admit she didn't think to let Mrs. Glow know that Erica would be leaving.

Mrs. Glow had planned to replace her smartphone and give Chloe the old one. Given the evening's events, she needed to rethink that. The Glow family would definitely be discussing cell phone rules and posting them on the bulletin board before they let Chloe use one.

FOURTH-GRADE ACADEMICS

It's here! Fourth grade—the year reading becomes a tool for learning rather than a skill to master. Themes in science and social studies will integrate math and language arts, so your child will use all the skills learned in the previous grades and build on those concepts in context.

This is an exciting year of widening eyes and exclamations like "Oh, *now* I get it."

Social Studies

Fourth-grade social studies curriculum usually focuses on state history and current events. Your child will learn about indigenous peoples, patterns of immigration, key events, political leaders, common industries, and the development of the state economy where you live. You'll probably get asked a variety of thoughtful questions to help process all this new information.

Science

The science curriculum will expand a great deal this year. Your child will likely explore forces of motion, including opposite poles in magnetism and electricity, energy conduction, and conservation. Other common areas of study are properties of physical matter, how rocks undergo change, the Earth's place in the universe, fossils, plants, and animals, molecular biology regarding how foods, vitamins, and minerals get used in the body, and the effects of physical exercise.

Standardized Subject Tests

Schedules vary from state to state, but standardized subject tests are usually added to the annual math and language assessments in fourth or fifth grade. Your child may be taking a science exam, for example, to see how well she's learning how to make a hypothesis, test ideas, draw conclusions, and understand key concepts. Some states also give social studies exams, and most assess students' physical fitness toward the end of fourth or fifth grade too.

Your child's teacher will probably keep you informed. You can also visit the website of the district or school where your child attends, or type into a search engine the name of the state where you live and "education standards K–12."

New Learning Demands and Downtime

Your child will be expected to learn more independently, applying and building on prior knowledge. The teacher will assign research projects, which may include collecting and interpreting data, making multimedia presentations, and writing longer essays with attention to spelling and grammar. Math will expand to three-digit multiplication, long division, equivalent fractions, percentages, decimals, elapsed time, and lines and angles. Your fourth-grader will be expected to keep up with daily work as well as complete larger projects due on future dates.

This year, downtime will be more important than ever before! Do your best to make sure your fourth-grader gets at least an hour a day to completely unplug: no TV, cell phone, computer, homework, or extracurricular activity. Brains need space for deeper thinking, even if subconsciously, to process and recharge.

According to Sandra Bond Chapman, PhD (2014), founder and chief director of the Center for Brain Health at the University of Texas at Dallas, "Temporarily cutting ties with technology . . . can . . . [im-prove] brain health. . . . The key . . . lies largely within our remarkable frontal lobe and its deep connections to other brain areas. Our brain can focus on vast details, but it was built to do so much more, like in-novative thinking, appreciating different perspectives, and figuring out new plans."

Collaboration

Your fourth-grader will likely be involved in more group projects and be responsible for specific tasks within a larger presentation. Ideally, the teacher will provide a handout outlining the structure for group work so you can refer to it if your child comes home with complaints. If you don't receive that information and a problem arises, email the teacher and ask for a list of rules and procedures.

You'll want to talk to your child about social turbulence and provide coaching for annoyances like disagreements on how to do something, bossy kids, distracted ones, undependable classmates who don't do their part, and so on. Helping your child learn to deal with these issues now will make group projects more fun and satisfying through high school.

FOURTH-GRADE ACADEMIC SKILLS

Language Arts

- Read fourth-grade text with accuracy and fluency to support comprehension.

- Determine meanings of words and phrases based on context, pho-nics, and word analysis.

- Summarize and analyze text, including themes, characters, settings, and events—or determine the main idea, supported by details—us-ing examples and inferences from the text.

- Compare points of view in first- and third-person fiction and narrative nonfiction stories.

- Explain historical, scientific, or technical material based on the information in a text.

- Analyze stories with similar themes and genres from various cultures.

- Compare reports on an event from primary and secondary sources.

- Write opinion pieces, informational essays, and fiction and nonfiction narratives.

- Use standard writing conventions—spelling, capital letters, commas, ending punctuation—as well as proper grammar.

- Use sensory details in writing (e.g., visual, smell, texture, sound, and taste), specific nouns (e.g., Toyota pickup vs. car), and active verbs (sprinted or trotted vs. was going).

- Use keyboarding and other technology to produce writing and collaborate with others.

- Use multiple resources (e.g., articles, charts, graphs, videos, and books) to take notes, categorize information, and provide a list of sources on a topic for short research projects.

- Comfortably write both long-term projects (over days or weeks, requiring research) and short-term essays (drafted and revised in one or two sittings).

- Research topics to engage in partner, small-group, and classroom discussions.

- Develop articulate collaborative and individual presentations using media and other visual aides to illustrate points.

Mathematics

- Understand place value to one million and use patterns to solve problems.

- Solve multi-digit addition, subtraction, multiplication, and division problems.

- Order fractions by size and equivalence, change fractions to have like denominators for addition and subtraction, and multiply fractions by whole numbers.

- Know the relationship between decimals and fractions, and calculate conversions.

- Compare whole numbers, decimals, and fractions using symbols: <, >, and =.

- Analyze and classify geometric shapes based on properties (e.g., sides, angles, and symmetry).

- Grasp units of measurement in time, money, distance, weight, and volume, and use knowledge to solve word problems (e.g., to find area and perimeter of the playground).

- Draw models to solve multiple-step word problems that include various operations.

- Collect and represent data (e.g., in a line plot) to interpret and draw conclusions.

- Generate number sequences based on rules, such as n + 3, beginning with 0: {0, 3, 6, 9 . . .}, and discuss patterns—e.g., every other number is even, and every other is odd.

- Determine all factor pairs for whole numbers from 1 to 100, and identify prime numbers.

- Argue strategies and troubleshoot others' ideas in collaborative problem-solving.

To find out what your child will be expected to master in your area, type into a search engine the name of your state and "education standards K–12." Skills may appear in a different grade in your state's standards.

FOURTH-GRADE HIGH-FREQUENCY WORDS

Fourth-graders officially read to learn this year, and they write a lot more too. The combined word lists in *Brain Stages* from kindergarten to fourth grade make up about 60 percent of writing vocabulary at this age. Imagine how much easier the transition to upper grades will be if your child can automatically read and spell these words.

Have your fourth-grader make flash cards, assemble Scrabble tiles, and spell the words with alphabet cereal for a special snack. Offer a reward that your child can strive for, and lavish praise for mastering all six lists.

65 High-Frequency Words—Fourth Grade

across	anything	area	behind	believe
between	breakfast	brought	catch	caught
circle	close	clothes	cried	direction
easy	explain	friend	guess	half
heavy	height	interest	listen	maybe
measure	medium	minutes	neighbor	noise
nothing	ocean	ourselves	person	please
possible	problem	quickly	quiet	reason
receive	record	remember	rough	safety
several	since	solution	solve	special
square	straight	surprise	though	thought
tomorrow	travel	tried	true	voice
week	while	whisper	world	yesterday

6 WAYS TO KICK-START FOURTH-GRADE LANGUAGE ARTS

1. **Explore historical fiction books.** Reading a story that takes place in a given period imparts historical events and customs in a way that can't be learned from a textbook. For a list of titles, type into a search engine "fourth-grade historical fiction."

2. **Visit museums and landmarks that bring state history to life.** School field trips to museums are great, but they don't take the place of exploring state history with family. The more intimate setting allows kids and parents to read information posted around display cases and talk about what it was like to live in their state a long time ago.

3. **Go to the natural history museum.** Find a local museum or other establishment that shows science in action: plant and animal cycles, conservation, weather and atmospheric changes, geology, electricity, and magnetism. Kids love to read about and discuss the marvels they experience.

4. **Throw a thematic birthday party.** Brainstorm science or social studies themes with your child. When you choose a theme, search online together to come up with fun games to play. For example, if you live in California, you might choose a Gold Rush theme and have partygoers "pan for gold" in your backyard or at the local park. If you live in Massachusetts, you could set up an obstacle course to simulate Paul Revere's wild ride. Websites like Science Buddies (science-buddies.org) make planning science parties a snap with all kinds of simple experiments kids love, like lighting a bulb using the energy in a potato.

5. **Play chess.** Age 9 or 10 is a great time to teach a child to play chess. Fourth-graders' brains are getting better at connecting cause and effect and planning with a future outcome in mind. Chess exercises these fledgling skills for use in real life.

6. **Take the next step with Treasure Hunt (page 143) or Story Starter (page 190).** If your child makes up oral adventures or becomes interested in doing so, encourage her to type stories on the computer. For a story your child gets particularly excited about, suggest experimenting with illustrations. Print it out and provide art materials. For a passionate, budding author, go to youidraw.com to build computer-generated illustrations without downloading software—many services are free.

6 FUN WAYS TO KICK-START FOURTH-GRADE MATH

These activities are great for both gifted students and those needing practice and can be adjusted according to interest and ability.

1. **Play Buzz.** This game not only reinforces number patterns, multiples, and strategy, but offers hilarious family fun. Our kids learned this game in fourth grade, and we played through high school while taking long car rides or waiting in line. Two or more people take turns counting, beginning with number 1. When a player lands on a multiple of 7 or a number with a 7 in it, the player says "Buzz" in place of the number. Here is an example: "1, 2, 3, 4, 5, 6, Buzz, 8, 9, 10, 11, 12, 13, Buzz, 15, 16, Buzz, 18, 19, 20, Buzz, 22, 23, 24, 25, 26, Buzz, Buzz, 29, 30 . . ."

   See how high you can count before someone messes up, and then the next person takes a turn and starts over with number 1. To add variety and further bolster math skills, use different multiples for this game—for example, say "Buzz" when a player lands on a multiple of 6 or a number that ends with 6.

2. **Double the recipe.** There's no better way to transform confusing fractions into usable tools than to change a recipe while cooking

or baking. You can bring to life equivalent fractions and the need for common denominators by assisting your child in doubling the amount of sugar—for example, from 3/4 cup to 6/4 cup. Reduce the fraction by dividing the numerator and denominator by 2 to get 3/2, or 1½ cups.

Making sure the cookies for a birthday party will have enough sugar is powerful motivation. Manipulating recipes is also a useful skill for future projects, like tripling the recipe for the chili cook-off or cutting the recipe in half to make homemade soup with the vegetables left in the fridge.

3. **Earn your gizmos.** By fourth grade, kids need to earn their own money to buy items like video games, clothing accessories, a toy they saw on TV, or sports equipment, or to go to a special event with a friend. They may need to be reminded to multiply the cost of that newfangled skateboard by the percentage of sales tax (if your state charges tax). This is great motivation to use decimals, a big topic in fourth grade. Your child will also build self-confidence and a sense of personal responsibility upon reaching his goal.

4. **Play Jenga.** This game requires manipulation of three-dimensional shapes, supports fourth-grade geometric concepts, and provides practice in strategic planning to reach a goal (also suggested for third-graders on page 194).

5. **Take a poll.** When family and friends are faced with a decision—what campground to stay in together during spring break, for example—have your child work with a cousin or friend to take a poll. In this example, the kids might collect everyone's preferences for facility features, location, and price, and then make a chart to represent the data. Real-life application of math concepts, such as data collection and synthesis, gets sent to the hippocampus for long-term memory.

6. **Play Farkle (or the 10,000 game).** Although there's a hefty element of chance, this game gives kids an opportunity to devise strategies to beat opponents and it can keep them busy having fun for hours. Plus, they get to clarify and cement place value concepts. Using six dice and as few as two players (though it's more fun with three or four), the object is to be the first to hit 10,000 points. For more detailed instructions, see dicegamedepot.com. *Hint:* If you already own Yahtzee, you can simply add one more dice and print instruction and score cards from dicegamedepot.com.

Focus, Focus, Focus

In fourth grade, given the jump in academics and pressure to develop social skills, the ability to be attentive and stay on task is more critical than ever before. For some kids, though, they get bored easily and have to grow into the responsibility of paying attention—even when a lesson or project is less than exciting. Some fourth-graders' brains are still defining neural pathways to lengthen their attention spans.

Other kids find sitting in a chair for more than a few minutes a challenge, and their knees bounce or their fingers tap on their desks. Still other kids' brain chemicals cause brain waves to cycle too fast or too slow, making their minds flit from one thing to the next or zone out while the teacher gives directions or they're supposed to be working.

The great thing about 9- and 10-year-olds is that they've generally formed enough neural connections, myelin coating to insulate pathways, and supportive glial cells to improve communication between hemispheres, organs, and lobes within the brain (Semrud-Clikeman, n.d.). Whether your child needs healthy habits to focus a typically functioning brain or tools to compensate for attention deficits or other disabilities, fourth grade is the sweet spot for developing focusing skills.

Here are four ways you can help.

4 GREAT TOOLS TO HELP UPPER-GRADERS FOCUS

1. **Weekly planner.** Get your child a weekly planner where homework assignments, long-term projects, and school events can be logged. Encourage him to fill out the planner daily, and check entries until he has been consistent with the planner for two to three weeks. Then pick a regular day of the week to check the planner to stay abreast of classroom activities and support your child in keeping up with daily entries.

2. **One earplug.** I don't have scientific evidence to support this, but I've found giving kids one earplug in class has worked wonders. The subtle white noise produced from one earplug and the slightly reduced volume in the environment seem to relax them and help maintain focus. The brand that has worked best for me is Hearos with a noise reduction range (NRR) of 33 decibels (the blue ones). Follow the directions on the package and practice with your child at home for best results.

3. **A colored dot.** Have your child stick a colored dot on her pencils and other writing instruments as well as on the e-tablet she uses to complete schoolwork (if applicable). When your fourth-grader feels her mind slipping off somewhere, she can purposely stare at the dot for a second to help her take responsibility for paying attention and refocus. (I've found blue and green dots work best—red and yellow are bright enough to cause greater distraction.)

4. **A focusing contract.** For some kids, especially those whose brains function differently, such as children with attention issues or learning disabilities, a more structured approach to focus in class may be needed. For example, the teacher can track 20- to 30-minute intervals daily on a Post-it, marking each one with a symbol. Parents can then offer a reward for a predetermined number of days with mostly

checkmarks or happy faces and no X's or sad faces. Revisit page 49
to create a contract between your child, you, and the teacher, and
establish regular communication between home and school. *Note:*
If your child has an IEP (page 156), this focusing agreement could be
included.

Elementary Health Education

Although some districts begin in third grade and others in fifth, students often begin to learn in fourth grade about how their bodies will
change over the next few years. The unit usually consists of three to five
gentle lessons, and boys and girls are usually separated for instruction.

The lessons help kids understand physical changes associated with
puberty that sometimes begin to happen this early, ready or not (don't
worry, sex usually doesn't get discussed in clinical terms until sixth
grade). The idea of your little one getting exposed to bodily changes
so soon may make you uncomfortable, but be assured that information is presented tactfully.

If the school employs such a program, your child's teacher will
likely mention this short health unit at the beginning of the school year,
and you will be asked to sign a permission slip to allow your child to
participate.

Upper Elementary Fitness Test

Beginning in fourth or fifth grade, fitness tests are required in most
states toward the end of the school year. Typical exams include measures for flexibility, upper body and abdominal strength (minimum
specified number of varying forms of pull-ups and sit-ups), and aerobic
endurance (a one-mile walk/run or something similar).

If your child has been physically active, he will require little preparation to pass. If not, don't wait until a week before the assessment to get
your fourth-grader involved in regular exercise. Kids are sensitive, and
failing a test like this can cause them to make judgments about them-

selves that last decades—even lifetimes. They may believe themselves weak, uncoordinated, fat, unathletic, and a myriad of other disparaging adjectives. For helpful how-tos and a great way to get unmotivated kids into fitness, see "Fourth-Grade Exercise" on page 262.

Visit the school or district website to find out fitness requirements your child will be expected to accomplish this year. If you have a fourth-grader with physical challenges (other than excess weight that isn't part of a medical condition), speak with the teacher and administration to develop a modified list of physical tasks to meet her needs.

Homework in Fourth Grade

This is an age of developing autonomy, yet your 9- or 10-year-old will likely need to learn how to balance a heavier workload between daily and long-term assignments. A stressed-out fourth-grader may say something like "How am I supposed to get my math done, write an essay about the story we read today, and still have time to work on that stupid science project? My teacher gave us only two weeks to make the PowerPoint, and I don't wanna talk in front of the class anyway."

Resist the temptation to provide too much direct help with assignments—developing independence this year is important in preparing for later grades. Instead, assist in setting up a system to make increased homework responsibilities manageable, and support your child in sticking to it. Remember, brains work best when kids feel safe, and having a consistent plan of action can dissipate anxiety.

Experiment to find the most effective way to organize a long-term project. Maybe your fourth-grader works best in short periods. Try having your child choose a specific daily quarter or half hour, say 5:30 to 6:00, to get work on the project out of the way before dinner. Then the daily homework can be done after the dishes are cleared or at whatever time you agree on. The routine will be comforting and the assignments less overwhelming.

Your child may prefer to get long-term projects done in one or two sittings. If that's the case, make sure he marks a couple of dates on the calendar so he knows when he'll be doing those marathon work sessions. Having a plan will relieve the stress of a looming assignment. The days your child chooses should be well before the due date. That way, if something goes wrong or the assignment takes longer than expected, he won't panic.

By helping your child learn not to procrastinate now, you will avoid lots of drama through middle and high school. This is especially important if *you* put off doing things until the last minute. Your child watches you to see how to live life. Two procrastinators in the household can be overwhelming, and planning with your child may help you develop more productive habits as well.

You don't want your fourth-grader flying out of bed on Monday night, hysterical because she just remembered a big assignment due the next morning. Helping your fourth-grader learn how to budget time and plan for upcoming events is as important as coaching social interactions, skills that will improve your child's life for years to come.

4 STEPS TO MEETING UPPER-GRADE HOMEWORK DEMANDS

1. **Develop a system.** Reduce stress, frustration, and fatigue by helping your child come up with a plan to complete long-term projects along with daily assignments.

2. **Brainstorm a homework checklist together.** Minimize mistakes and missing work by asking your child to write a list of things that will make for a successful homework routine and have her post it somewhere in her work space. You might say, "You're in upper grades now, so you're going to have more homework. Let's think of some ways to make it easier." Guide your child to include the following items on her list:

   a. Have a snack and get a drink of water.

   b. Read (or finish reading) whatever the teacher assigned—pages in the textbook, articles, worksheets, web pages—and reread the notes from class.

c. Read the directions out loud. Directions often become clearer when we hear as well as see them, and reading aloud keeps us from skipping over words.

d. Take a quick break if needed. If your child gets frustrated or distracted, tell her it's okay to go to the bathroom or refill her water glass, and then come back to refocus. Sometimes a quick bout of jump rope or other physical activity works wonders to pump blood and a hefty dose of oxygen into the brain for a fresh perspective. But don't let her watch TV, use social media, or play a video game and lull her brain into languid alpha or theta waves (revisit brain waves on pages 16–26).

3. **Proofread essays and reports.** Point out the sentences that need fixing, ask your child if he can find his mistakes, and support him in correcting them.

4. **Review math facts.** Flip through flash cards and play math games occasionally to keep your child's math skills sharp.

THE REAL DEAL
In Trouble with My Daughter's Fourth-Grade Teacher

A few days before open house, the evening parents come to school to see what their kids have been doing all year, our younger daughter's fourth-grade teacher pulled me aside in the staff lounge. "Do you have a few minutes to talk after school?" he asked.

"Uh . . . sure," I said. His tone made me think I'd done something wrong.

As I taught my third-grade class that afternoon, the butterflies in my stomach picked up speed. By the time the bell rang to end the school day, I felt queasy. Two boys, the final stragglers, walked toward the door with their backpacks and jumped out of the way as my younger daughter burst into the room.

"Hey, Mom!" she shouted. "My teacher wants to talk to you."

One of the boys widened his eyes. "Ooh, Mrs. Wilkinson, what'd you do?"

"You think I've been naughty?" I chuckled, belying my nervousness. The other boy nodded solemnly. "It sorta sounds like it."

"You have to go now." My daughter grabbed my sleeve. "He has to leave soon."

I shrugged, though my heart beat faster. "Okay, everybody out." As I locked my door, my daughter ran in front of me and turned right, down the hall—away from her classroom. "Hey, where're you going?"

"He didn't ask to talk to me," she yelled over her shoulder, disappearing in the crowd of exiting students.

I walked into her classroom to see elaborate models of the California Missions lining the bookcases under the windows: one made of sugar cubes, another lit with battery-powered lights, and others assembled from expensive, prefabricated kits. I couldn't help but crack a smile when my eyes landed on my daughter's desk. Her prairie scene of lumpy clay animals she'd baked in the oven, painted, and arranged inside a large shoebox on a bed of moss depicted the landscape in the mid to late 1800s near the San Gabriel Mission—well, sort of.

"Wow," I said, embarrassed that my stubborn kid wouldn't let me help her. "It looks like parents did a lot of the work on these projects."

Her teacher put down his pen at the table in front of the room and glared up at me. "That was the assignment. Parents were *supposed* to participate. Did you read the instruction sheet?"

He knocked the wind out of me, especially since he was a teacher I dearly respected, one of the best I've ever known. I wandered down the aisle to pretend to get a closer look at the class projects so I could catch my breath.

"I tried to help her, but she wouldn't let me touch a thing after we got the materials at the craft store." I swallowed hard. "She said you would be proud of her for doing the project by herself." I walked to his table. "Have you read her report? She did all her own research and was careful to use action verbs." I crossed my arms. "Her prairie isn't fancy. But it was made with heart."

"Here I was worried she'd be upset that her model was—well . . ."

"Terrible?" I offered. "Hard to tell what the inside of that box is even supposed to be?"

At that we both laughed.

"I've been working on getting these kids to be independent all year." He smiled, his eyes sparkling behind his glasses. "I should have figured it was something like this. It's not like you're a neglectful parent." He glanced at his watch. "Thanks for coming in." He stood and grabbed his sport coat from the chair. "Gotta go. Have a great afternoon."

I think we were both glad he had an appointment. Here I'd always told parents to communicate with me to avoid such problems, and I never thought to mention to her teacher, someone I saw every school day, that our daughter was unwilling to let her dad or me contribute to her project. This humbling experience made me more understanding when my students' parents didn't think to tell me about an issue with a class project.

Test Anxiety

Upper elementary assessments, especially standardized tests, make a jump in difficulty compared to prior grades and stress out some fourth-graders. Brains full of worry can't do their best thinking, so your child may not earn the scores she deserves. If you have an anxious 9- or 10-year-old, practice tools to reduce trauma over tests—prior to middle and high school. If fear and nervousness before and during exams aren't addressed, they can worsen with time and haunt kids into adulthood.

5 TOOLS TO BUILD CONFIDENCE AND REDUCE TEST ANXIETY

1. **Preparation.** If material is available for review, quiz your child to build confidence that the information is in his head and that he'll be able to access it when the time comes to take the test.

2. **Catharsis.** Researchers found that students who wrote down their thoughts about an upcoming test improved their performance

(Ramirez and Beilock 2011). The morning before a test, set the timer for five minutes for your fourth-grader to scribble down his anxieties. When the timer goes off, he gets to crumple the paper and throw it away. If nerves resurface at school, he can remind himself that those issues he'd worried about are at home in the trash, where they can't touch him.

3. **Exercise.** Get your child's heart pumping by doing some rhythmic activity, like Zumba or jumping rope. Exercising reduces anxiety and causes the brain to produce dopamine, a neurotransmitter that facilitates working memory and the desire to do well (Godman 2014). An hour before bedtime, have your child work up a sweat for at least 20 minutes. This may also help her sleep, another stress reducer. Then have her work out again for 10 to 20 minutes in the morning before school. If the exam will take place in the afternoon, suggest aerobic activities she can do at recess so her brain will be ready to think.

4. **The magic of peppermint.** Studies indicate that some smells enhance performance, particularly peppermint, which seems to improve attention and focus (Barker et al. 2003). Send your child to school with an organic peppermint hand sanitizer or essential oil roll-on (and careful instructions regarding how much to use). The scent of the peppermint will improve recall and concentration. *Note:* Artificial scents include toxic petrochemicals and don't provide the positive effects of those scents derived from essential oils (Diamanti-Kandarakis et al. 2009).

5. **Deep breathing.** Borrow this gem from ancient yoga practice to restore calm and confidence: Ask your child to inhale as you count slowly from one to four and exhale the same way for two or three breaths. Have him repeat the process counting slowly in his head. If possible, practice several times over a few days before a test. Then suggest that your fourth-grader stop and breathe for a little recharge during the test if anxiety begins to distract him.

Family Organization in Fourth Grade

Some parents have the organization thing down by the time their kids get to fourth grade, but most of us need to do some regrouping each school year. With your child's increased academic demands, social changes, and a flurry of extracurricular activities, life sometimes gets overwhelming—and you still have to perform all the other roles you play, like partner, professional, or volunteer.

So don't try to set up the household schedule on your own. Make it a group effort—every family member must share the responsibility. You'll get better buy-in that way too.

Sit down together in the kitchen or living room with a large whiteboard. Divide it into seven sections for every day of the week, and mark each day with time slots. Then brainstorm a checklist, and guide the conversation to include the following:

1. Downtime after work and school (at least 30 minutes, preferably an hour—TV and computer games still don't count)
2. Homework
3. Extracurricular activities
4. Evening family meal (at least five days/week)
5. Lunch prep
6. Bedtime ritual
7. Reading before lights-out

When you finish adding all the items, hang the whiteboard in a common area for easy reference. Consider having each family member choose a different color when they fill out the weekly calendar with their extracurricular activities, events, or appointments. Remind them that this is a community effort, and ask them to help one another stay on task until the routine becomes a habit.

Here are four additional tips for successful family organization:

1. Make sure your fourth-grader chooses a readable color like green, blue, or purple to mark the family calendar. If he argues

yellow is his favorite color, tell him he can use yellow if he writes his information in black and circles the words in yellow.

2. Supervise your child marking dates on the calendar when long-term school projects are due. Have him pick benchmark dates to finish specific parts.

3. For the inevitable forgotten project(s), especially if your child has attention issues, consider stashing poster board, construction paper, glue, markers, stickers, and glitter in an art cupboard so you can avoid a midnight trip to Walmart.

4. If your child leaves an assignment at home, and you're able to bring it to her, explain that this is the only time you are willing to give her a pass. That way, if it happens again, she'll be ready for the consequences. Learning responsibility for homework can take a bit of suffering—and fourth grade is a much safer place to learn than in middle or high school.

FOURTH-GRADE OUTSIDE THE NORM

By now, if your child has a learning disability and qualifies for special education services (see page 156), you and school staff should have settled on an Individualized Education Plan, or IEP, to get your fourth-grader's needs met—or the meeting to establish an IEP should be coming soon. All you have to do at this point is keep reading to your child, encourage her to read independently, play some of the games in this book to help connect neural pathways, and monitor her progress at school.

But what if your fourth-grader struggles and doesn't qualify for services? What if your child did fine in third grade but is having difficulty with the transition to the upper grades?

Fourth-Grade Tortoises

Some children have trouble adjusting to the greater demands put on reading comprehension in fourth grade—even math assignments often include reading and writing. Deciphering information from a math, science, or social studies text is a different skill than understanding the plot in a novel. Luckily, with a little help from you, this problem has an excellent prognosis.

4 STEPS TO IRON OUT WRINKLES IN READING COMPREHENSION

Doing these four steps consistently with your child for three weeks will form habits of reading titles, scanning for key words, making predictions, and honing in on important details—things good readers do subconsciously. Instilling these tools will make school more fun, and you may never have to look back.

1. **Pre-reading preppers.** Ask your child to read aloud the title of the assigned article or chapter as well as the words or phrases in the text that jump out at him, including headings. Ask what he thinks he will learn and what he wants to know more about. If the assignment includes questions to answer, have him read them aloud *before* he begins reading the passage to keep him alert to important information.

2. **Troubleshooting.** Gently help your child decode and clarify unfamiliar, skipped, or incorrect words as he reads the assignment to you. Model sounding out words and deciding if a word makes sense in context.

3. **Thumb talk.** As your child reads aloud, have him give you a thumbs-up when he understands what he's reading, a sideways thumb if he kind of gets the gist, or thumbs-down if the words don't sink in at all. Try relating confusing passages to something in your child's experience to help him make sense of the material.

4. **Silly speed-reading.** Ask your child to reread all or part of the assignment aloud two or three more times. Make a game out of goading her into reading faster and faster. If your child likes racing against the clock, use a stopwatch to see how much faster she reads each time. Studies show repeated reading increases fluency and comprehension (Stevens et al. 2017), and silly speed-reading makes strengthening those skills more fun.

14 EXCITING AUTHORS TO KEEP FOURTH-GRADERS READING

Reading chapter books 30 minutes a day is still important in fourth grade. Novels, even fantasies, present social situations and facts for readers to process. And they're a relaxing, fun way to learn about the world. Check out this list of great books your child will look forward to reading.

1. Time Warp Trio swashbuckling series (16+ books) by Jon Scieszka—sends readers on a journey through events in history.

2. Magic School Bus series (167+ picture and chapter books) by various authors, including Joanna Cole—for kids who like science, cool illustrations, and quirky characters. Animated versions reinforce comprehension.

3. Hank the Cowdog series (68+ books) by John R. Erickson—a dog that always gets into trouble but saves the day in the end, a beloved ongoing series since 1982.

4. Little House on the Prairie series (9 books) by Laura Ingalls Wilder—historical fiction with lovable characters that children have enjoyed for generations.

5. *Matilda*, *James and the Giant Peach*, *George's Marvelous Machine*, *The BFG*, *The Witches*, and more by Roald Dahl—madcap clever books kids love.

6. Heroes of Olympus series (5 books) by Rick Riordan—hugely popular with the action-loving set, leveled for late third to early fifth grade for independent reading.

7. 39 Clues series (11 books) by various authors, including Rick Riordan—fantastic circumstances and nail-biting adventures kids can't put down.

8. *Charlotte's Web* and *Stuart Little* by E. B. White—longtime, beloved grade four stories.

9. Magic Shop series (5 books) by Bruce Coville—creepy, riveting stories (*The Monster's Ring*; *Jeremy Thatcher, Dragon Hatcher*; *Jennifer
   Murdley's Toad*, and *The Skull of Truth* are on fourth-grade reading
   level; *Juliet Dove: Queen of Love* is leveled for fifth grade).

10. Captain Underpants series (14 books) by Dav Pilkey—kooky stories
    with an unlikely hero who kids get a kick out of; most of the series is
    written on a fourth-grade reading level.

11. *The Miraculous Journey of Edward Tulane* by Kate DiCamillo—a toy
    rabbit gets lost and tossed into all kinds of crazy places and adven-
    tures. (DiCamillo has written several beloved stories at various read-
    ing levels.)

12. Spiderwick Chronicles series (4 books) by Tony DiTerlizzi—three
    siblings discover a field guide in the attic, left by their ancestor, that
    leads them to a dangerous parallel world.

13. Fudge series (5 books) by Judy Bloom—nine-year-old Peter is frus-
    trated by high-maintenance, hilarious little brother Fudge.

14. Wrinkle in Time series (5 books) by Madeleine L'Engle—one of the
    first science fiction fantasy series for children (1962), still beloved to-
    day; four books leveled for fourth grade.

Note: For more lists of favorite titles categorized by reading level, check
out these two sites: The Best Children's Books and Kids Book Series.

Checking In with Gifted Education

By fourth grade, most children have been placed in gifted programs if
they've met the local protocols (see page 161). If your child's school
hasn't assessed students yet, ask the teacher or administration when
the school plans to test and identify students who would benefit from
differentiated instruction appropriate to their abilities.

Gifted instruction should begin soon if it hasn't already. Your fourth-grader may be pulled out of the regular education classroom at a scheduled time to work on projects with other gifted students. He may receive special assignments that involve media, research, strategy, and presentation. Some schools have classrooms in each of the upper grades with a "gifted cluster," or a group of gifted kids who can collaborate on projects designed with their abilities in mind.

Fourth grade is critical for praising tenacity over intelligence. Assignments should require application of learned skills, logic, creativity, and ingenuity. Some children feel energized using more of their brainpower while others get discouraged. Gifted kids are often accustomed to catching on quickly, so projects specifically designed to be challenging can rattle them.

Keep an open dialogue to find out how your child is affected by the expectation of doing different, harder projects than most of the other kids. Talking through a project helps nervous fourth-graders process the expectation and feel confident about completing a challenging task. You can also allay fears by surfing the internet and looking at library resources together. It can ease your child's mind to know that whatever information she needs is at her fingertips.

Gifted Instruction

Teacher training for meeting gifted kids' needs is all over the map. Some teachers who have attended workshops and done research assign projects that develop higher-level thinking skills and help students devise systems for organization. Savvy teachers also provide guidance for collaborating with others. We've all known supersmart people who seemed scattered and socially awkward. Tools for interacting in a group and organizing stuff to keep it from getting misplaced are as important as layered assignments for exercising executive brain function. Such gifted programs can make the difference in keeping these kids interested in learning and motivated to do well in school.

Other well-meaning educators, however, who have had little training in supporting gifted students, have been known to assign extra math problems, spelling sentences, or worksheets to keep fast workers busy.

If your child complains of having to do a whole page of math problems when the rest of the class did only the odd numbers, or something similar, talk to the teacher. Your child likely needs less repetition of standard material, but is being asked to do more—the exact opposite of what he needs. You don't want your fourth-grader to feel punished for catching on to new concepts quickly or finishing assignments before the other kids, or he might mentally leave the classroom altogether.

Remember, you and the teacher are on the same side and want what's best for your child. Ask if the teacher would be open to not giving additional work of the same kind, but rather putting your heads together to come up with a more in-depth project in line with the curriculum that your fourth-grader can focus on after finishing classwork.

Have some ideas ready when you and the teacher brainstorm. For example, your child can do research on current science or social studies units to apply math and language concepts. If the teacher seems amenable to the idea, come up with some sort of presentation together that your child can do upon completion of the project. On the other hand, if the teacher seems overwhelmed, offer to provide materials and monitor the project yourself.

Thank the teacher for her time and effort, regardless of the outcome of the meeting, and offer Hoagies' Gifted Education Page (Carolyn K., n.d.) as a resource for a one-stop shop for information and project suggestions for kids like yours. This is a great website for parents and children too. You'll find books, software, games, and more.

The important thing is for your child to engage in learning. You've probably had to contribute to keeping that quick brain plugged in at school since kindergarten anyway. It will be a big help to continue doing the activities suggested in this book—your fourth-grader will subconsciously adjust them to accommodate the way his brain works.

FOURTH-GRADE CARE AND FEEDING

Throughout elementary school, children undergo constant growth. Fourth-graders still need 9 to 11 hours of sleep a night, but your child may squeak by with seven or eight. Be aware, though, that on the weekends following nights of skimped sleep, you'll probably have a grumpy kid on your hands. Organs, muscles, bones, blood—pretty much everything needs the brain to drop into delta waves to lull the body into repairing itself and growing bigger.

If your child has trouble sleeping, try foam earplugs. They will likely take a couple of nights to get used to, but the gentle sound of her heartbeat and muffled outside racket may slow her brain waves for the rejuvenation her body needs to face a new day. If your child can't get used to earplugs, try a white noise generator to help her tune out distractions. These small machines generally have a fan configured to generate adjustable sound without creating a draft.

Fourth-Graders Packin'—Lunches, That Is

Beware that fourth-graders seem to crave soda, cookies, candy, pizza, fries, and chips even more than other kids in the elementary grades. Those simple carbohydrates spike energy levels and then drop kids into lethargy—not to mention they pack on weight and have little nutrition.

By age 9 or 10, your child is perfectly capable of packing his own healthy lunch. Not only is this a good task to develop responsibility, but assembling nutritious lunches gets kids in the habit of making good food choices out in the real world.

You'll have to supervise for the first few weeks to make sure your child includes *water* and enough food to get through the day. After that, you'll want to periodically check the box or bag for water and nutrients needed to focus and think. To avoid rushed mornings, try getting your child into a routine of packing his lunch the night before.

Other kids may bring yummy empty calories to school to share, but you don't need to worry about occasional indulgences (unless your fourth-grader has physical health issues). If junk foods don't replace healthy ones, your child should be fine.

Having tasty healthy snacks on hand helps counteract the fourth-grade junk food cravings. For example, if your child isn't allergic, try keeping a big container of unsalted almonds or mixed nuts in the car. The fat and protein do a good job of tiding kids over until their next

meal, and the micronutrients help reboot fatigued brains. Keep a supply of water in the car too, especially for after-school sports practices
or games.

14 EASY BRAIN FOODS FOR FOURTH-GRADE LUNCHES

1. Any kind of fresh fruit adds nutrition and a little sweetness to the
   lunch box. Easy-peel oranges, rinsed grapes or berries, and sliced
   apples are thirst-quenching sources of potassium and vitamins. Apples even have phytonutrients that regulate blood sugar.

2. Dried fruit without added sugar when fresh fruit is unavailable will do
   in a pinch. Make sure to include water in the lunch box. Even without added sugar, dried fruit has natural sugar and can stick to teeth.
   Without a little rinsing, dried fruit can cause tooth decay.

3. Small pop-top cans of tuna are great for omega-3s and omega-9s for
   better thinking.

4. Finger Jell-O is surprisingly low in sugar, kids love to make and eat it,
   and the gelatin is great for hair, bones, and teeth.

5. Celery sticks and baby carrots have lots of fiber and a good crunch.

6. Sandwiches on whole wheat (for fiber) or sourdough (low sugar)
   pack lots of nutrition into one place. Encourage your child to add lettuce, avocado, cucumber, tomato slices, and/or sprouts. Guacamole
   is a nutritious alternative to mayonnaise, and any kind of mustard
   works. Turmeric (the yellow stuff) in mustard has antioxidants.

7. Hard-boiled eggs (you can even buy them cooked and peeled) provide protein, healthy fat, D and B vitamins, omega-3s, and omega-9s
   for a great pick-me-up to get kids through the rest of the school day.
   You and your child can also make egg salad as a delicious alternative. Slice in some celery for a refreshing crunch. Your child can eat it
   from a reusable container or on wheat bread.

8. Deli meat is easy to pack and has protein and B vitamins. Choose low sodium brands.

9. Prepackaged raw stir-fry vegetables are available in the produce section at the supermarket. They are colorful and healthy, and give a lunch some tasty crunch.

10. Hummus can be put in a small container and used as a protein-packed dipping sauce for raw veggies or put on wheat pita wedges.

11. Bagged salad from the produce section can be tossed into a container with other favorites, such as tuna, chunks of cheese, strawberries—kids love to get creative.

12. A banana and peanut or nut-butter burrito is fun to eat, easy to make, and contains healthy fiber, fat, protein, and carbs. For added deliciousness and protein, add a slice of bacon. *Note:* Check with the school to make sure nut products are allowed. Some children are violently allergic.

13. Brown rice with a fried egg and sliced avocado on top goes great in a container, is tasty, and provides more than 20 nutrients for brainpower including fiber, folate, potassium, Vitamin E, B vitamins, and folic acid.

14. Leftover dinner items—chicken, meatloaf, tuna casserole, green salad, pork fried rice, enchiladas—taste as yummy from a lunch box as they did at the table the night before and are quick to pack for the next day.

AND REMIND YOUR CHILD TO INCLUDE SOME WATER!

Fourth-Graders' Teeth

Most kids enjoy brushing and flossing autonomy by fourth grade, and parents often forget to check for sparkling smiles in the hustle of life. If your dentist put sealants on your child's molars in kindergarten or first grade, you have a better chance of pink gums and cavity-free choppers. Still, 9- and 10-year-olds use any excuse to scarf a cupcake at seemingly endless social events, and fourth grade can be a year of cavities, fillings, and caps.

Consider reviewing dental hygiene with your child. Go back to flossing and brushing in the mirror together, coaching a little where needed. Reinforce good dental care by asking the hygienist to do a quick workshop with your child at the next cleaning. Who knows—you may both learn something new that you can practice together.

★THE REAL DEAL★
My Fourth-Grade Mouth Full of Holes

The pink orb grew and grew until a sticky mess splatted across my nose and cheeks. I carefully peeled at the rubbery film, intent on blowing an even bigger, better bubble.

"Trishie, are you chewing bubble gum again?"

I jumped at my mom's voice behind me.

"Uh . . . what?" I pressed the wad inside my palm and turned to the doorway.

"We talked about this." Mom stepped into my room from the hallway. "Grinding sugar into your teeth is the best way to get cavities."

The sticky evidence left on my chin made denial ridiculous, so I reasoned instead, "I do a good job brushing." Maybe flossing wouldn't come up. Come to think of it, where *was* the dental floss?

Mom crossed her arms. "We have an appointment with Dr. Torgesen next week."

"Don't worry." I picked at the tacky spot on my chin. "My teeth are fine."

Adults worry about everything, I thought.

Except my teeth weren't fine. The dentist clipped my x-rays to the light board where he showed my mom and me *nine* dark smudges that he explained were cavities. My molars could have been Swiss cheese! Luckily, most of those molars would eventually fall out to be replaced by permanent teeth, but they had to be filled to protect the molars underneath.

That's when I learned Novocain shots hurt. A lot.

Fourth-Grade Exercise

By now, you understand how aerobic workouts strengthen the body and increase oxygen to the brain. If you have a kid who loves sports or dance and gets plenty of exercise, then you have nothing to worry about except making sure to provide lots of water. Kids get dehydrated faster than adults. Cramps, headaches, fatigue, or grumpiness after basketball practice could be the result of not enough hydration to replace the sweat (Van Pelt 2015).

But avoid passing out energy or sports drink. The American Academy of Pediatrics (2011) reports,

> Rigorous review and analysis of the literature reveal that caffeine and other stimulant substances contained in energy drinks have no place in the diet of children and adolescents. Furthermore, frequent or excessive intake of caloric sports drinks can substantially increase the risk for overweight or obesity in children and adolescents.

And according to KidsHealth (2014),

> The average young athlete can and should get all the necessary nutrients and hydration by eating healthy foods and drinking plenty of water before, during, and after exercise. During games and competitive events, drinks should be available at all times and regular water breaks should be scheduled about every 15 or 20 minutes.

The moral of the story: Pass out water bottles. It's cheaper and healthier.

Weight Training for Fourth-Graders

What if you have a child who isn't interested in sports or dance and would rather lounge on the couch? Strength training a couple of days a week may be your answer. Supervised weight training is great for young athletes too, but it is especially good for children who haven't been regularly active or are overweight. Light-weight repetitions fit perfectly into fourth-graders' natural preference to go full-throttle for 30 to 60 seconds and then stop to rest before picking up speed again. Even better, kids can experience an immediate sense of accomplishment when they successfully lift appropriate weights.

People used to think children would damage growing bodies if they worked out with weights, but it turns out that *supervised* weight training reduces injuries while playing sports, enhances bone development, and increases muscle strength (Westcott and Faigenbaum 2003).

It makes sense when you figure old people benefit from pumping a bit of iron. Why not kids?

Wayne Westcott, PhD, and Avery Faigenbaum, EdD, specialists in weight training for children, report there's never been a recorded injury in a strength training study, and in their 17 years of training kids, no child has gotten hurt. They've had the best results with the DeLorme-Watkins protocol, which includes the following:

> 10 repetitions performed at 50 percent of the 10-repetition maximum weight load; the second set . . . 10 repetitions . . . at 75 percent . . . and the final set . . . as many repetitions as possible with the 10-repetition maximum weight load. When a child can complete 15 repetitions, a higher 10-repetition maximum weight load is determined and the training protocol repeats. (Westcott and Faigenbaum 2003)

Westcott and Faigenbaum have found—and studies confirm this—that weight training twice a week builds confidence and fitness as well as helps with weight loss. If your child loves it, you can safely add a third day. You'll want to consult a trainer who has experience with children to establish the amount of weight, the best type of exercises, and the proper way to lift to avoid injury. Take your child with you to the gym a couple of days a week and spend quality time together. Or have a trainer establish individual routines for each of you, and lift free weights at home. Helping your child become fit may be just the incentive you need to get in better shape too.

If you can't work out with your fourth-grader, look for other options in your area. There may be kids' strength-training programs available at the local YMCA, community center, or the gym where you have a membership. Since your child will begin fitness tests either this year or next (see pages 244–245 and page 284), this is great preparation for success.

A lot of kids, even active ones, can't do enough calisthenics to pass, which demoralizes them rather than providing incentive to get stronger. Fourth-graders who lift weights build the strength necessary to pull their chins above the bar and do 15 consecutive sit-ups. Gaining strength incrementally will set up your child to pass the fifth-, sixth-, and seventh-grade fitness exams—not to mention boost self-esteem when she helps bring in groceries that no longer feel heavy.

WHERE DO YOU SEE YOURSELF?

Mr. Harrow rushes into the parking lot, a half hour late, to pick up Ryan from school. His fourth-grader barely jumps into the backseat of the sedan before he stomps on the accelerator to go get his daughter, Diana, an eighth-grader who has to be at lacrosse practice by 4:30.

Mr. Harrow must have been temporarily insane when he'd complained to his ex-wife that he never got to see the kids except on Wednesdays and every other weekend. Getting to work by 6:30 a.m. so he can leave early to pick up the kids two extra days a week is killing him. How has their mom managed to juggle work and the kids for the past three years?

He glances in the rearview mirror to see Ryan staring out the window. Oh man. Are those tears in his son's eyes? What happened this time? He doesn't remember all this drama when he was a kid. He slows the car to stop at a red light next to his daughter's middle school and wishes he didn't have to ask, but his kid looks so sad back there.

"Hey, Ryan." Mr. Harrow braces himself for a crying jag. "You all right?"

"I'm fine." His son's clipped tone doesn't sound convincing.

The light turns green, and he starts to hit the gas when the SUV in front of him slams on the brakes. He screeches to a halt an inch behind the bumper and shouts a four-letter word. If Ryan tells his mom, Mr. Harrow won't be driving the kids around anymore. Maybe that wouldn't be a bad thing.

Who's he kidding? Getting his daughter to lacrosse is a pain, but he likes going to practices to watch her, and Ryan's done much better in math since he started giving his son hints how to solve problems as they sit on the bleachers.

"Uh, sorry for the bad word, Ryan. I almost hit that idiot—"

Diana runs to the passenger side and hops into the front seat.

"Dad, our practice is at Cedar Park today," she says out of breath.

"Are you the reason that SUV almost made an accordion out of Ryan and me?"

"Yeah, but—"

"We could've crashed." He eases the car through the intersection, giving the SUV lots of room. "You're lucky you didn't get killed. What the hell is wrong with you?"

He hears sniffles in the backseat. Poor Ryan seemed on the edge before, and now this.

"I'm supposed to be at practice in—" Diana glances at the clock on the dashboard as she winds an elastic band around her brown ponytail "—two minutes."

"Why didn't you text me?"

"I left my phone in my locker so it wouldn't get taken away by one of my teachers." His eighth-grader gives him surly, narrowed eyes. "Would it have made a difference? You're late. You're always late."

She has no idea how hard it is for Mr. Harrow to get to his kids at all. He isn't supposed to leave work until 5, and he usually doesn't finish with paperwork and phone calls until 6 or 6:30. Even getting in early, it's practically impossible to get out of the office by 3.

Diana slams athletic shoes on her feet, scrunches below the windshield to switch from her blouse she wore to school to her lacrosse practice shirt, and wiggles out of her jeans to pull on her shorts. Ryan's sniffles from the backseat get louder—or is it that the car has gone deathly silent after his daughter scolded him for running late?

"Let me out here," demands his bossy daughter on the street outside the grass field at Cedar Park. She opens the door before the car comes to a complete stop and sprints across the sidewalk and down the field to meet her teammates.

Mr. Harrow glances at his white knuckles gripping the steering wheel. He plans to have a talk with his teenager later about respect and car safety.

He pulls into a parking space and looks over his shoulder to see his son wiping tears from his cheeks with his sleeves. "Ryan, buddy, what's wrong?"

"Nothing. I'm fine," his son says with a surprisingly steady voice.

Mr. Harrow knows he should press his son to talk about what's bothering him, but he's exhausted as it is, and it's only 4:35.

◉◉ Mr. Flutter pulls into the space on the end, near the playground and his daughter's fourth-grade classroom. His schedule is flexible since he does most of his work online. The bell rings. After five minutes, his foot starts tapping on the floorboard. A flexible schedule doesn't mean he's done with work by 3:15. He still has a project to send to a client before 5. In seven minutes, he gets out of the car and goes looking for her.

Mr. Flutter pokes his head into Shawn's classroom. All the children have left the room.

"Mr. Flutter, how are you?" Ms. Chu asks from her desk in the back corner of the room. "May I help you with something?"

"I'm looking for Shawn."

"That's strange." Ms. Chu gets up and walks toward him. "She was the first one out of the room when the bell rang."

Mr. Flutter's heart skips a beat. "Where could she be?"

He has seldom let Shawn out of his sight in the three years since they lost his wife to cancer. His heart starts to race, and he tries to inhale, but air doesn't seem to fill his lungs.

Ms. Chu's eyes soften with concern, and she walks past him, out the door, waving a hand for him to follow. "Let's go check the restroom," she says.

Past a few classrooms down the hall, they come to the restroom, and Ms. Chu opens the door. "Shawn, are you in here?"

"Ms. Chu?" Shawn's shaky voice comes from behind the door of the last stall.

"Shawn?" Mr. Flutter bursts into the restroom. "Honey, what's wrong?"

"Dad! My underwear is—I think I'm dying!" Shawn bursts into sobs that echo off the walls.

"Oh, God. No." The blood drains from Mr. Flutter's face.

Ms. Chu grabs his arm and whispers, "She's not dying. She started menstruating."

"But she's only 10," he whispers back.

"She's almost 11," Ms. Chu reminds him, releasing his arm.

Shawn repeated second grade after missing so much school the year her mother died.

"She's a little early." The teacher sighs. "I wish you had let her stay for our health education unit."

"That class about adolescence? She'll get there soon enough." Mr. Flutter's whisper amplifies just below a shout. "She's a child. She doesn't need her head filled with—"

"Da-ad." Shawn stretches the word into two syllables. "What's wrong with me?"

"You're not dying, sweetie," Mr. Flutter assures her.

"You're just growing up," Ms. Chu says. "I'll go get some things to help you."

"Dad?" Shawn's high-pitched panic sounds so young and innocent.

"Don't worry. We'll take care of this. You'll be all right." Mr. Flutter turns to Ms. Chu. "How could this happen already?"

"If I had to guess, I'd say early menses runs somewhere in the family," the teacher says. "I'll be right back."

"Thank you," Mr. Flutter mouths to Ms. Chu.

She nods as she hurries out the door. For the millionth time since Diane's passing, his chest aches with longing. Diane would have let Shawn participate in that health unit.

😇 Mr. Eagle Feather prepares celery and peanut butter at the kitchen counter, his daughter's favorite after-school snack. Well, anything with peanut butter: apple slices, bananas, baby carrots. He figures she'd brush her teeth with the stuff if they let her.

Although thrilled about the promotion to regional manager, he'd worried about the swing shift. He hadn't anticipated these treasured couple of hours after his fourth-grader got off the school bus, before he went to work. They talk and laugh and snack. He didn't think he would like helping with homework, but he's gotten into helping her plan her time to do the science project on electricity. She has been putting it together in stages for almost a month. And he likes to do his paperwork while Raina does her math, in case she gets stuck. The word problems have been fun to dissect and figure out together.

Mrs. Eagle Feather warns that he should slow down on the peanut butter since Raina has gained a little weight since he's been home in the afternoons, so he gives the celery a lighter touch without taking the fun out of it.

The front door slams. His body jolts with the noise. "What the—"

Seconds later, a bedroom door bangs down the hallway. He can guess which one. Licking the peanut butter from his fingers, he walks out of the kitchen to find out what happened with Raina's supposed friends on the playground *this* time.

He taps a gentle knuckle against her door. "Hey, rainbow girl, can I come in?"

"No." Her voice is muffled and teary. "You'll just get mad."

He opens the door anyway. "Seems like you're mad enough for both of us, so I'll try to keep my cool." He walks across her room and sits next to her on the twin bed. Curled on her side, she hides her face under her pillow with the Little Mermaid print. Why was his little girl getting so upset lately? "What's with slamming the door?" he asks.

"Robert sat next to me at lunch today . . ." She pauses to gulp a breath. "He traded me one of his chocolate chip cookies for one of my little oranges."

"Robert's the boy you kind of like, right? Why is that a bad thing?"

She pulls the pillow off her head and yells, "He doesn't like me because I'm fat."

"How do you know that?" he asks, and at the same time he thinks, *She has gained a few pounds, but it's not like she's grown out of her jeans.*

Raina bursts into choking sobs. "Dolores said . . . he just wants to copy off . . . my spelling test tomorrow."

"Ah. Dolores again." He puts a hand on her shoulder. "I know you think she's on your side—"

"We've been friends since kindergarten, Dad!"

"Do you think Robert gave you a cookie to copy off you?"

Raina sits up and folds her legs on the bed. "He sits in the group behind mine." Her head tilts. "How would he see my paper?"

"Good question." Mr. Eagle Feather crosses his arms. "Didn't you tell me Dolores likes this Robert kid too?"

"Yeah, but . . ." Raina's eyes widen and her mouth drops. Then she looks at her dad with pinched eyebrows. "She called me a fat ass."

He shrugs. "Okay, well, if you think that's being a good friend."

Raina shakes her head. "I wouldn't say that to anyone." She looks up at her dad with earnest dark eyes. "Even if I thought it."

"That's smart." He chuckles. "But you know, ever since I changed jobs, I've been hearing about a lot of mean things this girl does."

Her eyes drop to her lap. "She didn't used to be like this."

"Not until you started getting more confident and making new friends." He lifts Raina's chin with a gentle finger. "You and Dolores have been friends for a while, but it's okay to cut her loose. I mean, you're stuck with Mom and me. We're family. But you don't have to stay friends with someone who doesn't treat you right."

Raina blows between her lips. "We're in the same group in class, and we hang out at recess. What do I do?"

"Ask Mrs. Wyman to change your group." He puts his finger to his lips. "On the QT."

"How?"

"Email Mrs. Wyman. Tell her you've tried to work out stuff with someone all year, you talked to your dad, and you both think it would be best if you moved away from this person."

Raina looks past him and nods slowly. "What do I do about recess?"

"You said you have friends who like to play four square, and Dolores doesn't like that game." He smirks. "I say you go play four square."

"And if she tries to boss me around, I'll tell her she can play whatever she wants, but I'm playing four square."

"I think you'll be a lot happier." Mr. Eagle Feather gives his daughter's shoulder an encouraging squeeze, pleased he could help her let go of this longtime friend turned mean.

*   *   *

Did you recognize the busy parent who was too exhausted and hassled to deal with his fourth-grade son's emotions at that moment? This happens to the best of us. After all, parents are human too.

Once the moment passes, though, you may not be able to gently cajole your child into talking about a problem, especially with boys. I'm not being sexist. There are always exceptions, but based on my experience, and on the experiences of friends and family members who have sons, fourth-grade girls are generally more willing to talk out problems than their male counterparts.

Regardless of gender, if you can muster the energy to do the sometimes arduous task of persuading your child to share something upsetting that happened at school, you'll all be much better off. Otherwise, an unaddressed issue will reappear in an escalated version at a future date.

In difficult circumstances, such as the death of a partner, divorce, illness, or job loss, well-meaning parents often have damaging reactions. They can hover or get overprotective in dealing with their own guilt or grief, as Mr. Flutter does.

Even more harmful is when parents lose sight of the boundaries they've set with their kids. Dietary, bedtime, TV, video game, and homework rules get inconsistent or collapse altogether. Not only do children have to deal with the family hardship, but they also lose the security of clear guidelines—and the protective, reliable consequences for breaking rules. Especially in times of trouble, children need boundaries, a solid routine, and plenty of hugs.

If you find yourself in difficult circumstances, reach out to friends, family, a therapist, church members, a support group—anyone who can help you get through your own pain. Humans are pack animals. We do much better when we find positive influences to share our experiences with.

Partnering with your kids to forge a path together to find your way through a difficult situation can develop confidence in knowing "this, too, shall pass," and any challenge can be managed.

Lucky Mr. Eagle Feather gets a couple of hours a day with his daughter to snack, talk, and help organize her fourth-grade long-term and short-term homework assignments. Not all of us have that luxury, but most of us can help set up a homework routine on the weekend or some evening we can sit down after dinner.

The more regular conversations you can have with your child, after school and during or after the evening meal, the more effectively you'll be able to help with the social dramas that erupt in fourth grade. Open communication now will establish a habit that will become even more critical in your child through the sharp rocks and murky waters of adolescence.

CONCLUSION

Nine- and 10-year-olds' brains reach a point of neural connection that brings higher-level thinking into play, both academically and socially. For example, fourth-graders make the transition from learning to read to reading to learn. Lots of parents find that their kids' brains need extra reading practice to fine-tune those neural pathways and meet increased academic demands.

This is also an important year to provide tools to help children remain attentive or regain focus when their minds wander. Experimenting with ways to purposely "tune in" will be critical to meet new demands to develop higher-thinking skills in math and writing, absorb concepts in history and science, and know when projects are due.

Learning how to get organized and budget time this year is also a big deal. Fourth-graders need help figuring out how to complete daily homework as well as make progress on long-term projects. Fitting in downtime to process what they learn will be more important than ever. They also need space for independent reading, exercise, extracurricular activities, and eating healthy while still getting enough sleep. Fourth grade can be a juggling act.

Fourth-graders' more defined neural connections mean that parents will need to help their kids process philosophical questions and understand deeper emotions. You'll find yourself discussing less-than-comfortable subjects, like why a friend's clothes look too small, yet she keeps wearing them. Your questions, careful listening, guidance, and occasional practice through role-playing will be key in how your child learns to deal with the rest of the world. But after the pep talks, fourth-graders need to practice facing social situations on their own.

In fifth grade, relationships and social awareness will become even more acute as your child gets ready to enter those infamous middle school years.

8

FIFTH GRADE
Shaky Egos and "Where Do I Fit?"

Get ready for some chatting. Ten- and 11-year-olds love to talk. Not without exception, but often, even the kid who used to be considered "the quiet one" in the family starts voicing opinions, sticking up for friends or siblings, and asking questions. Fifth-graders can laugh heartily one minute and feel slighted or disrespected the next. If friends come home with your child to hang out ("playing" is no longer cool), you'll probably hear a lot of babbling in the next room—and not all conversations will be pleasant.

YOUR FIFTH-GRADER'S BRAIN

Boys' and girls' brains are fairly in sync until about the middle of fourth grade, when girls' frontal lobes start growing a bit faster. Before fifth grade, outside evidence of the difference is only slightly apparent. Then by age 10 or 11, not only do girls have more intense social tendencies than boys, but they also start to grow taller than their male peers, and their bodies may begin to reshape, getting ready for adolescence.

Conversely, although boys' voices may crack and get lower, growth spurts in frontal lobes and everywhere else generally wait for middle school. The variation in brain development might explain social clashes between genders at this age—their minds are quite literally in different places (Lenroot et al. 2007). Even so, similar developmental processes occur in both girls' and boys' brains in the fifth grade.

A Bit More Established

By this time, neurons reproduce and reorganize less often, decreasing the number of new connections. Scientists think this is the reason children who begin to learn a language at age 10 or 11 seldom totally lose their accents. On the other hand, myelin production, the white matter plasma that grows around neural highways to insulate them and make neurons better electrical conductors, shifts into a higher gear. Mental processes speed up as communication between sections of the brain becomes more efficient (Barkovich 2000).

This means your child's higher-level thinking skills will continue to increase. Expect your fifth-grader to get better at applying abstract ideas to solve problems, connecting information from various sources, using inference and deductive reasoning, and being socially aware. You may also notice a greater empathy for others.

Here's the catch: These things will happen on a continuum and be hit-and-miss.

Inevitable Inconsistency

The prefrontal cortex, or the rational part of the brain, will continue to grow, and myelination will become more refined in your child's brain until age 18 to 25. Before then, neural signals and mental processing will be inconsistent (Johnson et al. 2009).

In other words, grasping variables in math will seem obvious one day. Your child may even use the concept to figure out logistics for a birthday party. The next day, anything algebraic is a foreign language, and the following day or week, variables become usable tools again. Similarly, a friend at school makes a comment on Tuesday that makes your child laugh, but on Wednesday the same comment brings tears. And at home, your child may insist on making an independent decision and soon after need a warm, safe hug (maybe because of that decision). She might often disappear into a bedroom or the backyard just because she'd rather be alone.

Be patient as your fifth-grader goes through the many physical, emotional, and social changes typical of this year. Her moodiness is grounded in physiology as neural pathways get refined and insulated for efficient communication throughout the brain. But the roller coaster is a small price to pay for how fun loving and resourceful these kids can be.

FIFTH-GRADE SOCIAL TRAITS

Fifth-graders are generally upbeat and still enjoy the company of family, yet they sometimes get mouthy as they try to sort through feelings. The first time your child shouts "You just don't get it!" and stomps off, you'll wonder what happened to that sweet kid you knew yesterday.

Fragile Fifth-Graders

Ten- and 11-year-olds' progressively pruned neural pathways define them as individuals, and their increased ability for mental processing makes them acutely attuned to how others—or how they *think* others—perceive them. Clinical psychologist Bruce Dolin (2009b), author of *The Privilege of Parenting*, says, "I've seen many [10-year-old] kids develop a deepening sense of angst, alienation and despair. . . . And while we expect these feelings to emerge along with body hair, they are often subtle but overlooked in the years preceding puberty."

As "fitting in" with their peers becomes even more important than it was in fourth grade, your child may struggle with peer pressure, cliques, jealousy, and bullying. Children can become melancholy, anxious, and withdrawn.

Dr. Dolin (2009b) points out,

Given that all kids feel "different" to some extent and now that their self-concept is paired with a more powerful imagination (which can conjure awful scenarios of misery all the more vividly), they can suddenly seem very moody, disturbed, and more remote around this age. . . .

And since one of the hallmarks of angst and alienation is feeling alone and like no one truly understands us . . . we serve our ten-year-olds by deepening our compassion for how truly and deeply they may feel their human condition.

Collaboration

Although the process can get rocky, fifth-graders tend to thrive when working in groups—brainstorming ideas and putting their heads together to figure out an issue or create something. They're also good at memorizing facts and using them for higher-level quests, such as applying logic to solve mysteries or problems.

By resolving conflicts doing structured projects with peers, kids can improve their skills to deal with dicey social situations at recess or the lunch table.

Your Relationship

You can't shield fifth-graders from the need to find a place in their peer group, but you can provide an attentive ear, lots of hugs, and advice, pointing out your child's strengths to bolster a fragile ego.

Another way you can help is to engage in community service together. Your child's empathy and understanding are growing. Feeling a part of a wider world and making a positive contribution go a long way toward building confidence and learning effective ways to interact with people.

A Strange View of Expertise

You should probably know that kids this age find "experts" in the darndest places. The Scout leader knows everything about making spaghetti. The soccer coach is the world's authority on nutrition. A friend's mother knows more about colds, flu, and strep throat than the family doctor.

No need to argue, and please don't tease for flawed logic. In fact, discrediting one of these heroes may not only hurt feelings but also weaken your fifth-grader's opinion of you. Necessary truths will come out—maybe in an unrelated conversation with you later.

That being said, if your child comes home with a plan to eat a couple of beetles to get rid of a common cold, instead of refuting such sage advice, research together online for an effective alternative to crunchy insects.

Perception and Communication

You may find stinky clothes stuffed in the closet or shoved under the bed when you ask your child to clean his bedroom. Try not to get upset. If kids this age don't see the mess, it doesn't exist. In their minds, they've done what was asked of them. Your fifth-grader may seem mature due to all that myelin speeding up neural pathways, but 10- and 11-year-olds don't think like adults.

Discuss the benefits of having clean clothes to wear and a better-smelling room. Maybe have a race to see who can clean up faster: your child by cramming dirty clothes in obscure corners or you by tossing them in the bathroom hamper. Even if you lose by a second or two, giggling over such a silly competition will motivate your child to use the hamper more often.

Try asking open-ended questions and be patient with short answers. A response like "I dunno" doesn't mean your fifth-grader no longer trusts you or wants to talk to you. Your child may not have thought about what you asked or may not know how to articulate a feeling. Similarly, a promise to finish homework before playing video games may be an honest declaration—that goes right out of his head an hour later.

Establish rules and be consistent with predetermined consequences, but keep communication amicable. For instance, if you think your fifth-grader hopped onto the computer before finishing his homework or if the skimpy amount of time spent makes you suspicious about the quality of work, you might say, "Oh, cool. You finished your history project already. Can I see it?"

And don't take no for an answer.

In this example, if you were to find unfinished or substandard work, here is a positive way to handle the situation: "Well . . ." Sigh. "You know what this means . . ." Wait for your child to tell you the consequence for the infraction. If he doesn't, state it for him: "Turn off the computer. You'll get to play on it again in a week." If he starts to argue, say something like "Sorry. The rule hasn't changed since the last time this happened. You'll get your privileges back in a week."

It may not seem so in the moment, but children this age appreciate consistent rules. Knowing what's expected of them offers security. Avoid yelling, nagging, or name-calling. Remember, until children reach about 11 years old, their frontal lobes don't process negative correction (Van Duijvenvoorde et al. 2008). And even if your child has turned 11, studies show that positive redirection is still more effective.

Psychologist Linda Sonna, author of *The Everything Tween Book*, says, "Being called an idiot by an adult has terrible implications, since adults are thought to know the truth about who the idiots of the world really are" (2003, 6).

Not that fifth-graders are impeccably honest, but they seem to more conscientiously tell the truth as their views of right and wrong and what's "fair" come into sharper focus. They like to explain things and can listen attentively, although sometimes they need to be reminded to stay with the speaker and not think about what they want to say next (but then, we all know adults like that, right?).

Family

Your 10- or 11-year-old may be trying at times, but this sensitive, precious being will engage you in interesting conversations and still enjoy doing things together. One of my favorite things about our kids when they were in fifth grade was how fun dinners became. Jokes got funnier and cleverer. Questions, answers, and reports of what happened during the day got more layered and philosophical as our daughters' ability to process abstract concepts became more adept.

Sometimes angst came to the dinner table, and after bouncing around a situation to get everyone's input, we had occasional emotional eruptions, but usually our fifth-grader left feeling better, with a plan for handling the issue. Three cheers for myelination!

Fifth-graders tend to love family projects, such as building a doghouse or planting a vegetable garden. They also like to contribute to the household—help prepare a meal or clean up the yard for company. A science project inspired by a question that came up in conversation may engage them for weeks.

Although your hugs may no longer be welcome in public, most kids in this age group appreciate affection when no one else is around, including snuggling on the couch to watch a movie or share in a good book.

If your child hasn't given gifts to others yet, fifth grade is a good year to start. You may get resistance at first, but kids this age get a sense of satisfaction from buying gifts with their own money or making presents for family members and friends. They feel grown up and capable, which builds confidence for weathering future social storms.

5 SOCIAL LIFE HACKS TO HELP
YOUR FIFTH-GRADER RELATE WELL TO OTHERS

1. **Teach your child to be a good listener.** Remember "The Social Magic Bullet" (page 182)? Model asking your child questions, listening to responses, nodding, and repeating to check understanding. Role-play actual situations as well as hypothetical ones that include someone saying or doing something mean. Brainstorm disarming questions with your child and practice actively listening to responses. People seldom feel heard, and when someone truly listens, it feels like a gift. This skill will help your fifth-grader not only develop empathy for others, but also greatly improve his relationships and quite possibly turn his rivals into friends.

2. **Advise your child not to "give away his power."** If kids tease him, empathize by sharing a similar story of when you were his age. Then practice rolling your eyes, puffing air between your lips, and saying, "Whatever." Showing bullies they can't take your power (even if you hurt on the *inside*) takes the fun out of teasing.

3. **Do something fun.** If your fifth-grader comes home wounded, whether or not she'll talk about it, bake cookies together, ride bikes, or kick around the soccer ball. Reinforce that she has a safe place to turn when life gets unpleasant.

4. **Provide a snuggle opportunity.** Watch a movie on the couch together, read a book, or take a nap. Your child may seem bigger, but

10- and 11-year-olds generally appreciate safe physical contact, especially when upset—even boys if you're subtle about it.

5. **Encourage your fifth-grader to help a younger cousin, sibling,
   or friend.** Reading picture books aloud to little kids or helping with
   math problems can provide a much-needed ego lift as well as a way
   to practice skills that may have gotten a little rusty.

THE REAL DEAL

From Tragedy to Triumph

Lahnay kept to herself, listening, watching, and seldom raising her
hand in her fifth-grade class. Why did her dad have to take a new job?
A month into the school year, and she still hadn't made any friends.

At recess, Lahnay settled on a bench outside the classroom to read
when a boy flicked her book. "Hey, Brillo pad," he teased as he passed
to get to the playground.

"Brillo pad," repeated a girl. "That's what we should call you."

Lahnay's curly hair was soft and brown, not wiry and prickly. New
schools sucked.

When Lahnay got home, she pulled her library book from her backpack, sat at the kitchen table, and read with her forehead propped in
her hand. Dana, the family track star, in her junior year of high school,
pranced in to grab a banana and asked, "What's wrong, squirt?"

"Nothing." Lahnay winced at the fib, but Dana would tell her to
quit being so shy and stand up for herself.

"I'm going on a short run, just a couple of miles," Dana said. "You
want to come?"

"Yeah!" Lahnay jumped from her chair. Dana hardly ever invited
her to go places. "Lemme get my shoes."

On the dirt trail past the high school, leaves crunched underfoot
as Lahnay struggled to keep up with Dana's longer strides. The damp,
cold air felt heavy in her lungs. She wanted to stop and walk to catch

her breath, but if she did that, Dana might not ever ask her come along again.

"You know you're a great kid, right?" Dana said into the silence, not sounding the least bit winded. "You're smart and arty, way more creative than the rest of us."

"Thanks," Lahnay replied on a pant.

When the girls got home, spaghetti and salad waited on the table. Lahnay felt better after the jog with her sister. Still, she went to bed that night dreading another day of fifth grade.

The next morning, Lahnay tried to get out of bed, but she couldn't move. Her legs lay on the mattress like lifeless blobs, and pain sliced through her hips. Her heart raced as she grabbed her right thigh with both hands to push her leg over the side, and the momentum sent her body crashing onto the hardwood floor. Her pelvis burned white-hot. Struggling to catch her breath, she rolled onto her belly. Her cry for help came out little more than a whimper. The floor chafed her forearms as she dragged her dead legs to her parents' room in an army crawl.

"Mom!" she cried. "My legs won't work."

It took a little convincing, but once her parents realized Lahnay's legs truly couldn't hold her weight, her dad scooped her up, loaded her into the station wagon, and took off to the emergency room. Shortly after they arrived, Lahnay found herself in a hospital bed in the pediatric wing. Fever seemed to boil her from the inside out, and no amount of blood tests, examinations, or consults with physicians solved the mystery of her symptoms.

The sterile white walls seemed to close around her when Lahnay's mother left the hospital for the evening. She cried herself to sleep and dreamed of dancing and playing. Throughout the night, nurses took vital signs, jolting her awake to the crushing reality that she might never walk again. Finally, after 10 days of trial and error, her doctor managed to regulate her temperature and the pain, but her legs were still useless.

About that time, Lahnay received a manila envelope full of colorful construction-paper cards made by the kids in her class. Their funny pictures and sweet "get well" wishes made her laugh through tears.

The boy who'd teased her the most sent her a promise to be nice to her when she came back to school as well as a pair a "new legs" cut from peach paper.

Two weeks after she'd awakened paralyzed, the hospital released her to go home in a wheelchair. When she returned to school, the kids greeted her and fought over who got to wheel her up the ramp to the classroom. People talked to her without teasing, and for the first time, she felt a part of the group. But the change came from Lahnay too. While isolated in that hospital room, she'd come to realize that she hadn't made it easy for people to get to know her, so she purposely became friendlier.

One day, Angela, barely an acquaintance, asked her, "Can I roll you to lunch?"

"Yeah, thanks," Lahnay replied, amazed. "That'd be great."

Within a few days, Lahnay and Angela spent all their recesses and lunch periods together. They did homework, ate dinner, and watched movies at each other's houses. Other girls started joining them at recess, and they modified games like hopscotch, letting Lahnay roll into the squares in her wheelchair, so she could play too.

Though her social life improved, a month after she'd come home, Lahnay's fever spiked again. She ended up back in the hospital, and the doctor worried the mysterious infection or syndrome was spreading. He talked to her parents about amputating her legs to save her life. The image of stumps hanging off the edge of her wheelchair made Lahnay dizzy.

When her fever broke two days later, the doctor came into her room with a spring in his step. "I ordered another blood test," the doctor told Lahnay and her mom. "I read something in a journal, and I may have an idea."

In a couple of hours, he returned to her bedside with a wide grin. "It's osteomyelitis," he said. "You must have gotten scratched by someone who was infected. The bacteria that's been eating away at your bone marrow probably lay dormant for years—until you pumped up your heart rate so high on that run with your sister."

For the first time, Lahnay felt hopeful. "So, you won't have to cut off my legs?"

"Nope. We're going to give you strong antibiotics for 10 days to kill the infection and a special diet to help your bones reproduce the marrow you lost. You should be out of that wheelchair within the next couple of weeks."

Lahnay stood on her own at the dinner table less than a week later. Her whole family cried, happy that her legs were getting stronger—and that their frequent days eating catfish and brussels sprouts were numbered. She conscientiously took her pills, ate lots of plain yogurt, salad, and vegetables without complaint, and practiced wobbly walking until she got strong enough to stride into her classroom without help.

Her classmates erupted in whoops and applause. Never would she have guessed these fifth-graders could be so nice.

Angela talked her into practicing to compete in the 100-yard dash at Fifth-Grade Field Day at the end of the school year. When the big day came, Lahnay lined up with five other girls. The cap gun cracked the air and Lahnay took off. To her surprise, her whole class sprinted after her cheering, "You can do it, Lahnay! Go! Go!"

She crossed the finish line last, but Cheryl, the girl who came in first, gave Lahnay her blue ribbon and said, "You're the winner."

Lahnay had never felt so loved and couldn't hang onto the tears any longer. A bunch of girls in her class all hugged her at once, and she noticed some of them crying too.

Cell Phones in Fifth Grade

If you've decided this is the year your child will have access to a cell phone, set some ground rules to make it a happy family experience (see "5 Ways to Make Cell Phones a Help, Not a Headache" on page 230).

Though your fifth-grader will probably vie for a smartphone, keep in mind that a 10- or 11-year-old doesn't need the internet to communicate changed plans or to call for help.

Your child may be more emotional than in the past due to progressive myelination of neural pathways, brain chemistry, and social challenges with peers, so why give her the opportunity to get mired in social media on her cell phone? If you choose to get your fifth-grader a phone with the capacity to do more than call or text, please set filters in the settings.

Better yet, make the cell phone a valuable tool in your family by avoiding common problems. Purchase a parenting app, such as Net Nanny, MMGuardian, or Norton Family Parental Control to monitor and regulate your child's use. Parenting apps range from $20 to $50 a year, a small price to pay to keep track of how much and when the cell phone gets used for things apart from communicating with you, and to ensure your child's safety from unsavory websites or cyberbullying. MMGuardian even has an inexpensive one-time payment offer for permanent use. If you set cell phone boundaries from the beginning, your family will enjoy a much happier household!

FIFTH-GRADE ACADEMICS

In fifth grade, your child will be preparing for the transition to middle school. This year, kids need to take control of their education—get organized, be responsible for their learning, and seek help when they need it. Managing short- and long-term assignments will intensify and reading to learn will be in full swing.

Your child will be expected to write essays dissecting stories and articles in terms of theme, main ideas, components, and meaning. Fractions, decimals, and operations will all expand to higher place values. Skills learned in math and language arts will be applied to science projects on things like changes in matter, weather, habitats, and food chains. In social studies, your child will likely write a report on a state (other than your own) that discusses population, economics, and cultures and includes graphs, diagrams, and photos.

Regardless of whether your state began standardized exams in fourth grade for science and physical fitness, your fifth-grader will likely be given tests in these areas this year. The thing is, while academic expectations ratchet up, peers become even more important, and outside activities—sports, Scouts, music, or art lessons—compete for kids' time.

How You Can Help

Using self-discipline to keep up with schoolwork will take more energy than ever before. Your fifth-grader will probably need your support.

Reinforcing good work habits now will save painful lessons in middle school—which will be here before you know it. Revisit page 246 in chapter 7 for the "4 Steps to Meeting Upper-Grade Homework Demands" and update last year's system with your child to incorporate fifth-grade needs and current extracurricular schedules. The more consistent the time, place, and routine for working on assignments, the less stress and better results your fifth-grader will enjoy.

Trouble Focusing on Homework

If your child struggles with distraction and motivation while doing homework, pull out the timer and experiment. For example, agree upon an amount of time to work without interruption, maybe 15 minutes, set the timer, and have your child begin work. When the buzzer goes off, she can take three minutes to go to the bathroom, get a drink of water, do jumping jacks, jog in place, or dance to the song of her choice. Then have her set the timer for another 15 minutes. Repeat the process until the homework is finished.

Whether your child is ready to lengthen work periods from 15 to 20 or 30 minutes on the same day you start using the timer, the following week, or in three months, let her be the one to decide. Allowing your fifth-grader to tailor a system for herself will instill personal responsibility for learning and completing tasks.

Note: For more help, review "4 Great Tools to Help Upper-Graders Focus" on page 243.

When Distraction Becomes More Than a Focusing Problem

Sometimes fifth-graders get so caught up in other things—friends, a hobby, or a sport—they lose interest in learning. If your child's behavior changes—he stops doing work or does the minimum to get by—simply hoping your child will "grow out of it" can set him up for a slew of problems in middle and high school. Fifth-graders are considerably more malleable than middle-schoolers, and parents can encourage kids' passions to reignite an interest in learning.

HOW TO REKINDLE YOUR FIFTH-GRADER'S INTEREST IN SCHOOLWORK

Enlist the teacher in reigniting your child's motivation for doing well in school. Even if she can't dedicate much time, her support will be helpful in getting your son or daughter to participate in the process. Ask the teacher to meet with you and your upper-grader to discuss ways to involve music, sports, friends, or whatever your child loves across the curriculum.

If your fifth-grader is into baseball, the plan may look like this:

- He does his state report on New York, home of the Yankees, where his idol, Babe Ruth, played most of his career.

- A science group investigates the physics of hitting a baseball.

- With help from home, he applies decimal, fraction, percentage, ratio, and graphing skills to baseball players' batting averages and other statistics.

- He explores area and volume in terms of the dimensions of a regulation baseball diamond and compares teams' stadium volumes, both measurement and seating capacities.

- Your child does an online search to find books on baseball or players and commits to reading titles approved by the teacher.

Your child's teacher will no doubt want to help rekindle your child's interest in schoolwork. As a practical matter, however, with so many students in the classroom, the teacher can do only so much. You will help your child the most by participating in this effort and augmenting the plan at home if necessary.

Health Education

Your baby is growing up. Education about the physical changes people undergo during puberty often begins in fourth grade and continues in fifth (some programs don't start until fifth grade). Frankly, most programs are a bit hokey, using silly games or songs to get points across, and they deserve the kids' jokes. Still, the important information gets communicated: your body is changing (or it will soon), here's what's going on, it's nothing to be afraid of, treat yourself and others with respect.

Some schools separate genders and some do co-ed presentations. The material is presented clinically and in a professional manner, so unless you have religious objections, sign the permission slip and let your fifth-grader participate. Getting separated from the other kids is far more embarrassing than sitting through the program. If you decide not to allow your child to participate or you're homeschooling, make sure to provide the information in a safe environment where your child can ask questions.

FIFTH-GRADE ACADEMIC SKILLS

Language Arts

- Understand and use root words, prefixes, and suffixes to decode unfamiliar words.

- Use context to check understanding and reread as necessary.

- Summarize stories, poems, and articles and understand the five stages of plot.

- Explain themes or main ideas using quotes from the text.

- Determine the meaning of figurative language (e.g., metaphors, idioms, and similes) in a text.

- Compare stories in the same genre (e.g., mystery or fantasy) and articles regarding the same subject.

- Describe how the narrator's point of view influences a story or article.

- Explain people's interactions in historical and scientific events, citing evidence from text.

- Learn and use fifth-grade vocabulary relevant to science and social studies units.

- Show how an author supports a premise by including reasons, examples, and evidence.

- Use multiple sources to locate an answer to a question or solve a problem.

- Research several sources to assemble oral and written reports on a topic.

- Write opinion pieces supporting a point of view with reasons and information.

- Write organized informative essays, supported by authoritative sources on the subject.

- Write fiction and nonfiction narratives with descriptive language and a clear order of events.

- Demonstrate a command of grammar conventions.

- Plan, revise, and edit writing with feedback from adults and peers and self-evaluate.

- Use technology to produce and publish writing and collaborate with others.

- Build on others' ideas in discussions, offering facts from research and personal thoughts.

- Include multimedia and visual displays in presentations when appropriate.

Mathematics

- Add, subtract, multiply, and divide fractions and mixed numbers; compare fractions using <, >, = symbols; and use these concepts to solve word problems.

- Understand decimals to the 1,000ths place; compare using <, >, = symbols; use these concepts to solve real-world problems; and add, subtract, multiply, and divide to the 100ths place.

- Explain the pattern of 0s and multiply using powers of 10.

- Round whole numbers and decimals to any place.

- Multiply multi-digit whole numbers.

- Find quotients for up to four-digit dividends and two-digit divisors.

- Use parentheses, brackets, or braces in numeric expressions, and evaluate expressions.

- Convert measurement units (e.g., centimeters to meters, inches to feet, and centimeters to feet).

- Experiment with probability (e.g., predicting the outcome of a coin toss or dice roll).

- Organize statistical information (e.g., a line plot for a data set) and uses the information to solve problems.

- Graph points on a coordinate plane to solve real-world and mathematical problems.

- Understand the volume of solid figures and solve for cubic units.

- Classify two-dimensional figures into categories based on properties and find the area.

To find out what your child will be expected to master in your area, type into a search engine the name of your state and "education standards K–12." Skills may appear in a different grade in your state's standards.

165 FIFTH-GRADE HIGH-FREQUENCY WORDS
FOR BETTER READING AND WRITING

It's time to get out the Scrabble tiles again or play Hangman to ensure your child can read and spell this next set of high-frequency words. Your fifth-grader will be expected to have a greater command of written language, so there are more words in this chapter. Adding them to your fifth-grader's toolbox will make assignments easier and more fun. You'll also want to review the lists in previous chapters.

able	according	action	addition	against
age	ago	ahead	alone	already
although	amount	another	answer	attention
away	beautiful	become	began	below
beside	beyond	bird	black	blood
board	body	bought	brother	brown
center	century	certain	chance	check
child	choose	city	column	common
compare	complete	correct	decide	describe
different	direction	distance	down	drive
during	each	early	edge	equal
example	experiment	family	famous	farther
few	figure	finally	floor	follow
forward	found	game	general	girl
gone	government	great	group	happen(ed)
hear(d)	heart	history	hour	however
hundred	idea	important	include	information
instead	knowledge	language	large	least
leave	length	machine	material	method
might	movement	music	nature	necessary
notice	object	office	often	opposite

pattern	picture	piece	point	practice
probably	process	product	reach	ready
region	return	road	room	rule
school	science	section	sense	sentence
similar	straight	surface	system	talk
teacher	temperature	therefore	though	throughout
toward	travel	trouble	true	turn(ed)
twice	type	understand	United States	unless
until	usually	value	various	village
visit	voice	wait	watch	water
whether	which	while	whose	woman
women	world	write	yellow	you're

Note: If your child finds learning high-frequency words particularly helpful, especially for a student who reads via sight words rather than phonetically, visit the K12 Reader website for Fry's top 1,000 high-frequency words, broken into lists of 20.

5 FUN GAMES TO SUPPORT FIFTH-GRADE LEARNING

1. **Guess Who?** Take turns with your child describing characters in books or movies, political figures, family members, or kids in the Scout troop or on a sports team. State the category (e.g., book, movie, troop), and see how many clues it takes to arrive at the right person. This game is fun to play as you're driving or waiting in line, and it improves observation skills for science. You will also notice your child including more details in essays.

2. **Mad Libs.** Get the Mad Libs phone app for a dose of hilarity anytime anywhere. Mad Libs are stories with words left out for players to fill

in. The game asks for parts of speech (e.g., noun, adjective, verb, adverb), which clarifies grammar for kids and improves their writing. Best of all, the stories with random words are super funny.

3. **Idioms.** Install an idioms app on your phone to play with goofy sayings we take for granted, like "Quit pulling my leg" or "She has eyes in the back of her head." Then you and your child can "try your hand" at making up a few of your own. Playing with idioms can improve reading and writing and may stimulate areas of the brain used in problem-solving. Idiom play especially helps families learning English.

4. **Simile game.** Fifth-graders are expected to develop descriptive writing skills. Take turns making up comparisons using "like" or "as," the sillier the better, to help your child incorporate similes for clarity in her writing. Examples: Quiet as a burglar, she tiptoed across the carpet. His cheeks stuck out like bloated bubbles.

5. **"50 States Songs for Kids" video on YouTube.** In social studies this year, your child will learn about American history, the states, and their capitals. Check out this and other silly songs sung to great graphics for easy memorization.

12 GREAT SERIES TO KEEP FIFTH-GRADERS READING

Lots of wonderful novels and nonfiction books leveled for fifth grade aren't part of a series, but when kids find a book they enjoy, they'll go looking for more. These are also fun titles if you're a lucky parent who has a 10- or 11-year-old who still enjoys reading with you.

1. Tales of Magic series (7 books) by Edward Eager—characters wish into a magic book that fills in the pages of their lives with experiences that come true and get out of control.

2. Sammy Keyes series (18 books) by Wendelin Van Draanen—gutsy girl gets in trouble and finds her way out.

3. Percy Jackson and the Olympians series (5 books) by Rick Riordan—savvy kid finds out he's related to gods on Mount Olympus. Lots of beings threaten the world—and him.

4. Chronicles of Narnia series (7 books) by C. S. Lewis—kids discover a secret world.

5. Anne of Green Gables series (8 books) by L. M. Montgomery—orphan girl and her adoptive family.

6. Artemis Fowl series (8 books) by Eoin Colfer—12-year-old criminal mastermind. Colfer describes the series as "*Die Hard* with fairies."

7. Ranger's Apprentice series (12 books) by John Flanagan—boy finds himself on adventures to save the kingdom of Araluen from an evil lord bent on destroying it.

8. City of Ember series (4 books) by Jeanne DuPrau—teens in a subterranean city look for a way to return to Earth's surface to save their people.

9. Mysterious Benedict Society series (4 books) by Trenton Lee Stewart—intelligent kids must infiltrate a dangerous organization to solve a mystery with global ramifications.

10. A. I. Gang series (3 books) by Bruce Coville—smart, wacky kids solve problems created by unstable adults.

11. My Side of the Mountain series (5 books) by Jean Craighead George—a boy makes his way on his own in the wilderness and trains a peregrine falcon.

12. Brotherband Chronicles series (6 books) by John Flanagan—survivalist action series, a spin-off of the Ranger's Apprentice series.

5 FUN ACTIVITIES TO KICK-START FIFTH-GRADE MATH

1. **Let's Party!** You can involve your child in real-life math when planning birthday, scouting, or sports team parties. By fifth grade, he's accumulated a lot of tools, and *using* math concepts gives them meaning. Have your child estimate how many guests based on the possible number and current RSVPs. Collaborate on setting a budget, creating shopping lists, and deciding how much to buy (he'll use multiplication, addition, and problem-solving). Put your child in charge of collecting receipts to figure the total cost (he'll use addition and decimals).

2. **Crazy Poker.** Together with your child, come up with huge, uneven amounts to assign to the chips. For example, red chips could be worth $1,052.55, blue $255.33, and white $98.75. At the end of each hand, have your child estimate the amount of "money" she has in chips and then calculate the exact amount to see how close she came with her guess.

3. **Measuring Tape Madness.** Challenge your child to measure the dining room table, find the area in square inches, and figure out how many plates would fit side by side on the table. Then have him find the volume of the couch, measuring length x width x height in cubic inches. (*Note:* Your child must solve for two volumes and add them together: one for the base, where people sit, and one for the back support.) Fractions are big in fifth grade, so encourage exact measurements. Use these activities as a springboard for others as they come up—measuring to install a window covering, for example.

4. **Battleship.** Do you remember strategically placing plastic ships on a grid when you were a kid and trying to sink the other player's ships by guessing their coordinates? Your child will do a lot of graphing, plotting coordinates, and interpreting data in fifth grade, and playing Battleship is a fun way to sharpen these skills.

5. **Online math games.** If you're slammed with work and life and can't squeeze in time to play with your fifth-grader right now, websites like mathplayground.com provide fun games for each grade level (type "math games for fifth grade" into a search engine for lots more options). Is he behind in math—or ahead? No problem. Clicking on a grade lower or higher will give your child hours of practice or enrichment. Remember, though, experts say no more than two hours of screen time a day for kids (Jary 2018).

FIFTH-GRADE OUTSIDE THE NORM

Kids who don't fit into the bulk of the bell curve sometimes stop caring about schoolwork in fifth grade. Some get tired of catching on quickly to new concepts and having to sit through the remainder of the lesson with the rest of the class. Occasionally, these kids get into mischief, and parents get calls from the teacher or administration. Other kids decide they're done struggling with learning disabilities, working longer and harder than their peers to understand the same material.

If your "outlier's" interest wanes, talk to the teacher and refer to "How to Rekindle Your Fifth-Grader's Interest in Schoolwork" (page 286). Be sure to check with the district as well for additional programs or clubs that might motivate your child.

Also, look for opportunities at the local community center, parks and recreation department, museum, or nature center. Private organizations in your area may also offer intriguing programs. Pick up a regional magazine or search online for activities nearby that might spark your child's curiosity and incorporate skills he's learning in class.

FIFTH-GRADE CARE AND FEEDING

Due to social pressures and increased academic expectations, fifth-graders can be prone to bouts of the blues. Take a look at "15 Ways to Get Your Fifth-Grader Out of a Funk—or Prevent One" on pages 297–300. Lots of things on the list are good reminders for raising happy, healthy fifth-graders anyway, but some of them may prepare you for situations you didn't anticipate.

Sometimes kids this age are accused of acting "hormonal," but their emotional nature stems more from inconsistencies in myelination of neural pathways (Johnson et al. 2009). For an irritable or withdrawn fifth-grader, chances are that upping sleep, nutrition, and hydration, having heart-to-heart talks, and getting in free playtime will improve your child's outlook.

But if you don't see much improvement after a week or two of taking steps to raise your child's spirits, make an appointment to see the pediatrician. Prolonged sadness or crabbiness can be caused by hypothyroidism or other medical conditions (Spiro, n.d.). If your doctor can't find a physical problem, you may get a referral to a mental health professional for an evaluation (McInerny 2013).

The Federal Drug Administration cautions that if your child lacks energy and enthusiasm and becomes withdrawn, irritable, sulky, and possibly sad, anxious, or restless, these may be signs of depression (FDA 2014). Other symptoms include no longer enjoying favorite activities, gaining or losing weight, sleeping too much or too little, having frequent head or stomachaches, experiencing feelings of worthlessness, and not caring about the future (McInerny 2013).

The Anxiety and Depression Association of America (n.d.) reports: "As many as 2 to 3 percent of children ages 6 to 12 . . . may have serious depression." Getting your child thoroughly assessed is key since depression indicators can also be caused by anxiety, a learning disability, or other factors (Spiro, n.d.).

Ideally, your 10- or 11-year-old will sail through fifth grade on an even keel. In case your child is like most kids, though, the "15 Ways to Get Your Fifth-Grader Out of a Funk—or Prevent One" on the next page will give you tools and reminders to gracefully deal with ups and downs. The tips will also set up your family for the exciting, challenging middle school years.

15 WAYS TO GET YOUR FIFTH-GRADER
OUT OF A FUNK—OR PREVENT ONE

1. **Acknowledge your child's behavior and ask open-ended questions.** Sit next to him on the bed and say something like "You look kind of sad lately. What's going on?"

2. **Be patient and persistent.** If he says, "Nothing. I'm fine," gently call him out: "Honey, I've known you a long time. Something's bothering you. I love you, and I want to help."

3. **Resist interruptions.** When your child begins to talk, do everything in your power not to get interrupted—either by other family members or by your own thoughts. Once there's a break in the conversation, you may have trouble getting him to open up again.

4. **Ask about bullying and grief.** Maybe he had a falling out with a friend or lost at a sport or academic competition. Maybe someone called him names. Help your child process the problem and figure out what to do about it.

5. **Be prepared to be part of the problem.** Kids, heck, humans are sensitive. If your home life has undergone turmoil—arguments within earshot, alcohol or other substances, separation or divorce, job loss—your child shares in the family stress.

6. **Reduce pressure.** This may require talking to the teacher about modifying assignments, reducing obligations in the family schedule, working with siblings to be kinder, and looking at your own behavior to see if you can make the household a more relaxing environment.

7. **Do a diet check.** Fifth-graders are growing (whether we can see it or not). They crave chips, pizza, pasta, and cookies for quick calorie dumps to accommodate the extra energy their bodies need. The trouble is, processed carbohydrates don't provide the nutrients kids

require. *What we put into our bodies has a lot more influence on our moods than most people realize.*

Amp up the fruits, vegetables, and lean proteins while limiting sugar and processed carbohydrates. Research nutrition together so your child understands *why* his body needs vitamins, minerals, protein, and healthy fats. Show him how eating wholesome foods will make his body work more efficiently to help him think better and feel better too. Then go grocery shopping, and let your child choose nutritious items to stock the fridge. You might be amazed at your child's new outlook!

8. **Make sure your child is hydrated.** Taking regular swigs from a water bottle may vastly improve your child's attitude. Drinking water, although simple, produces big dividends. Researchers for the Department of Nutrition at the University of North Carolina found that "mild levels of dehydration can produce disruptions in mood and cognitive functioning . . . [including] concentration, alertness and short-term memory in children" (Popkin et al. 2010).

   Our bodies need water for cooling the brain, maintaining body temperature, dispersing oxygen and nutrients to cells, and eliminating waste. In short, getting enough water is an easy way to improve thinking and feeling.

9. **Work out how to get adequate sleep.** Although individuals vary, 10- and 11-year-olds generally need 9 to 11 hours of sleep *nightly*. Their brains need delta waves to continue connecting, coordinating, and insulating neural pathways as well as to orchestrate their physical growth. If your child isn't getting enough snooze time, adjust schedules, change the bedtime routine, or recreate one. "If a person is deprived of sleep, it can lead to tremendous emotional problems," says Dr. Steven Feinsilver, director of the Center for Sleep Medicine at Icahn School of Medicine at Mount Sinai in New York City (Miller 2015).

10. **Allow for unstructured, unsupervised playtime.** Playing outside or making forts inside on rainy or snowy days can do a world of good for kids (screen time doesn't count—it's the potato chips of free time).

    Dr. Peter Gray (2010), professor at Boston College and author of *Free to Learn*, says it best:

    > By depriving children of opportunities to play on their own, away from direct adult supervision and control, we are depriving them of opportunities to learn how to take control of their own lives. We may think we are protecting them, but in fact we are diminishing their joy, diminishing their sense of self-control, preventing them from discovering and exploring the endeavors they would most love, and increasing the odds that they will suffer from anxiety, depression, and other disorders.

11. **Get your child moving.** Set your fifth-grader loose to run around outside: take a walk, ride bikes, or train for a 5K to support a charity. Indoor options: dance, go to the gym and lift weights, or do a kickboxing class. Scientists have found that exercise gets FNDC5 protein active in the hippocampus, which improves mood as well as overall wellness (Servick 2013). The US Department of Health and Human Services (2008, 15) recommends that kids get at least one hour of exercise *daily* for healthy growth, development, and future well-being as an adult.

12. **Give gentle praise for constructive, engaged behavior.** Remember, kids this age generally respond to positive feedback (Van Duijvenvoorde et al. 2008).

13. **Point out specifics about your child's strengths.** Instead of saying "You're a good artist," say something like "The way you shaded that tree looks so real!"

14. **Help your child relax with creative activities.** Writing in a journal, listening to calm music, and doing yoga (especially deep breathing) can significantly reduce stress.

15. **Break down tasks, schoolwork or otherwise, into smaller steps.** When projects seem overwhelming, help your child focus on one aspect at a time. Accomplishing small victories, one by one until an activity is completed, is much more manageable than looking at the whole venture at once.

Note: If your child's irritability or blues persist, make an appointment with your pediatrician.

Fifth-Graders' Teeth: A Quick Word

Your child is older now and quite capable of doing a good job flossing and brushing her teeth. Dental hygiene should be one thing you can leave to her without having to think about it. Still, her classmates will bring candy and chips to school, and they'll share boxes of Girl Scout cookies. Kids this age adore junk food. Casually checking up on your 10- or 11-year-old's technique and coaching when necessary may save a lot of future pain, heartache—and expense.

WHERE DO YOU SEE YOURSELF?

😖 Ms. Larz does her best to be a conscientious mom. Her son, Joe, begged her to get him a cell phone last year in fourth grade—after all, he argued, his friends had one, so he should get one too. She saw no reason to buy him a phone when her part-time job got her home minutes before the bus dropped Joe at the street corner. He didn't need to get into trouble playing games under the desk or posting pictures on Instagram. She knew her son.

During the summer, though, she and her husband separated. It had been a long time coming, but his move out of state was a shock. Joe had been devastated.

At the beginning of the school year, she gave in and bought her fifth-grader a phone to use only for specific purposes, but Joe's good at bending rules. On the plus side, his dad calls before bed most nights, which seems to have helped their son adjust to the new family arrangement. Frankly, she's the one having the most trouble—being a full-time mom *and* dad, not to mention expanding her job to a 40-hour week to make the bills.

Ms. Larz glances at the clock above her desk: 4:50. Joe's supposed to let her know when he gets home from school. He forgot to send a text again, that little squirt.

At least, she hopes he forgot, and he hasn't gotten himself stuck under the bed again—or worse.

She calls Joe and gets his voicemail. "He's fine," she reassures herself, but she rushes to get out the necessary emails, puts the papers on her desk into her "active" file in the bottom drawer, and gets up to leave at 4:57.

"You're leaving already?" It's that petty Janice in the next cubicle. She'll probably let the early exit slip to their boss, but Ms. Larz has to be sure Joe didn't get himself into some kind of trouble.

Driving the minivan a little too fast to get home, Ms. Larz passes the grocery store. Their empty pantry makes her think of "Old Mother Hubbard," but life keeps getting in the way of shopping.

The tires screech into the driveway. "Come on, come on," she coaxes the garage door, wondering if it always lifted this slowly. She leaps from the car and bursts into the kitchen. No Joe. He's supposed to be doing his homework at the table when she gets home.

"Joe?" she calls on the way through the living room and gets no answer. She's sure he's stuck again under the bed frame. That boy needs some exercise—and to start making healthy lunches again, the way he did in fourth grade, if she could just get to the darn store—and to eat dinners at home instead of out of a window. Come to think of it, her pants fit tighter too.

The trek to his bedroom at the end of the hall has Ms. Larz's heart pounding. She trips over his tennis shoes in the doorway and stops short when she sees him on his bed, thumbs tap, tap, tapping, staring at the screen on his phone.

"Joseph Drake Larz," she scolds, and he jumps, startled. "Didn't you hear me call you?"

"You mean on the phone?" His brown lashes flutter, and he rubs an eye with his fist like he's waking from a nap. "I thought if I answered it, I'd lose points."

"I *meant* calling your name in the house just now! You were so busy playing games on your phone—which you're not even allowed to do—you didn't text me when you got home from school *or* pick up when I called. I've been worried sick! We've talked about this." Ms. Larz stomps over the dirty clothes strewn on the floor and grabs the cell phone from Joe's hand.

"Mom!" He scuttles off the bed and tries to grab it from her. "It's only on pause. Let me save the game!"

"There is no game, buster." She yanks the cell out of his reach. "This phone's job is to make sure we can communicate, and since you don't seem to be able to use it for its purpose, you have no phone until further notice."

His chocolate eyes fill with tears. "But what about when Dad calls?"

"I'll answer your phone and tell him to call you on Skype." She knows how to lock Joe out of her laptop unless he's doing homework or talking to his dad.

"But his internet always cuts out."

"I'm sorry, Joe. You should have thought about that before you decided to break the cell phone rules again." She turns and starts to walk toward the door.

"No!" Joe screams in full panic and grabs her around the waist from behind. "I'll text you, I swear, and I won't play games on my phone." He sobs against her, dampening her blouse between her shoulder blades. "I don't want to miss Daddy. Please!"

Ms. Larz's anger drains like a flushed toilet as her little boy gulps air in short bursts at her back. Not for the first time, she wants to kick herself.

If only she'd taken the time to install one of those parental control apps so she could check his activity. She would have known he was playing a game instead of answering her call. They could have had a civil conversation before she limited his phone use. Instead, she caught him red-handed and reacted by cutting him off from his father.

She turns in his arms and holds him tight.

"I'll let you talk to your dad on your phone. That will be the one thing you can do with it." Ms. Larz kisses her son's dark curls. "Come on, let's go get a pizza."

"My tummy hurts," Jenny groans, rolling over in her bed.

How many stomachaches does that make this month? Mrs. Jackson thinks, putting a hand on her daughter's tepid forehead. "You don't have a fever, honey. Let's get a piece of toast in you and take you to school. We have an appointment this morning to talk to the teacher about your state report."

"Toast'll make me puke." Jenny puts the pillow over her messy blonde head. "I'm not going."

"Get up." Mrs. Jackson snatches Jenny's pillow and bumps her head on the hanging plant above her daughter's bed, one of the many all over the house.

"Nooo!" her daughter screams, and hides under the covers.

Mrs. Jackson rubs her scalp, scowling at Jenny, the mound under the rainbow comforter. At least Jenny stopped all that macramé and growing plants from clippings. The house looks like a jungle. And typical of kids, Jenny stopped watering them several weeks ago. They'd have a dead jungle if Mrs. Jackson hadn't taken over the chore.

She grabs the edge of the comforter and rips it from her daughter's upper body. "As it is, you won't get the achievement award this semester, and if you keep missing school, we'll never catch up. At this rate, you'll have to repeat fifth grade!"

"I don't care. I—" A gag interrupts. Then another one. Jenny hangs her head off the side of the bed, but there's nothing in her stomach. Dry heaves.

Mrs. Jackson sits at the foot of the twin bed and puts her face in her hands. "I guess I'll go talk to Mr. Putnam alone then." She notices the cell phone on the carpet, amid the crumpled jeans, and wonders if the problems started after she and her husband bought Jenny's phone.

Later, outside the fifth-grade classroom, Mrs. Jackson stares at the green door. A crisp breeze rattles her shoulders in her navy peacoat. She'd blamed the teacher for Jenny's poor grades this year. If Mr. Putnam made his class more interesting, Jenny would be doing better, she'd thought.

Then she volunteered to help with a science experiment where the kids mixed household items to cause chemical reactions. The groups made hypotheses and were thrilled at the foam bubbling out of their plastic bottles. They wrote equations and drew conclusions—except for Jenny, who sat off to the side.

No amount of cajoling would get Jenny to participate with the three other fifth-graders in her group. That night, Mrs. Jackson had to stand over her daughter to get her to finish the lab report that most students finished before the bell rang to go home.

Jenny used to enjoy school, she thought. *When will she snap out of this?*

Mrs. Jackson pokes her head into Jenny's classroom. "Good morning, Mr. Putnam." She walks beyond the clusters of desks, soon to be filled with students, and meets the teacher sitting at a kidney-shaped table, tapping a stylus on an e-tablet.

Mr. Putnam puts down his e-tablet and raises his brows. "Where's Jenny?"

"She woke up with another stomach bug, so I came in to get her things and ask the questions we had about her state report."

"Jenny's missed a lot of school this year." Mr. Putnam folds his hands on the table.

Mrs. Jackson exhales and sits across from the teacher. "I know. The blood tests came back negative for all the things Dr. Hernandez thought might be causing the stomach cramps and headaches." She pauses. Will he judge her if he knows the rest? "The doctor gave us the number of a shrink," she confesses, not knowing what else to do. "But Jenny's symptoms are real. She's not crazy."

The teacher leans back in his plastic chair with his hands in his lap. "I agree, and I bet the doctor does too. But Jenny isolates herself more and more—"

"This is a phase. She'll grow out of it, like she grew out of her thing for macramé."

The teacher smiles. "Jenny did macramé?"

Mrs. Jackson chuckles. "You should see our house and patio. Jenny's hung plants in her hemp creations everywhere. Lots of the plants, she grew herself from clippings."

Until I started making them too. Could it be my fault she stopped growing and hanging plants? But that doesn't make sense . . . does it?

Mr. Putnam's eyes widen. "People losing interest in something they enjoyed is a symptom of depression. I know because my son went through something similar in fifth grade. He withdrew from family and friends and stopped building airplane models." The teacher pauses and leans his forearms on the table. "It turned out our son had a chemical imbalance that a psychiatrist treated with medication and therapy. He helped him through his depression and also helped my wife and me improve our relationship with all three kids. Our whole family has gotten closer, and the doctor weaned our son off the meds last year in eighth grade."

"Did he start making model airplanes again?"

Mr. Putnam laughs. "He's set on becoming an aircraft engineer. The best thing we ever did was go see a child psychiatrist."

Mrs. Jackson dares to feel hopeful—for the first time in months.

😇 Austin Wu asks his parents on Wednesday if Justin can sleep over Friday night. Justin's parents have to go to a funeral Saturday morning, and Austin wants his friend—and the team's starting pitcher—to make it to their playoff game. Mr. and Mrs. Wu give their permission with two stipulations: first, their son will clue in his friend about the household rules, and second, the boys will be asleep by 10.

Austin agrees, but when everyone sits down to eat dinner on Friday, Justin brings his cell phone to the table. Austin sees his father scowl at the top of Justin's brown curly head as his friend texts under the table. "Um, Justin," Austin says, "I think you forgot your cell phone goes in the basket."

Mr. Wu nods approval to Austin.

"Uh-huh, just a minute," Justin says, continuing to tap the screen with both thumbs. A second later, he laughs, and his thumbs get going again.

Austin leans sideways toward his friend and whispers, "Dude, we're about to eat."

"Fine. I'm done." Justin puts the phone on the table next to his plate.

Austin nods toward the front door. "The basket, remember?"

Justin lifts a brow like, *Are you kidding me?*

He turns his head and winces at Mr. and Mrs. Wu's stares across the table, plates of steaming meat and vegetables in the center, waiting to be served. "Uh, sorry. I just had to . . ." Justin's voice trails off, and he jumps up from the table. "I'll be right back."

The Wu family sits quietly, waiting for his return, without the cell phone. "Would you like some broccoli beef?" Mrs. Wu asks as she hands Justin the platter of food.

The 11-year-old stares, confused, but he takes the dish with a tentative hand and spoons some food onto his plate. "You want some, dude?" Justin asks and hands off the platter to Austin.

Mixed vegetables and chicken have traveled around the table in the opposite direction, and Justin serves himself last. Austin smiles at the look of awe and satisfaction on his friend's face. Justin usually brags that he won't eat vegetables, but he's powering down Mrs. Wu's cooking. Who could blame him?

"So what did you do today?" Mr. Wu asks Austin, who described how his group in science measured the shadows of trees on the playground at different times.

Justin passes when Mr. Wu asks him about his day. Mrs. Wu, a pediatric nurse, tells a funny story about a kid who slipped through everyone's fingers, and they had to chase him down the hall to give him his shot. His dad complains that a coworker wants to change the specs on his design for the drainage ditch at the city park to save money.

Justin is the first member of what Mr. Wu calls "the clean plate club."

"Feel free to have seconds, Justin," Mrs. Wu says. "We want you to be full of energy for tomorrow's game." She winks at him, and Austin notices his friend stops chewing. Justin's whole body goes tense. Mrs. Wu must see it too and adds, "Although if you guys lose, we'll be done for the season and won't have to cart you all over the county." Austin's mom and dad laugh.

"You guys," Austin scolds and then looks at his friend. "They don't mean it."

Justin sighs and slumps on the back of his chair. "I wish Coach Rodriguez felt like that."

"You'll both do great," Mr. Wu says. "Now tonight, after dinner, we're making ice cream sundaes for dessert."

"Seriously?" Justin sits up in his chair.

"After you guys clear the table and put the dishes in the dishwasher," Mr. Wu says. "I set the table."

"Deal." Justin reaches diagonally across the table and shakes Austin's dad's hand.

"Oh, and you have to be in bed by 9 to read, lights out at 9:30," Mrs. Wu says.

"But, Mom," Austin whines, "you said we didn't have to go to bed until 10."

"We said you had to be *asleep* by 10. No one wants a sleepy pitcher or first baseman." She dabs her mouth with her napkin and puts it on her empty plate. "It's only 6:30. You guys have plenty of time for sloppy sundaes and to hang out afterwards." She scoots her chair from the table. "I'll tell you what. It's a special night. I'll help you clean up the kitchen."

* * *

Do you see glimpses of your parenting in any (or possibly all) of these scenarios? This "raising happy kids" thing doesn't seem so easy at times. By fifth grade, hopefully, you've instilled some good habits your children can apply to relationships with friends, such as how Austin handled Justin bringing a cell phone to the dinner table.

It can be tricky to figure out how to keep a hand near the wheel to keep your child from crashing, without pushing her out of the way to steer yourself. On the other hand, you won't want to let go altogether, fool yourself into thinking that kids are better off deciphering relationships all on their own. Wouldn't it be nice if there were a solid formula for how much involvement in your child's life is too much or too little? The thing is, every kid has different needs and traits, so a certain amount of trial and error is necessary.

The truth is, you *will* mess up sometimes, but that's the beauty of raising kids. If you continue to play together and listen to and respect one another, no one has to be perfect. You'll love each other despite your humanness.

CONCLUSION

Fifth-graders are fun loving, talkative, and energetic. At the same time, they can be sensitive folks. Emotional ups and downs take wider swings as kids battle insecurities with friends and doubts in their own abilities. Parents need to set consistent boundaries because clearly defined rules and consequences provide a sense of order in a seemingly chaotic world. Talking to your child politely, correcting disrespectful behavior in a calm manner with a predetermined consequence, will help maintain open communication, crucial in the middle school years.

In addition to providing predictable outcomes for behaviors, you'll want to ask questions and be an attentive listener and a thoughtful coach. This year will be particularly important for teaching and practicing good nutrition and hygiene. You'll have to police computer games and a cell phone (if you choose to provide one this year) and make sacrifices to create space for downtime and adequate sleep.

Though fifth-graders need independence, they also require attention and not necessarily when it's convenient. You may be exhausted from a tough day at work, yet your child needs you to help mentally process a drama that happened on the playground. Worse, you might sense something's wrong, but your 10- or 11-year-old won't cop to it.

You may feel she's holding out on you when really she doesn't know how to explain what's bothering her. Sometimes you'll probe for clues too soon, and she'll escape into her room. Other times you'll give her space before asking gentle leading questions to help bring a situation into focus and find out she's mad because she wanted you to help her before.

If you're a dad talking to a daughter, she may not think you'll understand. If you're a mom talking to a son, you may get a similar reaction. Fifth-graders are unpredictable, but they're also enthusiastic and full of wonder. Be kind to yourself and your child, and enjoy the ride.

✦ 9 ✦

READY FOR MIDDLE SCHOOL

Where did the time go? You've read together, played games, gone places, and tried new things. What your child loved to do one month, or year, fell away as experiences sparked new interests.

You learned how to capitalize on each stage of your child's brain growth. Things your child said and did that could have been annoying, even insufferable, became tolerable because you knew that neurons misfire as parts of the brain develop.

You have fed your child's self-confidence by consistently enforcing rules, helping with organization, assigning chores to create a sense of belonging and responsibility, and communicating openly. And you've enjoyed deep conversations, laughed and cried, and role-played to give your child tools to deal with the next uncomfortable social situation.

Adjusting your parenting according to your child's maturation has been an ongoing process that will continue throughout middle and high school. One of your greatest gifts will be the strong academic, social, and emotional base you've helped your child develop in the elementary school years. It's amazing how much you've learned on your child's journey too, isn't it?

You may be in for some emotional roller coaster rides in the future, but you'll enjoy watching how your child applies and builds upon the skills you've worked on together in these early years.

Every kid is different. Your child may struggle with academics but get along great with other people. Maybe adjusting to schoolwork has been easy, but managing social scrapes has been a continuing topic at your house. Whether your child is full of energy or a challenge to get off the couch, artistic or analytical, extroverted or introverted, be confident that you are *exactly* the parent your child needs to be a happy kid and, someday, become a well-adjusted adult.

Join the Brain Stages community!

Visit **theBrainStages.com** for:

- Free printables
- More research-based tips and activities
- Upcoming speaking events
- Brain Stages workshops

ACKNOWLEDGMENTS

Infinite thanks to Professor Frischknecht's children, particularly Amalie, who were instrumental in realizing Jackie's dream of getting brain research into parents' hands to help them raise successful children. It felt like your mom was writing along with me, sharing my laptop, whispering in my head, and guiding me throughout this journey. I am profoundly grateful for the opportunity to immortalize her legacy in *Brain Stages*.

Heartfelt thanks also go to Sandra Jonas of Sandra Jonas Publishing. Without her sharp instincts, willingness to think outside the box, attention to detail, and superior production, *Brain Stages* would still be my "someday" wish to support parents in having fun while raising happy kids in this complicated world. And I'd like to give a special nod to Jill Tappert for her wise, meticulous editing.

I'm grateful to my husband, Chuck, for coming up with the idea a decade ago for me to write a grade-by-grade book for parents. His steady encouragement and support through every phase of my transition, from teaching in the classroom to becoming a professional writer, has been nothing less than amazing. I'm so grateful to have been able to work at home during our girls' adolescent years. I love you so much, Charlie!

Big hugs to our daughters, Alia and Paige, for their cheerleading and constant support. You ladies are awesome. I'm such a lucky mom!

Warm appreciation goes to the many parents who read chapters and gave their feedback to make this book the best possible resource. Also, a huge thanks to those who allowed me to make videos of them playing games with their children to post on the *Brain Stages* website (thebrainstages.com). If a picture is worth a thousand words, how many is a video worth?

REFERENCES AND
FURTHER READING

The following list is divided into two sections: the "References" section contains the works cited in this book, and the "Further Reading" section contains additional works consulted during the research process.

REFERENCES

Adolphus, Katie, Clare L. Lawton, and Louise Dye. 2013. "The Effects of Breakfast on Behavior and Academic Performance in Children and Adolescents." *Frontiers in Human Neuroscience* 7 (August 8): art. 425. https://doi.org/10.3389/fnhum.2013.00425.

American Academy of Pediatrics, Committee on Nutrition and Council on Sports Medicine and Fitness. 2011. "Sports Drinks and Energy Drinks for Children and Adolescents: Are They Appropriate?" Reaffirmed July 2017. *Pediatrics* 127, no. 6 (June 2011). https://doi.org/10.1542/peds.2011-0965.

American Federation of Teachers. 2004. "Waiting Rarely Works: 'Late Bloomers' Usually Just Wilt." *American Educator*. Fall 2004. https://www.aft.org/periodical/american-educator/fall-2004/waiting-rarely-works-late-boomers-usually-just-wilt.

American Heart Association. 2011. "Understanding Childhood Obesity: 2011 Statistical Resource Book." Accessed October 31, 2016. https://www.heart.org/idc/groups/heart-public/@wcm/@fc/documents/downloadable/ucm_428180.pdf.

Anderson, Gabrielle E., Angela D. Whipple, and Shane R. Jimerson. 2003. "Grade Retention: Achievement and Mental Health Outcomes." CDL: Center for Development and Learning (website). January 1, 2003. http://www.cdl.org/articles/grade-retention-achievement-and-mental-health-outcomes/.

Anxiety and Depression Association of America. n.d. "Anxiety and Depression in Children." Anxiety and Depression Association of America (website). Accessed February 22, 2017. https://www.adaa.org/living-with-anxiety /children/anxiety-and-depression.

Barker, Shannon, Pamela Grayhem, Jerrod Koon, Jessica Perkins, Allison Whalen, and Bryan Raudenbush. 2003. "Improved Performance on Clerical Tasks Associated with Administration of Peppermint Odor." *Perceptual and Motor Skills* 97, no. 3 (December 1): 1007–10. https://doi.org /10.2466/pms.2003.97.3.1007.

Barkovich, A. James. 2000. "Concepts of Myelin and Myelination in Neuroradiology." *American Journal of Neuroradiology* 21, no. 6 (June 1): 1099–109. http://www.ajnr.org/content/21/6/1099.long.

Bedard, Kelly, and Elizabeth Dhuey. 2006. "The Persistence of Early Childhood Maturity: International Evidence of Long-Run Age Effects." *Quarterly Journal of Economics* 121, no. 4 (November 1): 1437–72. https:// doi.org/10.1093/qje/121.4.1437.

Bergland, Christopher. 2013. "Why Is Dancing So Good for Your Brain? Dancers Maximize Cognitive Function and Muscle Memory through Practice." *Psychology Today* (website). October 1, 2013. https://www .psychologytoday.com/blog/the-athletes-way/201310/why-is-dancing-so -good-your-brain.

Bergmann, Jeroen H. M., Joan Fei, David A. Green, Amir Hussain, and Newton Howard. 2017. "A Bayesian Assessment of Real-World Behavior during Multitasking." *Cognitive Computation* 9, no. 6 (August 12): 749–57. https://doi.org/10.1007/s12559-017-9500-6.

Birch, Leann, Jennifer S. Savage, and Alison Ventura. 2009. "Influences on the Development of Children's Eating Behaviours: From Infancy to Adolescence" *Canadian Journal of Dietetic Practice and Research*. Author manuscript PMC 2678872. May 7, 2009. Published in final edited form *Canadian Journal of Dietetic Practice and Research* 68, no. 1 (2007): s1–s56. https://www.ncbi.nlm.nih.gov/pmc/articles/PMC2678872/#R43.

Bradberry, Travis. 2014. "Multitasking Damages Your Brain and Career, New Studies Suggest." *Forbes* (website). October 8, 2014. https://www.forbes .com/sites/travisbradberry/2014/10/08/multitasking-damages-your-brain -and-career-new-studies-suggest/#3b3d32ba56ee.

Bui, Sa, Steven Craig, and Scott Imberman. 2012. "Poor Results for High Achievers: New Evidence on the Impact of Gifted and Talented Programs." *Education Next* 12, no. 1 (Winter): 70–76. http://educationnext .org/poor-results-for-high-achievers/.

Chaddock, Laura, Kirk I. Erickson, Ruchika Shaurya Prakash, Jennifer S. Kim, Michelle W. Voss, Matt VanPatter, Matthew B. Pontifex et al. 2010. "A

Neuroimaging Investigation of the Association between Aerobic Fitness, Hippocampal Volume, and Memory Performance in Preadolescent Children." *Brain Research* 1358 (October 28): 172–83. https://doi.org/10.1016/j.brainres.2010.08.049.

Chapman, Sandra Bond. 2014. "Do Brain Games Really Boost Brainpower? See If Crossword Puzzles, Sudoku, and Brain Training Websites Are Worth the Hype." *Psychology Today* (website). March 4, 2014. https://www.psychologytoday.com/blog/make-your-brain-smarter/201403/do-brain-games-really-boost-brainpower.

Chen, Xiaoli, May A. Beydoun, and Youfa Wang. 2008. "Is Sleep Duration Associated with Childhood Obesity? A Systematic Review and Meta-Analysis." *Obesity* 16, no. 2 (February): 265–74. https://doi.org/10.1038/oby.2007.63.

Children's Defense Fund. 2010. "Child Nutrition Fact Sheet." July 2010. http://www.childrensdefense.org/library/data/child-nutrition-factsheet.pdf.

Cooper, Harris, Jorgianne Civey Robinson, and Erika A. Patall. 2006. "Does Homework Improve Academic Achievement? A Synthesis of Research, 1987–2003." *Review of Educational Research* 76, no. 1 (Spring): 1–62. http://ueeval.ucr.edu/teaching_practices_inventory/CooperRobinsonPatall_2006.pdf.

Cradduck, Susan. 2016. In-person interview with author Patricia Wilkinson. July 26, 2016.

Degree Prospects. n.d. "Other Health Impairment." Special Education Guide (website). Accessed February 28, 2017. http://www.specialeducationguide.com/disability-profiles/other-health-impairment/.

Diamanti-Kandarakis, Evanthia, Jean-Pierre Bourguignon, Linda C. Giudice, Russ Hauser, Gail S. Prins, Ana M. Soto, R. Thomas Zoeller, and Andrea C. Gore. 2009. "Endocrine-Disrupting Chemicals: An Endocrine Society Scientific Statement." *Endocrine Review* 30, no. 4 (June 1): 293–342. https://doi.org/10.1210/er.2009-0002.

Dolin, Bruce Steven. 2009a. "Orchid Children." *Privilege of Parenting* (blog). November 23, 2009. http://privilegeofparenting.com/2009/11/23/orchid-children/.

Dolin, Bruce Steven. 2009b. "Ten-Year-Olds and Their Changing Brains." *Privilege of Parenting* (blog). July 31, 2009. http://privilegeofparenting.com/2009/07/31/ten-year-olds-and-their-changing-brains/.

Eagleman, David. 2015. *The Brain with David Eagleman.* Episode 2, "Inside a Child's Brain." Aired October 21, 2015, on PBS. https://www.pbs.org/show/brain-david-eagleman/.

Education Commission of the States. 2014. "50-State Comparison: Kindergarten Entrance Age." Education Commission of the States. March 2014. http://ecs.force.com/mbdata/mbquestRT?rep=Kq1402.

El Nokali, Nermeen E., Heather J. Bachman, and Elizabeth Votruba-Drzal. 2010. "Parent Involvement and Children's Academic and Social Development in Elementary School." *Child Development* 81, no. 3 (May/June): 988–1005. https://doi.org/10.1111/j.1467-8624.2010.01447.x.

FDA: U.S. Food and Drug Association. 2014. "FDA: Don't Leave Childhood Depression Untreated." FDA: U.S. Food and Drug Association (website). September 10, 2014. https://www.fda.gov/ForConsumers/ConsumerUp dates/ucm413161.htm.

Figueiro, Mariana G., Andrew Bierman, Barbara Plitnick, and Mark S. Rea. 2009. "Preliminary Evidence that Both Blue and Red Light Can Induce Alertness at Night." *BMC Neuroscience* 10, no. 1 (August 27): 105. https://doi.org/10.1186/1471-2202-10-105.

Furnham, Adrian. 2014. "Secrets to Eye Contact, Revealed." SCRIBD (website). December 10, 2014. https://www.scribd.com/document/337964127 /Eye-Gaze.

Gaines, James. 2016. "This School Replaced Detention with Meditation. The Results Are Stunning." Upworthy (website). September 22, 2016. http:// www.upworthy.com/this-school-replaced-detention-with-meditation-the -results-are-stunning?g=2&c=ufb1.

Gale, Jonathan. 2009. Telephone interview with author Patricia Wilkinson. June 11, 2009. http://npino.com/psychologist/1700089372-dr.-jonathan -d-gale/.

Georgiou, Harris V. 2017. "Intrinsic Dimension Estimation of the fMRI Space via Sparsity-Promoting Matrix Factorization: Counting the 'Brain Cores' of the Human Brain." Paper presented at the 21st Pan-Hellenic Conference on Informatics, Article No. 20, Larissa, Greece. September 28–30, 2017. https://doi.org/10.1145/3139367.3139391.

Godman, Heidi. 2014. "Regular Exercise Changes the Brain to Improve Memory, Thinking Skills." Harvard Health Publishing (website). April 09, 2014. http://www.health.harvard.edu/blog/regular-exercise-changes-brain -improve-memory-thinking-skills-201404097110.

Golan, Natali, and Giora Pillar. 2004. "The Relationship Between Attention Deficit Hyperactivity Disorder and Sleep-Alertness Problems." Abstract. *Harefuah* 143, no. 9 (September): 676–80, 693. https://www.ncbi.nlm.nih .gov/pubmed/15521685.

Goleman, Daniel. 2006. *Social Intelligence: The New Science of Human Relationships*. New York: Bantam Dell.

Gray, Peter. 2010. "The Decline of Play and Rise in Children's Mental Disor-

ders." *Psychology Today* (website). January 26, 2010. https://www
.psychologytoday.com/blog/freedom-learn/201001/the-decline-play-and
-rise-in-childrens-mental-disorders.

Gregory, Alice M., Terrie E. Moffitt, and Richie Poulton. 2009. "Sleep Problems in Childhood Predict Neuropsychological Functioning in Adolescence." *Pediatrics* 123, no. 4 (April): 1171–1176. https://doi.org/10.1542
/peds.2008-0825.

Guyer, Amanda E., Koraly Pérez-Edgar, and Eveline A. Crone. 2018. "Opportunities for Neurodevelopmental Plasticity from Infancy through Early
Adulthood." *Child Development* 89, no. 3 (May): 687–97. https://doi.org
/10.1111/cdev.13073.

Hatfield, Bobbie. 2008. In-person interview with author Patricia Wilkinson.
August 12, 2008.

Hitti, Miranda. 2008. "More Sleep, Less Childhood Obesity." webMD (website). February 12, 2008. https://www.webmd.com/children/news/2008
0212/more-sleep-less-childhood-obesity#1.

Hoogeveen, Lianne, Janet G. Van Hell, and Ludo Verhoeven. 2012. "Social-
Emotional Characteristics of Gifted Accelerated and Non–Accelerated
Students in the Netherlands." *British Journal of Education Psychology* 82,
no. 4 (December): 585–605. https://doi.org/10.1111/j.2044-8279.2011
.02047.x.

Hughes, Christopher, and Jeffrey A. Dean. 2016. "Mechanical and Chemo-
therapeutic Home Oral Hygiene." In *McDonald and Avery's Dentistry for
the Child and Adolescent*, 10th ed., edited by Jeffrey A. Dean, David R.
Avery, and Ralph E. McDonald, 120–37. St. Louis: Elsevier.

Influence Central. 2016. "Kids and Tech: The Evolution of Today's Digital
Natives." Influence Central (website). http://influence-central.com/kids
-tech-the-evolution-of-todays-digital-natives/.

Jabr, Ferris. 2013. "The Reading Brain in the Digital Age: Why Paper Still
Beats Screens; E-readers and Tablets Are Becoming More Popular as Such
Technologies Improve, but Reading on Paper Still Has Its Advantages."
Scientific American (website). November 2013. https://www.scientific
american.com/article/the-reading-brain-in-the-digital-age-why-paper-still
-beats-screens/.

Jary, Simon. 2018. "How Much Screen Time Is Healthy for Children?"
Tech Advisor from IDG (website). February 23, 2018. https://www
.techadvisor.co.uk/feature/digital-home/how-much-screen-time-for-kids
-3520917/.

Jensen, Eric. 2005. "Movement and Learning." In *Teaching with the Brain
in Mind*, 2nd ed., 60–67. Alexandria, VA: Association for Supervision &

Curriculum Development. http://www.ascd.org/publications/books/104
013/chapters/Movement-and-Learning.aspx.

Jeong, Se-Hoon, and Yoori Hwang. 2016. "Media Multitasking Effects on
Cognitive vs. Attitudinal Outcomes: A Meta-Analysis." *Human Communication Research* 42, no. 4 (October 1): 599–618. http://doi.org/10.1111
/hcre.12089.

Jimerson, Shane R. 2001. "Meta-Analysis of Grade Retention Research: Implications for Practice in the 21st Century." *School Psychology Review* 30,
no. 3: 420–37. https://eric.ed.gov/?id=EJ667518.

Johnson, Sara B., Robert W. Blum, and Jay N. Giedd. 2009. "Adolescent Maturity and the Brain: The Promise and Pitfalls of Neuroscience Research in
Adolescent Health Policy." *Journal of Adolescent Health* 45, no. 3 (September): 216–21. https://doi.org/10.1016/j.jadohealth.2009.05.016.

Jones, Pat. 2016. Telephone interview with author Patricia Wilkinson. November 25, 2016. http://www.teacher-support-force.com/.

K., Carolyn. n.d. Hoagies' Gifted Education Page. Accessed June 14, 2018.
http://www.hoagiesgifted.org.

K12 Reader. n.d. "Fry Word List—1,000 High Frequency Words." K–12
Reader. Accessed February 20, 2017. http://www.k12reader.com/subject
/vocabulary/fry-words/.

Kell, H. J., D. Lubinski, and C. P. Benbow. 2013. "Who Rises to the Top?
Early Indicators." *Psychological Science* 24, no. 5 (May): 648–59. https://
doi.org/10.1177/0956797612457784.

Kharitonova, Maria. 2010. "The Relationship between Individual Differences
in Working Memory and Filtering Task-Irrelevant Information, in Children and Adults." PhD thesis, University of Colorado. https://scholar
.colorado.edu/psyc_gradetds/6.

KidsHealth. 2014. "Sports and Energy Drinks." With review by Mary L.
Gavin. KidsHealth (website). October 2014. https://kidshealth.org/en
/parents/power-drinks.html.

Kitsaras, George, Michaela Goodwin, Julia Allan, Michael P. Kelly, and Iain
A. Pretty. 2018. "Bedtime Routines Child Wellbeing and Development."
BMC Public Health 18, no. 1 (March 21): 386. https://doi.org/10.1186
/s12889-018-5290-3.

Klein, Denise, Kelvin Mok, Jen-Kai Chen, and Kate E. Watkins. 2014. "Age of
Language Learning Shapes Brain Structure: A Cortical Thickness Study of
Bilingual and Monolingual Individuals." *Brain and Language* 131 (April
24): 20–24. https://doi.org/10.1016/j.bandl.2013.05.014.

Klein, Helen Altman. 2000. "Self-Esteem and Beyond." *Childhood Education*
76, no. 4 (Summer): 240. http://link.galegroup.com/apps/doc/A63089280
/AONE?u=deschutes&sid=AONE&xid=aafbe479.

Kredlow, M. Alexandra, Michelle C. Capozzoli, Bridget A. Hearon, Amanda W. Calkins, and Michael W. Otto. 2015. "The Effects of Physical Activity on Sleep: A Meta-Analytic Review." *Journal of Behavioral Medicine* 38, no. 3 (June): 427–49. https://doi.org/10.1007/s10865-015-9617-6.

Leiden University. 2008. "Learning from Mistakes Only Works after Age 12, Study Suggests." Science Daily (website). September 27, 2008. https://www.sciencedaily.com/releases/2008/09/080925104309.htm.

Lenroot, Rhoshel K., Nitin Gogtay, Deanna K. Greenstein, Elizabeth Molloy Wells, Gregory L. Wallace, Liv S. Clasen, Jonathan D. Blumenthal et al. 2007. "Sexual Dimorphism of Brain Developmental Trajectories during Childhood and Adolescence." *NeuroImage* 36, no. 4 (July 15): 1065–73. https://doi.org/10.1016/j.neuroimage.2007.03.053.

Lightfoot, Cynthia, Michael Cole, and Sheila R. Cole. 2009. *The Development of Children*, 6th ed. New York: Worth Publishers.

Lin, Fuchun, Yan Zhou, Yasong Du, Lindi Qin, Zhimin Zhao, Jianrong Xu, and Hao Lei. 2012. "Abnormal White Matter Integrity in Adolescents with Internet Addiction Disorder: A Tract-Based Spatial Statistics Study." *PLoS ONE* 7, no. 1 (January 11): e30253. https://doi.org/10.1371/journal.pone.0030253.

Lin, Lin, Deborah Cockerham, Zhengsi Chang, and Gloria Natividad. 2016. "Task Speed and Accuracy Decrease When Multitasking." *Technology, Knowledge and Learning* 21, no. 3 (October): 307–23. http://dx.doi.org/10.1007/s10758-015-9266-4.

MacArthur, Britt, Dawn Coe, Allison Sweet, and Hollie Raynor. 2014. "Active Videogaming Compared to Unstructured, Outdoor Play in Young Children: Percent Time in Moderate- to Vigorous-Intensity Physical Activity and Estimated Energy Expenditure." *Games for Health Journal* 3, no. 6 (November 25): 388–94. https://doi.org/10.1089/g4h.2014.0017.

Makel, Matthew C., Michael S. Matthews, Scott J. Peters, Karen Rambo-Hernandez, and Jonathan A. Plucker. 2016. "How Can So Many Students Be Invisible? Large Percentages of American Students Perform Above Grade Level." Johns Hopkins School of Education, Institute for Education Policy (website). August 16, 2016. http://edpolicy.education.jhu.edu/how-can-so-many-students-be-invisible-large-percentages-of-american-students-perform-above-grade-level/.

Matsudaira, Izumi, Susumu Yokota, Teruo Hashimoto, Hikaru Takeuchi, Kohei Asano, Michiko Asano, Yuko Sassa, Yasuyuki Taki, and Ryuta Kawashima. 2016. "Parental Praise Correlates with Posterior Insular Cortex Gray Matter Volume in Children and Adolescents." *PLoS ONE* 11, no. 4 (April 21): e0154220. https://doi.org/10.1371/journal.pone.0154220.

McInerny, Thomas K. 2013. "Recognizing Signs of Childhood and Teen De-pression." On *Healthy Children* podcast, hosted by Melanie Cole, aired on RadioMD. January 9, 2013. Audio, 9:44. http://radiomd.com/show /healthy-children/item/9042-recognizing-signs-of-childhood-and-teen -depression#.UO3DEHdX98E.

Miendlarzewska, Ewa A., and Wiebke J. Trost. 2013. "How Musical Training Affects Cognitive Development: Rhythm, Reward, and Other Modulating Variables." *Frontiers in Neuroscience* 7:279. https://doi.org/10.3389/fnins .2013.00279.

Mikkonen, Denise. 2010. In-person interview with author Patricia Wilkinson. July 15, 2010.

Miller, Sara G. 2015. "The Spooky Effects of Sleep Deprivation." Live Science (website). October 27, 2015. http://www.livescience.com/52592-spooky -effects-sleep-deprivation.html.

Mueller, Claudia M., and Carol S. Dweck. 1998. "Praise for Intelligence Can Undermine Children's Motivation and Performance." *Journal of Personality and Social Psychology* 75, no. 1 (July): 33–52. https://doi.org/10.1037 /0022-3514.75.1.33.

Musiek, Eric S., and David M. Holtzman. 2016. "Mechanisms Lining Circa-dian Clocks, Sleep, and Neurodegeneration." *Science* 354, no. 6315 (No-vember 25): 1004–8. https://doi.org/10.1126/science.aah4968.

Myrberg, Caroline, and Ninna Wiberg. 2015. "Screen vs. Paper: What Is the Difference for Reading and Learning?" *Insights* 28, no. 2 (July 7): 49–54. http://doi.org/10.1629/uksg.236.

National Association for Gifted Children. 2010. "Position Statement: Re-defining Giftedness for a New Century: Shifting the Paradigm." March 2010. https://www.nagc.org/sites/default/files/Position%20Statement Mandated%20Services%20for%20Gifted%20and%20Talented%20 Students.pdf.

National Association for Gifted Children. 2013. "Position Statement: Man-dated Services for Gifted and Talented Students." September 2013. https:// www.nagc.org/sites/default/files/Position%20Statement/Redefining%20 Giftedness%20for%20a%20New%20Century.pdf.

National Education Association. n.d. "Research Spotlight on Homework: NEA Reviews of the Research on Best Practices in Education." Accessed November 15, 2016. National Education Association (website). http:// www.nea.org/tools/16938.htm.

Page, J. S. 2010. "Challenges Faced by 'Gifted Learners' in School and Be-yond." *Inquiries Journal/Student Pulse* 2, no. 11. http://www.inquiries journal.com/a?id=330.

Palmer, David. 2011. "Gifted Kids with Learning Problems: The 'Twice-

Exceptional' Child." *Psychology Today* (website). December 26, 2011. https://www.psychologytoday.com/blog/gifted-kids/201112/gifted-kids -learning-problems.

Payne, Jessica D., Matthew A. Tucker, Jeffrey M. Ellenbogen, Erin J. Wams- ley, Matthew P. Walker, Daniel L. Schacter, and Robert Stickgold. 2012. "Memory for Semantically Related and Unrelated Declarative Informa- tion: The Benefit of Sleep, the Cost of Wake." *PLoS ONE* 7, no. 3 (March 22): e33079. https://doi.org/10.1371/journal.pone.0033079.

Perry, Susan. 2010. "Glia: The Other Brain Cells." BrainFacts.org (website). September 15, 2010. http://www.brainfacts.org/archives/2010/glia-the -other-brain-cells.

Peterson, Lloyd R., and Margaret Jean Peterson. 1959. "Short-Term Retention of Individual Verbal Items." Journal of Experimental Psychology 58, no. 3 (September): 193–98. http://dx.doi.org/10.1037/h0049234.

Popkin, Barry M., Kristen E. D'Anci, and Irwin H. Rosenberg. 2010. "Water, Hydration, and Health." *Nutrition Reviews* 68, no. 8 (August): 439–58. https://doi.org/10.1111/j.1753-4887.2010.00304.x.

Ramirez, Gerardo, and Sian L. Beilock. 2011. "Writing about Testing Wor- ries Boosts Exam Performance in the Classroom." *Science* 331, no. 6014 (Jan 14): 211–13. https://doi.org/10.1126/science.1199427.

Reinberg, Steven. 2009. "Sedentary Kids May Take Longer to Fall Asleep: But Active Kids Need More Sleep and Get It More Easily, Expert Says." Health Day (website). July 23, 2009. https://consumer.healthday.com /fitness-information-14/misc-health-news-265/sedentary-kids-may-take -longer-to-fall-asleep-629310.html.

Riebl, Shaun K., and Brenda M. Davy. 2013. "The Hydration Equation: Up- date on Water Balance and Cognitive Performance." *ACSM's Health and Fitness Journal* 17, no. 6 (November/December): 21–28. https://www.ncbi .nlm.nih.gov/pmc/articles/PMC4207053/.

Romeo, Rachel R., Julia A. Leonard, Sydney T. Robinson, Martin R. West, Allyson P. Mackey, Meredith L. Rowe, and John D. E. Gabrieli. 2018. "Beyond the 30-Million-Word Gap: Children's Conversational Exposure Is Associated with Language-Related Brain Function." *Psychological Science* 29, no. 5 (May): 700-10. https://doi.org/10.1177/0956797617 742725.

Rubenking, Neil J., and Ben Moore. 2018. "The Best Parental Control Soft- ware of 2018." PCMag (website). June 6, 2018. http://www.pcmag.com /article2/0,2817,2346997,00.asp.

Rubino, Michael. 2016. "Teens, Tweens, and Cell Phones: Advice for Par- ents." Pleasant Hill Patch (website). September 14, 2016. http://patch.com /california/pleasanthill/teens-tweens-cell-phones-advice-parents.

Sacheck, Jennifer, Catherine Wright, Virginia Chomitz, Kenneth Chui, Christina Economos, and Nicole Schultz. 2015. "Active Bodies, Active Minds: A Case Study on Physical Activity and Academic Success in Lawrence, Massachusetts." The Boston Foundation (website). January 2015. https://www.tbf.org/~/media/TBFOrg/Files/Reports/Active%20Bodies%20Active%20Minds.pdf.

Sadeh, Avi. 2007. "Consequences of Sleep Loss or Sleep Disruption in Children." *Sleep Medicine Clinics* 2, no. 3 (September): 513–20. https://doi.org/10.1016/j.jsmc.2007.05.012.

Scholastic. n.d. "Patricia Polacco." Accessed November 18, 2016. http://www.scholastic.com/teachers/contributor/patricia-polacco.

Semrud-Clikeman, Margaret. n.d. "Research in Brain Function and Learning: The Importance of Matching Instruction to a Child's Maturity Level." American Psychological Association (website). Accessed October 29, 2016. http://www.apa.org/education/k12/brain-function.aspx.

Servick, Kelly. 2013. "How Exercise Beefs Up the Brain." Science (website). October 10, 2013. http://www.sciencemag.org/news/2013/10/how-exercise-beefs-brain.

Sheikholeslami, C., H. Yuan, E. J. He, X. Bai, L. Yang, and B. He. 2007. "A High Resolution EEG Study of Dynamic Brain Activity during Video Game Play." Paper presented at the Annual International Conference of IEEE Engineering in Medicine and Biology Society, Lyon, France. August 22–26, 2007. https://doi.org/10.1109/IEMBS.2007.4352833.

SickKids Hospital Staff. 2011. "Cognitive Development in School-Age Children." AboutKidsHealth (website). December 14, 2011. http://www.aboutkidshealth.ca/En/HealthAZ/DevelopmentalStages/SchoolAgeChildrenPages/Cognitive-Development.aspx.

Simmons, J. G., O. S. Schwartz, K. Bray, C. Deane, E. Pozzi, S. Richmond, J. Smith et al. 2017. "Study Protocol: Families and Childhood Transitions Study (FACTS) – A Longitudinal Investigation of the Role of the Family Environment in Brain Development and Risk for Mental Health Disorders in Community Based Children." *BMC Pediatrics* 17, no. 153 (June 30). https://doi.org/10.1186/s12887-017-0905-x.

Smith, Hallie. 2013. "The Benefits of Downtime: Why Learners' Brains Need a Break." Scientific Learning (website). December 17, 2013. http://www.scilearn.com/blogbenefits-of-downtime-why-learners-brains-need-a-break.

Sonna, Linda. 2003. *The Everything Tween Book: A Parent's Guide to Surviving the Turbulent Preteen Years.* Avon, MA: Adams Media.

Spiro, Linda. n.d. "The Most Common Misdiagnoses in Children: When Symptoms Have Multiple Causes, Mistakes Are Made." Child Mind Insti-

tute (website). Accessed February 23, 2017. https://childmind.org/article
/the-most-common-misdiagnoses-in-children/.

Stencil, Annie. 2008. In-person interview with author Patricia Wilkinson. October 9, 2008.

Stevens, Elizabeth A., Melodee A. Walker, and Sharon Vaughn. 2017. "The
Effects of Reading Fluency Interventions on the Reading Fluency and
Reading Comprehension Performance of Elementary Students with Learning Disabilities: A Synthesis of the Research from 2001 to 2014." *Journal
of Learning Disabilities* 50, no. 5 (September/October): 576–90. https://
doi.org/10.1177/0022219416638028.

Stiles, Joan, and Terry L. Jernigan. 2010. "The Basics of Brain Development."
Neuropsychology Review 20, no. 4 (December): 327–48. https://doi.org
/10.1007/s11065-010-9148-4.

US Department of Health and Human Services. 2008. "Active Children and
Adolescents." In *2008 Physical Activities Guidelines for Americans*, 15–
20. Washington, DC. October 2008. https://health.gov/paguidelines/pdf
/paguide.pdf.

Van Duijvenvoorde, Anna C. K., Kiki Zanolie, Serge A. R. B. Rombouts,
Maartje E. J. Raijmakers, and Eveline A. Crone. 2008. "Evaluating the
Negative or Valuing the Positive? Neural Mechanisms Supporting Feed-
back-Based Learning across Development." *Journal of Neuroscience* 28,
no. 38 (September 17): 9495–503. https://doi.org/10.1523/JNEURO
SCI.1485-08.2008.

Van Pelt, Jennifer. 2015. "Hydration in Young Athletes." *Today's Dietitian*
(website). April 2015 (vol. 17, no. 4, p. 28). http://www.todaysdietitian
.com/newarchives/040715p28.shtml.

Vartanian, Lenny R., Marlene B. Schwartz, and Kelly D. Brownell. 2007.
"Effects of Soft Drink Consumption on Nutrition and Health: A Systematic Review and Meta-Analysis." *American Journal of Public Health* 97,
no. 4 (April): 667–75. https://doi.org/10.2105/AJPH.2005.083782.

Vermeulen, Marije C. M., Kristiaan B. Van der Heijden, Hanna Swaab, Eus J.
W. Van Someren. 2018. "Sleep Spindle Characteristics and Sleep Architec-
ture Are Associated with Learning of Executive Functions in School-Age
Children." *Journal of Sleep Research* (October 18): e12779. https://doi
.org/10.1111/jsr.12779.

Wallace, Taylor C., and Victor L. Fulgoni. 2017. "Usual Choline Intakes
Are Associated with Egg and Protein Food Consumption in the United
States." *Nutrients* 9, no. 8 (August 5): 839. https://doi.org/10.3390
/nu9080839.

Westcott, Wayne, and Avery Faigenbaum. 2003. "Strength Training for
Kids: Practical Guidelines and Recommended Resistance Exercises You

Can Use Today to Improve Youth Muscle Strength by as Much as 74 Percent!" *IDEA Health Fitness Source* (website). April 1, 2003 (vol. 2004, no. 4). http://www.ideafit.com/fitness-library/strength-training-for -kids.

FURTHER READING

Academy of Nutrition and Dietetics. 2017. "Water: How Much Do Kids Need?" With review by Mary Mullen and Jo Ellen Shield. Eatright: Academy of Nutrition and Dietetics (website). May 2, 2017. http://www.eat right.org/resource/fitness/sports-and-performance/hydrate-right/water-go -with-the-flow.

Adodo, S. O., and J. O. Agbayewa. 2011. "Effect of Homogenous and Heterogeneous Ability Grouping Class Teaching on Student's Interest, Attitude, and Achievement in Integrated Science." *International Journal of Psychology and Counselling* 3, no. 3 (March): 48–54. http://www.academic journals.org/article/article1380364076_Adodo%20and%20Agbayewapdf.

Basch, Charles E. 2011. "Healthier Students Are Better Learners: A Missing Link in School Reforms to Close the Achievement Gap." *Journal of School Health* 81, no. 10 (October): 593–98. https://doi.org/10.1111/j.1746-1561 .2011.00632.x.

Bjelland, Mona, Bart Soenens, Elling Bere, Éva Kovács, Nanna Lien, Lea Maes, Yannis Manios, George Moschonis, and Saskia J. te Velde. 2015. "Associations between Parental Rules, Style of Communication, and Children's Screen Time." *BMC Public Health* 15 (October 1): 1002. https:// doi.org/10.1186/s12889-015-2337-6.

Constantinidis, Christos, and Torkel Klingberg. 2016. "The Neuroscience of Working Memory Capacity and Training." *Nature Reviews Neuroscience* 17 (May 26): 438–449. https://doi.org/10.1038/nrn.2016.43.

Davis, Catherine L., Phillip D. Tomporowski, Colleen A. Boyle, Jennifer L. Waller, Patricia H. Miller, Jack A. Naglieri, and Mathew Gregoski. 2007. "Effects of Aerobic Exercise on Overweight Children's Cognitive Functioning: A Randomized Controlled Trial." *Research Quarterly for Exercise and Sport* 78, no. 5 (December): 510–19. https://doi.org/10.1080/0270 1367.2007.10599450.

DiMaria, Christine. n.d. "What You Should Know about Your Child Losing Baby Teeth." Colgate (website). Accessed December 30, 2016. http:// www.colgate.com/en/us/oc/oral-health/life-stages/childrens-oral-care /article/what-you-should-know-about-your-child-losing-baby-teeth-0414.

Dolin, Bruce. 2011. *Privilege of Parenting*. Beverly Hills, CA: PoP the World Publishing.

Education.com. 2009. "Your 4th Grader's Social Life." Education.com (website). November 10, 2009. https://www.education.com/magazine/article /On_Playground_Fourth_Grade/.

Fadda, Roberta, Gertrude Rapinett, Dominik Grathwohl, Marinella Parisi, Rachele Fanari, Carla Maria Calò, and Jeroen Schmitt. 2012. "Effects of Drinking Supplementary Water at School on Cognitive Performance in Children." *Appetite* 59, no. 3 (December): 730–737. https://doi.org/10 .1016/j.appet.2012.07.005.

Fiedler, Ellen D., Richard E. Lange, and Susan Winebrenner. 2002. "In Search of Reality: Unraveling the Myths about Tracking, Ability Grouping, and the Gifted." *Roeper Review* 24 (3): 108–11. https://doi.org/10.1080/02783 190209554142.

Gearing, Mary E. 2015. "Natural and Added Sugars: Two Sides of the Same Coin." With figures by Shanon McArdel. Science in the News, Harvard University, Graduate School of Arts and Sciences (website). October 5, 2015. http://sitn.hms.harvard.edu/flash/2015/natural-and-added-sugars -two-sides-of-the-same-coin/.

Ghezzi, Patti. n.d. "4th Grade Academics: What to Expect." School Family (website). Accessed February 2, 2017. https://www.schoolfamily.com /school-family-articles/article/869-fourth-grade-academics-what-to-expect.

Ghezzi, Patti. n.d. "4th Grade Social Changes: What to Expect" School Family (website). Accessed January 29, 2017. http://www.schoolfamily.com /school-family-articles/article/870-fourth-grade-social-changes-what-to -expect.

Giedd, Jay N., Jonathan Blumenthal, Neal O. Jeffries, F. X. Castellanos, Hong Liu, Alex Zijdenbos, Tomáš Paus, Alan C. Evans, and Judith L. Rapoport. 1999. "Brain Development during Childhood and Adolescence: A Longitudinal MRI Study." *Nature Neuroscience* 2, no. 10 (October 1): 861–63. https://doi.org/doi:10.1038/13158.

GreatSchools Staff. 2016. "Developmental Milestones: Your 7-Year-Old Child." GreatSchools.org (website). March 16, 2016. http://www.great schools.org/gk/articles/developmental-milestones-your-7-year-old-child/.

Health & Medicine Week. 2015. "Researchers from University of Louisville Report Findings in Pediatric Psychology and Psychiatry (Parental Perfectionism and Overcontrol: Examining Mechanisms in the Development of Child Anxiety)." *Health & Medicine Week*. April 24, 2015. http://go.gale group.com/ps/i.do?p=AONE&sw=w&u=deschutes&v=2.1&id=GALE %7CA415389072&it=r&asid=b33894929bf10d751330f5958bd3942a.

Herrman, Ned. 1997. "What is the Function of the Various Brainwaves?" *Scientific American* (website). December 22, 1997. https://www.scientific american.com/article/what-is-the-function-of-t-1997-12-22/.

Indiana State University. 2013. "Students Perform Well Regardless of Reading Print or Digital Books." ScienceDaily (website). May 24, 2013. https://www.sciencedaily.com/releases/2013/05/130524160710.htm.

Jenuwine, Hannah R. 2014. "Third Grade Reading and Retention Policies to Improve Education Outcomes." *Inquiries Journal/Student Pulse* 6, no. 10. http://www.inquiriesjournal.com/a?id=928.

Johnson, Ben. 2011. "Student Learning Groups: Homogeneous or Heterogeneous?" Edutopia: George Lucas Educational Foundation (website). August 2, 2011. https://www.edutopia.org/blog/student-grouping-homogeneous-heterogeneous-ben-johnson.

Kempton, Matthew J., Ulrich Ettinger, Russell Foster, Steven C.R. Williams, Gemma A. Calvert, Adam Hampshire, and Fernando O. Zelaya et al. 2011. "Dehydration Affects Brain Structure and Function in Healthy Adolescents." *Human Brain Mapping* 32, no. 1 (January): 71–79. https://doi.org/10.1002/hbm.20999.

Kharitonova, Maria, Warren Winter, and Margaret A. Sheridan. 2015. "As Working Memory Grows: A Developmental Account of Neural Bases of Working Memory Capacity in 5- to 8-Year Old Children and Adults." *Journal of Cognitive Neuroscience* 27, no. 9 (September): 1775–88. https://doi.org/10.1162/jocn_a_00824.

Lee, Katherine. 2018. "Fourth Grade: What You & Your Child Can Expect: How Your Fourth Grader Will Grow This Year." VeryWellFamily (website). February 9, 2018. https://www.verywell.com/what-you-can-expect-in-4th-grade-620861.

Live Science Staff. 2010. "Meditation Boosts Attention Span." Live Science (website). July 14, 2010. http://www.livescience.com/10726-meditation-boosts-attention-span.html.

Malik, Vasanti S., and Frank B. Hu. 2012. "Sweeteners and Risk of Obesity and Type 2 Diabetes: The Role of Sugar-Sweetened Beverages." *Current Diabetes Reports* 12, no. 2 (April): 195–203. https://doi.org/doi:10.1007/s11892-012-0259-6.

Matsudaira, Izumi, Susumu Yokota, Teruo Hashimoto, Hikaru Takeuchi, Kohei Asano, Michiko Asano, Yuko Sassa, Yasuyuki Taki, and Ryuta Kawashima. 2016. "Parental Praise Correlates with Posterior Insular Cortex Gray Matter Volume in Children and Adolescents." *PLoS ONE* 11, no. 4 (April 21): e0154220. https://doi.org/10.1371/journal.pone.0154220.

Medina, John. 2008. *Brain Rules: 12 Principles for Surviving and Thriving at Work, Home, and School.* Seattle: Pear Press.

Medina, John. 2014. *Brain Rules for Baby: How to Raise a Smart and Happy*

Child from Zero to Five, 2nd ed. Edited by Tracy Cutchlow. Seattle:
Pear Press.

Mersch, John. n.d. "Young Children: Child Development (6–8 Years Old)."
With medical edit by David Perlstein. MedicineNet.com (website). Accessed November 2, 2016. http://www.medicinenet.com/young_children
_child_development/article.htm.

Morin, Amanda. n.d. "Developmental Milestones for Typical Fourth and Fifth
Graders." With review by Molly Algermissen. Understood: For Learning
and Attention Issues (website). Accessed May 31, 2018. https://www
.understood.org/en/learning-attention-issues/signs-symptoms/developmen
tal-milestones/developmental-milestones-for-typical-fourth-and-fifth
-graders.

Morin, Amanda. n.d. "Fourth-Grade Learning Challenges for Kids with
Learning and Attention Issues." With review by Bob Cunningham. Understood: For Learning and Attention Issues (website). Accessed June 7, 2018.
https://www.understood.org/en/school-learning/choosing-starting-school
/moving-up/learning-challenges-of-fourth-grade.

Munoz, Lisa M.P. 2015. "When Children Try to Remember Many Things at
Once." Cognitive Neuroscience Society (website). May 18, 2015. https://
www.cogneurosociety.org/workingmemory_children_may15/.

Newton, Phil. 2009. "What is Dopamine? The Neurotransmitter's Role in
the Brain and Behavior." *Psychology Today* (website). April 26, 2009.
https://www.psychologytoday.com/blog/mouse-man/200904/what-is
-dopamine.

Nierenberg, Cari. 2016. "Not So Sweet: New Sugar Limits for Kids Announced." Live Science (website). August 22, 2016. http://www.livescience
.com/55843-new-sugar-limits-for-kids-announced.html.

Norton, Sally. 2016. "Fruit Juice—Healthy or Unhealthy." *Huffington Post*
(website). September 13, 2014. http://www.huffingtonpost.co.uk/dr-sally
-norton/fruit-juice-healthy-or-un_b_5586825.html.

Pellissier, Hank. 2017. "Inside the 4th Grader's Brain: What Insights Can
Neuroscience Offer Parents about the Mind of a Fourth Grader?" GreatSchools.org (website). August 9, 2017. http://www.greatschools.org/gk
/articles/fourth-grader-brain-development/.

Pevzner, Holly. n.d. "Brain Development in Children: An Age by Age Guide to
Child Mental Growth." Parenting (website). Accessed December 5, 2016.
http://www.parenting.com/article/brain-development-children.

Salimpoor, Valorie N., Iris van den Bosch, Natasa Kovacevic, Anthony Randal McIntosh, Alain Dagher, and Robert J. Zatorre. 2013. "Interactions
between the Nucleus Accumbens and Auditory Cortices Predict Music Re-

ward Value." *Science* 340, no. 6129 (April 12): 216–19. https://doi
.org/10.1126/science.1231059.

Samani, Ashna, and Matthew Heath. 2018. "Executive-Related Oculomotor
Control Is Improved Following a 10-Min Single-Bout of Aerobic Exercise:
Evidence from the Antisaccade Task." *Neuropsychologia* 108 (January 8):
73–81. https://doi.org/10.1016/j.neuropsychologia.2017.11.029.

Schmidt, Mirko, Fabienne Egger, Valentin Benzing, Katja Jäger, Achim Con-
zelmann, Claudia M. Roebers, and Caterina Pesce. 2017. "Disentangling
the Relationship between Children's Motor Ability, Executive Function, and Academic Achievement." *PLoS ONE* 12, no. 8 (August 17):
e0182845. https://doi.org/10.1371/journal.pone.0182845.

Teacher Support Force. n.d. "Brain Exercises and Physical Coordination Are
Benefits of Physical Education." Teaching Support Force (website). Accessed November 16, 2016. http://www.teacher-support-force.com/brain
exercises.html.

Trudeau, François, and Roy J. Shephard. 2008. "Physical Education, School
Physical Activity, School Sports, and Academic Performance." *Interna-
tional Journal of Behavioral Nutrition and Physical Activity* 5, no.10
(February 25). https://doi.org/10.1186/1479-5868-5-10.

University of Tennessee at Knoxville. 2015. "Active Video Gaming Compared
to Unstructured Outdoor Play." ScienceDaily (website). June 12, 2015.
https://www.sciencedaily.com/releases/2015/06/150612143655.htm.

Vahabzadeh, Arshya. 2013. "Diagnosing ADHD by Brain Waves? A New
Brainwave Test for ADHD Diagnosis Has Gained FDA Approval." *Psychology Today* (website). July 21, 2013. https://www.psychologytoday
.com/blog/spectrum-theory/201307/diagnosing-adhd-brain-waves-0.

Winch, Guy. 2011. "How Much Homework Is Too Much? Are Schools Assigning Too Much Homework?" *Psychology Today* (website). October 19,
2011. https://www.psychologytoday.com/blog/the-squeaky-wheel/201110
/how-much-homework-is-too-much.

Yale University. 2016. "Video Games Can Have Lasting Impact on Learning."
ScienceDaily (website). September 20, 2016. https://www.sciencedaily.com
/releases/2016/09/160920104225.htm.

INDEX

ABOUT THE AUTHORS

PATRICIA WILKINSON, mother of two, taught grades kindergarten through sixth for 23 years, in both public and private schools. She earned a BA in recreation from California State University, Long Beach, and did graduate work at California State Universities, Los Angeles and Chico, to earn a Clear Multiple-Subject Teaching Credential and Language Development Specialist certificate from the State of California.

Today, Trish facilitates life-changing workshops for parents and teachers. It's amazing what can happen when years of creativity and practical experience merge with thousands of hours of brain research. She lives in Bend, Oregon, with her awesome husband, Chuck, and their rambunctious golden retriever, Alice. Visit her at thebrainstages.com.

JACQUELINE FRISCHKNECHT, mother of three, earned a BA in education from the University of Colorado, and an MA in library science and a PhD in communication from the University of Denver. Beginning her career as a first-grade teacher, she ultimately became a professor of speech communication at University College in Denver and served as dean of academic affairs. She authored or coauthored eight books on education, including *Asking Smart Questions* and the SMART Studying series.

Sadly, Jackie passed away in 2015 while working on *Brain Stages*. Passionate about family and learning, she would have been so excited to see her life's work and mission come to fruition in this book.

Made in United States
North Haven, CT
17 February 2024

48867552R00196